The Employer's Payroll Question and Answer Book (2021)

Author: Paul E. Love

Other Books by the Author:

The Employer's Payroll Question and Answer Book (2019)
The Employer's Guide to Surviving Payroll and Human Resource Audits (2019)
Professional Employer Organizations: Can They Help You Grow Your Business?
The Employer's Guide to In-House Payroll Software
The Business Insurance Question and Answer Book

Apollo 10: The Moon Landing That Wasn't
NASA's Artemis Program: To the Moon and Beyond
NASA's Artemis Program: The Next Step – Mars!

Computers: The Early Years
Rescue Me: Animals in Need
Healthcare and Medical Apps
Want a Job in IT? Here's Your Guide
Cowboy Shooting Sports
Virtual Robotics: Robotics on a Budget
The Volunteer's Guide
The Pet Menagerie

Building a No-code/Low-code Web Application On Airtable, Zoho Creator, Bubble and Caspio
Anatomy of a Zoho Creator Project (Building a Payroll Entry Application)
Anatomy of an Airtable Project (Building a Payroll Entry Application with Airtable)

CONTENTS

5

Introduction

Once upon a time payroll was pretty simple. Figure each employee's gross pay, subtract federal, state and local taxes (and possibly three or four other deductions) and write a check for the net amount. Nothing stays simple for long though -- pretty soon along came direct deposit, 401(k) plans, cafeteria plans, vehicle allowances, the Earned Income Tax Credit, garnishments, third party sick pay, paycards, and a raft of other complications.

For many small companies, payroll went from taking an hour or so each pay period to a process that can consume a whole day or more. And that's just to produce the paychecks -- there are usually various files to be written and reports to be filled out as well.

Unless you have an accountant or a payroll service to handle things payroll can be a very confusing, time-consuming task. For a new employer it can be frustrating just figuring out how to get started; and even employers who've been at it for a while can run into problems when new situations arise or payroll laws change.

The purpose of this book is to give a quick overview of what every employer needs to know about payroll. There are a number of sources of information for employers that can provide more detailed explanations of different topics (IRS Publication 15 or "Circular E" being the most important one). Appendix A lists a few additional sources and many others can be found using internet search engines.

NOTE: The information in this book deals primarily with payroll laws and practices in the United States.

Summary of Federal Law Payroll Changes for 2021

- The due date for submitting 2020 W-2s to the SSA is February 1, 2021, the same due date as the deadline for providing W2s and 1099s to recipients.

- The due date for filing the new (resurrected) form 1099-NEC (for 1099s that include non-employee compensation) is February 1, 2021. All other 1099 forms must be submitted by February 28, 2021 (or March 31, 2021 if filing electronically).

- Social Security Rate and Wage Base – The employee rate will remain at 6.2% for 2020, the same as the employer's matching contribution rate. The social security wage base increases to $142,800 for 2021, while the Medicare tax rate stays at 1.45% of taxable wages.

- Again in 2021 individuals who earn $200,000 or more per year in FICA (Social Security and Medicare) taxable wages will have to pay additional Medicare tax. An additional 0.9% must be withheld for Medicare as soon as an employee reaches $200,000 in FICA taxable earnings for the year (for a total Medicare rate of 2.35% instead of the usual 1.45%). Note: the additional Medicare tax does not affect the employer match, which stays at 1.45% for Medicare and 6.2% for Social Security for a total of 7.65% (up to the Social Security wage limit and 1.45% thereafter).

- The IRS has issued guidance to employers on how to compute federal withholding tax for employees whose current W-4 form dates back to 2019 or earlier. According to the draft version of Publication 15 (Circular E), this "computational bridge" works like this:

1. Select the filing status in step 1(c) of a 2020 or later Form W-4 that most accurately reflects the employee's marital status on line 3 of a 2019 or earlier Form W-4. Treat the employee as "Single or Married filing separately" on a 2020 or later Form W-4 if the employee selected either "Single" or "Married, but withhold at higher single rate" as their marital status on their 2019 or earlier Form W-4. Treat the employee as "Married filing jointly" on a 2020 or later Form W-4 if the employee selected "Married" as their marital status on their 2019 or earlier Form W-4. You

can't convert an employee to a filing status of "head of household" using this computational bridge.

2. Enter an amount in step 4(a) on a 2020 or later Form W-4 based on the filing status that you determined in (1) above when you converted the employee's marital status on a 2019 or earlier Form W-4. Enter $8,600 if the employee's filing status is "Single or Married filing separately" or $12,900 if the employee's filing status is "Married filing jointly.".

3. Multiply the number of allowances claimed on line 5 of an employee's 2019 or earlier Form W-4 by $4,300 and enter the result in step 4(b) on a 2020 or later Form W-4. 4. Enter the additional amount of withholding requested by the employee on line 6 of their 2019 or earlier Form W-4 in step 4(c) of a 2020 or later Form W-4.

- The FUTA (Federal Unemployment Tax Act) tax rate stays at 6% for 2021.

- Reminder: Under the new DOL standard, any salaried employee earning less than $684 per week (or $35,568 per year) has to be paid overtime pay for working more than 40 hours per week. Up to 10% of the salary may be in the form of "incentive pay" including non-discretionary bonuses, commissions and other incentive payments. An employee who doesn't make the minimum salary by the end of a 52-week calendar period may either be paid a "catch up" payment to cover the difference (which has to be paid within the first pay period after the 52-week cutoff) or the employee can be downgraded retroactively to a non-exempt employee and paid all the overtime accrued for the year.

- Reminder: Employers must use the new W-4 form introduced in 2020 for new employees or employees who make changes to their W-4 information after January 1, 2020. Note: Some states have developed their own IRS-approved W-4 form – check with your state revenue agency.

- The supplemental wage federal tax withholding rate decreased in 2018 from 25% to 22% and remains at that rate for 2021. Note: If an employee receives more than one million dollars in supplemental wage payments during the year, the excess is subject to the tax rate of the highest tax bracket for that year (currently 39.6%).

- Employees participating in a 401(k) or 403(b) (or most 457plans) can contribute a maximum of $19,500 for 2021,the same as for 2020 (the $19,500 elective deferral limit is also known as the 402(g) limit, named after the relevant tax code section). For employees who are 50 years old or older the "catch-up" contribution limit stays at $6,500 for 2021 for a maximum annual employee contribution of $26,000. Note: Even if you don't turn 50 until December 31, 2021 you can still contribute the additional $6,500 catch-up for the year. Also, if you contribute to two or more 401(k) plans, the contribution limits above apply to the total of your contributions.

- The annual contribution limit (employee + employer) for a defined 401(k) plan increases from $57,000 to $58,000 for 2021 ($64,500 for those age 50 and over).

- The annual compensation limit for calculating employer contributions to a qualified 401(k) plan increases from $285,000 for 2020 to $290,000 for 2021. That is, employers can't make any more matching contributions to an employee once that employee's compensation for the year reaches $290,000.

- Key employees' compensation threshold for nondiscrimination testing remains at $185,000 for 2021.

- Highly compensated employees' threshold for nondiscrimination testing stays at $130,000 for 2021.

- For 2021, the maximum annual benefit that may be provided through a defined benefit plan stays at the lesser of 100% of the participant's average compensation for his or her highest 3 consecutive calendar years or $230,000.

- The limit on contributions to either a Traditional or Roth IRA remains the same at $6,000 for 2021 with an additional $1,000 "catch-up" limit for individuals who are age 50 or over.

- Taxpayers can deduct contributions to a traditional IRA if they meet certain conditions. If during the year either the taxpayer or his/her spouse was covered by a retirement plan at work, the deduction may be phased out (reduced over a specified income range) until it is eliminated, depending on filing status and income. For individuals covered by a workplace retirement plan (such as a 401(k) plan) the income phase-out amounts stay the same for 2021. For single and head-of-household taxpayers the deduction is phased out for those who have an AGI (Adjusted Gross Income) between $65,000 and $75,000. For married tax payers filing jointly the deduction is phased out for AGI amounts between $104,000 and $124,000 and for couples where only the spouse is covered by a workplace plan, the AGI limits are $196,000 to $206,000.

- The 2021 income "phase-out" range for Roth IRA deductions is $125,000 to $140,000 for single and head-of-household taxpayers, up from $124,000 to $139,000.6,000 to $206,000 for married taxpayers. For married individuals filing a separate return, if they lived with their spouse at any time during the year, the phase-out range remains $0 to $10,000.

- For SEP (Simplified Employee Pension) IRA plans the total contribution limit for 2021 increases to $58,000 from $57,000 or 25% of the employee's salary, whichever is smaller. Employees who are 50 or over can contribute an additional $6,500 for a total of $64,500.

- For SIMPLE IRA or SIMPLE 401(k) plans the 2021 contribution limit stays at $13,500 (with a $16,500 limit for those who are age 50 or over).

- 2021 Health Savings Account contribution limits are $3,600 for individuals (with a catch-up limit of $4,600 for those 55 and over) and $7,200 for families (with a limit of $8,200 for those 55 and over). Minimum deductible amounts are $1,400 for individuals and $2,800 for families, with maximum out-of-pocket amounts of $7,000 for individuals and $14,000 for families. Note: Employer contributions to an HSA need to be reported on the W-2 in Box 12, code W.

- The 2021 contribution limit for employee contributions to health flexible spending accounts (health FSAs), made pretax through salary reductions stays at $2,750.

- The 2021 maximum tax exclusion for adoption assistance and the maximum adoption credit is $14,400 per child (for individuals with Adjusted Gross Income below $211,160), up from $14,300.. Phase-out of excludible income begins at $214,520 and ends at $254,520. Employer adoption assistance payments are generally excluded from federal withholding but are subject to Social Security, Medicare and FUTA tax.

- The federal standard mileage rate for business travel is expected to stay at 57.5 cents per mile for 2021.

- The 2021 monthly limit on the amount that may be excluded from an employee's income for qualified parking benefits stays at

$270 (IRS Code Section 132(f) allows employers to offer a qualified transportation benefit program to their employees on a tax-free basis).

- The general definition of a "highly-compensated" employee for the 2021 plan year is anyone who receives annual compensation from the business of $130,000 or more. A key employee is defined as anyone who receives annual compensation of $185,000 or more.

- For 2020, the average annual wage level at which the small business health care tax credit begins to phase out for eligible small employers will be $27,800 (up from $27,600). The maximum average annual wages to qualify for the credit as an "eligible small employer" for 2021 will be twice this amount, i.e., $55,600 (up from $55,200).

- Affordable Care Act:

  - Mandatory employer reporting requirements for the Affordable Care Act (Obamacare) went into effect in 2015. Information reporting is similar to Form W-2 reporting in that an information return (Form 1095-B or 1095-C) will need to be prepared for each applicable employee and copies of those returns have to be filed with the IRS at the beginning of the next calendar year. For 2020 the deadline for providing 1095-C forms to employees has been extended to March 2, 2021. The deadline for submitting forms to the IRS is February 28, 2021 if filing paper forms or March 31, 2021 if filing electronically. Note: Employers with more than 250 employees must file their returns electronically.

  - For 2020 reporting the IRS has again extended "good faith" transition relief to employers that report incorrect or incomplete information when they show that they made good-faith efforts to comply with the information-reporting requirements, both for furnishing forms to individuals and for filing them with the IRS. This relief applies to missing and inaccurate taxpayer identification numbers and dates of birth, as well as other information. The relief does not apply to forms that were untimely furnished to individuals or filed with the IRS.

  - Under the Affordable Care Act regulations employers with 50 or more full-time or full-time equivalent employees who don't offer affordable health insurance that provides minimum value to their full-time employees and their dependents may be subject to a penalty if one or more full-time employees receive a Premium Tax Credit in the Health Insurance Marketplace. Note: in this case a "full-time" employee is one who works an average of 30 hours or more per week. Employers with 50 or more full-time and full-time equivalent employees have to offer affordable, minimum essential coverage at minimum value to their full-time employees and their dependents or be subject to penalties.

- The ACA specifies that employers with 50 or more full-time and full-time equivalent employees won't be assessed penalties if they offer acceptable coverage to at least 95% of their employees in 2020. Employers who fail to offer coverage to at least 95% of full-time employees and dependents in 2020 may be subject to a penalty (under IRS Code Section 4980H(a)) of $2,570 multiplied by the number of full-time employees minus 30. Even employers who offer coverage may still be subject to a penalty if the coverage is not affordable or does not provide minimum value.

- A health plan meets the minimum value standard if it pays at least 60% of the total cost of medical services and includes substantial coverage for physician and inpatient hospital services.

- Assuming an ALE (Applicable Large Employer) meets the offer requirements but the coverage is either unaffordable or doesn't provide minimum value, the 2020 penalty under Code Section 4980H(b) will be increased to $3,860 for each full-time employee who receives subsidized coverage on the Exchange, an increase from $3,750 in 2019.

- Just a reminder – small employers (with less than 50 full-time and full-time equivalent employees) who provide health insurance to their employees still have a reporting requirement under the ACA. If the employer uses an insurance company, the insurer must supply 1094-B and1095-B forms to be distributed to employees and filed with the IRS. For companies that are self-insured the employer has to provide the 1094-B and 1095-B forms.

- Based on the ACA's affordability standard as adjusted for inflation, health coverage will satisfy the requirement to be affordable in 2021 if the lowest-cost self-only coverage option available to employees does not exceed 9.83 percent of an employee's household income, up from 9.78 in 2020.

For 2021 calendar-year plans using the federal poverty level (FPL) safe harbor to determine affordability, an employee's premium payment can't exceed $104.53 per month, up from $101.79 per month in 2020.

- Because employers don't know their employees' household incomes, there are three affordability safe harbors that employers can use that are based on information the employer does have. The safe harbors, any of which can be used, are:

    - The employee's W-2 wages, as reported in Box 1, generally as of the first day of the plan year

    - The employee's rate of pay—his or her hourly wage rate multiplied by 130 hours per month—as of the first day of the plan year.

    - The individual federal poverty level (for a household of 1) as of six months prior to the beginning of the plan year (since the FPL isn't published for a given year until January).

- The Tax Cuts and Jobs Act of 2017 included an important change in the ACA, the removal of the penalty for not having health insurance. As a result, some states are starting to implement their own individual mandates to control healthcare costs. New Jersey and the District of Columbia are the first to enact state-level ACA reporting, but other states are working on similar plans. The appearance of state-level ACA reporting means employers will need to monitor ACA developments in the states where they operate the same as they do for state and local tax withholding regulations.

- A reminder – Employers must pay all federal taxes online or by phone using the Electronic Federal Tax Payment System (EFTPS). The only exception is for employers who owe $2500 or less at the end of a quarter – those employers can send their tax payment along with their 941 form (Employer's Quarterly Federal Tax Return) or with their annual 943 or 944 form.

- New Federal Tax Tables – The IRS has issued new withholding tables for 2019 - see IRS Publication 15 (2019) and Appendix J.

- Employers with 250 or more employees in 2020 are required to file W-2s electronically using the Social Security's Business Services Online system. You can request a waiver from this requirement by filing Form 8508 with the IRS at least 45 days before the February 1, 2021 due date for filing W-2s with the Social Security Administration..

- Beginning with the 2012 W-2's all employers with 250 or more employees in the preceding year were required to report the total cost of all "applicable employer-sponsored health care coverage" provided to an employee on the employee's W-2 (box 12, code DD). **However, the IRS has granted transition relief to most employers until further guidance is provided.** The cost of employer-sponsored coverage is basically the total of employer and employee contributions to any group health care plan made available to an employee that is non-taxable to the employee. Types of coverage excluded from the overall calculation include: coverage under an HRA (Health Reimbursement Arrangement), long-term care coverage, stand-alone vision or dental coverage, contributions to an Archer MSA or Health Savings Account, salary reduction contributions to a health FSA, and any coverage not excludible from gross income. For further details see IRS Notice 2011-28.

- The small business healthcare tax credit (part of the Affordable Care Act) is available to certain small employers. See details at: https://www.irs.gov/affordable-care-act/employers/understanding-the-small-business-health-care-tax-credit.

- At this time the tax treatment of health insurance premiums paid to an employee/owner remains the same for C corporations and S corporations. For C corporations the amount of health insurance premiums paid for or reimbursed to an employee who is also an owner has to be treated as taxable wages for income tax and FICA purposes. For a 2% or more owner in an S corporation the total of the premiums is treated as taxable wages for income tax but not for FICA or FUTA tax (if the payments are made under a plan that makes provision for all or a class of employees or employees and their dependents).

- Standard U.S. Per Diem amounts for Oct. 1, 2019 through Sep. 30, 2020 are $96 per day for lodging and $55 for meals and incidental expenses. There are 332 non-standard areas that have rates higher than the standard rate (see https://www.gsa.gov/travel/plan-book/per-diem-rates/fy-2018-per-diem-highlights for details).

- Due to standard end-of-year close out, employers will experience a delay in receiving payments associated with Forms 7200, Advance Payment of Employer Credits, processed between late-December and mid-January.

  The IRS will continue to accept and process valid Forms 7200 during this time, but the processing of payments of valid requests will begin January 21, 2021. Employers will also still receive Letter 6312, Form 7200 Response, if their Form 7200 can't be processed.

- Note: You can download IRS and SSA forms at any time from www.irs.gov. All downloaded forms can be filed with IRS with the exception of copy A of forms W-2, W-3, W-2C and W-3C – the Social Security Administration only accepts the red ink copies of those forms (or an approved substitute).

- The federal minimum wage will stay at $7.25 in 2021, but 29 states and Washington, D.C. will have a minimum wage rate that's higher than the federal minimum wage. As an employer, you need to comply with the highest applicable minimum wage (including any applicable city or county laws) so be sure you're up-to-date on the local minimum wage laws that apply to you.

- There are no FUTA credit reduction states for 2020.

Changes Due to COVID-19

The effects of COVID-19 on employers throughout the United States triggered the passage of two major pieces of legislation designed to help businesses and their employees survive the pandemic. The Families First Coronavirus Response Act (FFCRA) and the Coronavirus Aid, Relief and Economic Security (CARES) Act have been enacted to provide aid for workers in the form of employee and family paid leave, along with incentives for employers to continue paying all employees in spite of a suspension of business or reduced company income. The legislation also provides help for employers to help offset the costs of dealing with COVID-19.

Q: **What are the main provisions of the CARES Act?**
A: Specifically, the CARES Act provides an employee retention tax credit for qualified employers and it also allows employers to defer payment until 2021 and 2022 of whatever 2020 Social Security payroll tax liabilities they incur following the passage of the CARES Act.

Note: On August 8, 2020, the president issued an executive order stating that the employee's portion of Social Security tax could be deferred effective September 1, 2020, through December 31, 2020. This option only applies to employees making $104,000 or less per year. Workers who take advantage of this option must repay at least half of the deferred tax by December 31, 2021 and the remainder by December 31, 2022.

Q: **What is IRS Form 7200?**
A: The IRS has issued Form 7200 to allow qualifying employers to file in advance to receive the refundable tax credits for qualified sick and family leave and the employee retention tax credit.

Q: **What are the main provisions of the Families First Coronavirus Response Act (FFCRA)?**
A: The FFCRA was signed into law on March 18, 2020 to provide relief for employees and their families who are affected by the pandemic. It created two new laws: the Emergency Paid Sick Leave Act (EPSLA) and the Emergency Family and Medical Leave Expansion Act (EFMLEA). The EPSLA mandates paid sick leave for employees who are missing work for reasons related to the COVID-19 pandemic. The EFMLEA expands the Family and Medical Leave Act (FMLA) temporarily to cover leave and loss of income for employees who have to stay home to care for children because of COVID-19 related school and childcare closures. Provisions of the FFCRA will remain in effect until December 31, 2020.

*** **Notice:** The stimulus package passed by Congress on December 20th apparently includes an extension of the FFCRA paid leave provisions and the payroll tax subsidy for employers offering workers paid sick leave. If the FFCRA leave provisions are extended into 2021, see Appendix M for frequently asked questions about FFCRA paid leave.

Note: Employers with fewer than 50 employees are subject to the new EFMLEA even though they;re exempt from FMLA regulations. Also, employers with less than 50 employees may qualify for exemption from the entire FFCRA if meeting the act's requirements would jeopardize the employer's ability to stay in business.

You can find more information on the new laws by searching the Internet. Here are a few resources with detailed explanations of the provisions of the FFCRA and the CARES Act:

- https://www.irs.gov/forms-pubs/employee-retention-credit-for-employers-subject-to-closure-due-to-covid-19-crisis
- https://www.irs.gov/newsroom/covid-19-related-tax-credits-for-required-paid-leave-provided-by-small-and-midsize-businesses-faqs
- https://ogletree.com/insights/the-families-first-coronavirus-response-act-faqs-the-fmla-amendments-and-paid-sick-leave-requirements-of-the-new-law/
- https://www.irs.gov/newsroom/coronavirus-related-relief-for-retirement-plans-and-iras-questions-and-answers
- https://www.plantemoran.com/explore-our-thinking/insight/2020/04/comparison-of-covid-19-employer-tax-incentives
- https://www.cdflaborlaw.com/coronavirus

Passage of the new laws has also required the IRS to make major changes in Form 941 (the Employer's Quarterly Federal Tax Return). New fields have been added to permit reporting of FFCRA paid leave payments and tax credits, FFCRA emergency family leave payments and tax credits, and CARES Act payroll tax deferrals and employee retention tax credits. Additional changes have been made to allow reporting of advance payment of tax credits, requested by employers on Form 7200. The new Form 941 takes effect beginning with the quarter ended June 30, 2020.

There are 23 new fields in the draft version of Form 941 that are related to the COVID-19 tax credits. The new data fields include:

- Total refundable and nonrefundable credits for payment of qualified sick and family leave wages.
- Total refundable and nonrefundable employee retention credits.
- The deferred amount of the employer share of social security taxes.
- Total advances received for the quarter from filing Form 7200, Advance Payment of Employer Credits Due to COVID-19.

Specific changes include:
- Added line 5a(i) for calculation of the employee Social Security tax portion of qualified sick leave wages.
- Added line 5a(ii) for calculation of the employee Social Security tax portion of qualified family leave wages.
- Added line 11(b), for entry of the nonrefundable portion of the credit for qualified sick and family leave wages (calculated on Worksheet 1).
- Added line 11(c) for entry of the nonrefundable portion of the employee retention credit (calculated on Worksheet 1).
- Added line 13(b) for entry of the deferred amount of the employer share of social security tax.
- Added line 13(c) for entry of the refundable portion of the tax credit for qualified sick and family leave wages (calculated on Worksheet 1).
- Added line 13(d) for entry of the refundable portion of the employee retention credit (calculated on Worksheet 1).
- Added line 13(f) for entry of advances received from filing Form 7200 for the quarter.
- Added line 19 for entry of qualified health plan expenses allocable to qualified sick leave wages.
- Added line 20 for entry of qualified health plan expenses allocable to qualified family leave wages.
- Added line 21 for entry of qualified wages for the employee retention credit.
- Added line 22 for entry of qualified health plan expenses allocable to qualified employee retention credit wages.
- Added line 23 for entry of credit received from filing Form 5884-C, Work Opportunity Credit for Qualified Tax-Exempt Organizations Hiring Qualified Veterans, for the quarter.

- Added line 24 for entry of qualified wages paid for the employee retention credit from March 13, 2020 through March 31, 2020. This line should only be used for the second quarter of 2020. **This line is marked as "reserved for future use" on the 2021 Form 941.**

- Added line 25 for entry of qualified health plan expenses allocable to wages reported on line 24 (use this line only for the second quarter of 2020). **This line is marked "reserved for future use" on the 2021 Form 941.**

- The addition of Worksheet 1. Employers reporting tax credits under the CARES Act and/or the FFCRA have to complete Worksheet 1, Credit for Sick and Family Leave Wages and the Employee Retention Credit. The three-step worksheet allows employers to accurately calculate the refundable and nonrefundable portions of the credits,

You can find the new 941 form at:
https://www.irs.gov/pub/irs-pdf/f941.pdf
and instructions for the new form at:
https://www.irs.gov/pub/irs-dft/i941--dft.pdf

State Employment Law Changes for 2021

Changes in state employment laws for 2021 that employers should be aware of include:

- **California**

  Due to the number and complexity of employment law changes in California, employers should contact the Labor Commissioner's Office for details.

- **Colorado**

  - SB 20-170: Provides that employees forced to leave work for domestic violence-related safety reasons, may still be eligible for unemployment benefits; expands definitions of family members; permits severance pay to be deducted from unemployment compensation.

  - SB 20-205: This law allows employees to accrue at least one hour of paid sick and safe time leave for every 30 hours they work, up to a maximum of 48 hours per year. *The law will apply to employers with 16 or more employees starting January 1, 2021, and then apply to all employers on January 1, 2022.

  - SB 19-085 Prohibits wage discrimination based on sex and gender identity; prohibits employers from seeking an applicant's salary history and from barring current employees from disclosing or discussing their wages. Also mandates transparency in wages and advancement and provides damages for non-compliance.

- **Connecticut**

  - P.A. 19-25: This law, enacted in 2019, established a Family and Medical Leave Insurance Program. The program doesn't begin until January 2022. However, employers need to begin making payroll deductions to fund the program starting in January 2021.

- **Georgia**

  - SB 288: Allows rehabilitated individuals to petition the court to restrict and seal certain criminal records, and prohibits the use of an employee's criminal history information in an action against an employer.

- SB 443: Limits the amount of wages that can be garnished for student loan repayment to 15% of garnishee's weekly disposable earnings.

- **Hawaii**

  - SB 2638: Modifies the documents that an employer may request in order to verify that an employee is a victim of domestic or sexual violence.

- **Iowa**

  - SB 2296: Establishes the circumstances under which certain independent contractors are not considered employees for purposes of various laws.

- **Louisiana**

  - SB 68: Defines what makes a worker an "employee" and what excludes independent contractors from that definition for the purpose of receiving unemployment benefits.

- **Maine**

  - LD 369 (SP 110): Entitles employees to accrue one hour of paid leave for every 40 hours worked, up to 40 hours per year. The law applies to employers who have more than 10 employees.

  - 12-170 Ch. X: Creates procedures for accruing paid leave, providing notice of the need to use leave, scheduling use of leave, and penalizing denial of paid leave.

- **Maryland**

  - Montgomery County Bill 12-19: Requires certain employers to provide a minimum work week of at least 30 hours for each employee who performs janitorial services while working as a janitor, building cleaner, security officer, concierge, doorperson, handyperson, or building superintendent

- **Massachusetts**

  - All private Massachusetts employers must provide covered individuals with paid family and medical leave, funded through a payroll tax.

- **Minnesota**

- Minneapolis Ord. No. 2019-00699: Creates the Freelance Worker Protection Ordinance; requires contracts for service to be set forth in writing and provides an enforcement mechanism for failure to pay a worker as agreed upon in the contract.

- **Missouri**

  - St. Louis Ord. No. 71074: Prohibits employers from basing hiring or promotion decisions on an applicant's criminal history, unless the employer can demonstrate its relevance to the employment-related decision.

- **Nevada**

  - SB 119: Expands mandatory safety training to include employees performing work at sites primarily used for trade shows, conventions and related activities.

  - SB 481 (BDR 788): Establishes requirements for obtaining a certificate of authority for self-funded multiple employer welfare arrangements.

- **New York**

  - SB 2328: Enables employees who have chosen direct deposit to receive electronic confirmation of direct deposit instead of paper pay stubs. Takes effect 4-05-2021.

- **Virginia**

  - HB 1407 (SB 744): Presumes that a worker is an employee, unless either party proves independent contractor status under federal IRS guidelines. Prohibits worker misclassification, providing civil penalties and prohibiting contract awards from public bodies and covered individuals for violations.

- **Washington**

  - HB 1645: Prohibits denying employment to a care provider or licensing to an early childhood educator where a background check reveals that the individual has a finding of child abuse or neglect in their record, but has since obtained a certificate of parental improvement, as defined in the new chapter.

  - Seattle Council Bill No. 119810: Imposes a local payroll tax on employers doing business within the City of Seattle.

Getting Started (For New Employers)

Q: **What's First?**

A: Before you do anything else, if you have just started a new business you need to apply to IRS for an Employer Identification Number or EIN. Your EIN identifies your company and appears on every form you send to the federal government. You apply for an EIN by filling out Form SS-4. You can call IRS at (800) 829-4933 and request a form or you can go to the IRS website (at www.irs.gov), click the link regarding a federal EIN and fill out a Form SS-4 online. You can also obtain an EIN by calling the IRS's Tele-TIN line (1-800-829-4933) which allows you to apply for and receive an EIN over the phone (you still need to fill out an SS-4 and send it in). Once your SS-4 has been processed you should receive a packet from IRS with a copy of IRS Publication 15 (Employer's Tax Guide or "Circular E"), which contains federal withholding tax tables, rules on making your tax deposits, and other essential information. If you don't receive a copy of Publication 15 you can download one at www.irs.gov. Note: You can find additional information on Employer ID numbers at:
https://www.irs.gov/businesses/small-businesses-self-employed/employer-id-numbers

Q: **What's next?**

A: You also need to register your company with the state (or states) where you're doing business. You can find links to various state government web sites at: https://www.irs.gov/businesses/small-businesses-self-employed/state-government-websites or https://www.payroll-taxes.com/state-tax. You will probably need a state identification number and it's usually helpful if you've already received your federal EIN. In any case you will need information about state withholding tax and state unemployment tax requirements (some states may also have additional requirements such as disability insurance withholding and reporting).

Q: **What about payroll taxes?**

A: Your payroll tax liability primarily consists of the Social Security, Medicare, federal and state income taxes withheld from your employees' wages plus the employer's matching share of Social Security and Medicare taxes. Social Security tax is calculated as 6.2% of the employee's FICA taxable wages (wages which are subject to Social Security and Medicare tax) while Medicare tax is calculated as 1.45% of FICA taxable wages. In addition, the employer pays an amount equal to the combined total of the Social Security and Medicare taxes. Social

Security tax also has an annual wage limit (which changes from year to year) and Social Security tax withholding stops once an employee reaches that limit. Medicare tax on the other hand has no wage limit. **Note:** When an employee reaches $200,000 in FICA taxable earnings for the year, the employer has to withhold an additional 0.9% in Medicare tax from that person's wages, making the employee's Medicare tax rate 2.35%. However, the employer's Medicare matching rate stays at 1.45% - the increased rate only applies to the employee.

In some cases employers may have to withhold a city, county, school district or other local tax based on where the company is based or where the employee lives. Be sure to check with your state agency for information on what local taxes you may be subject to, what your withholding rate is and what reports you may need to file.

In addition to the taxes mentioned above, employers normally have to pay state and federal unemployment taxes (SUTA and FUTA). The current FUTA rate is 6.0% of your employees' taxable wages but you can take a credit of up to 5.4% for SUTA taxes that you pay (unless the state you operate in is a "credit reduction" state). There is also a $7,000 taxable wage limit on FUTA, which means you stop paying FUTA tax on an employee once his or her FUTA taxable wages reach $7,000 for the year. Generally, your SUTA tax rate is based on the number of unemployment claims filed by employees that you have terminated, but you need to check with your state about the rate assigned to you and your state's SUTA taxable wage limit (both of which may change from year to year). Some states may also have additional withholding requirements – for example, Alaska, New Jersey, and Pennsylvania require employers to withhold state unemployment insurance from employee wages. There are also a few states that don't currently have a state withholding tax including: Alaska, Florida, Nevada, New Hampshire, South Dakota, Tennessee, Texas, Washington and Wyoming.

Q: **What do I do about paying payroll taxes?**
A: Social Security, Medicare and federal income tax amounts that have been withheld from employees' wages normally have to be deposited on either a monthly or semiweekly schedule (which schedule you use for the current calendar year is based on the amount of taxes you reported during the four quarters of a "look-back" period determined by the IRS. For details on look-back periods refer to Chapter 11 of Publication 15 - Employer's Tax Guide). Under the monthly schedule taxes on wages paid during a calendar month have to be deposited by the 15th of the following month (or if the 15th is a holiday, by the next business day following the 15th). For semiweekly depositors, taxes on wages paid on

Wednesday, Thursday or Friday must be deposited by the following Wednesday (which means you have to set the payment either by phone or on the Internet by Tuesday). Taxes on wages paid on Saturday, Sunday, Monday or Tuesday must be deposited by the following Friday (which means you have to set the payment by Thursday). If the due date for a semiweekly deposit falls on a holiday you have until the next business day to make your tax deposit. Whether you are a monthly or semiweekly depositor, if you have a tax liability of $100,000 or more for a particular pay date (even if it's the total of multiple payrolls – say a regular and a bonus payroll) you must make your deposit on the next business day - and if you were a monthly depositor, you automatically become a semi-weekly depositor for the remainder of the calendar year and for the following calendar year. **Note:** If your tax liability is less than $2,500 a quarter you can submit your tax payment with your Form 941 or Form 944 (if filed on time). Refer to IRS Publication 15 (Circular E) and Publication 966 (Electronic Federal Tax Payment System). **Note2:** If you you forget to schedule your tax payment until the day it's due, some banks can now make a same day payment – check with your bank beforehand to find out if that's a possibility and if so, what you would need to do to make a same-day payment.

Q: **How do I make payroll tax payments?**
A: Normally, all federal tax deposits have to be made electronically. Electronic fund transfers are usually made using the Electronic Federal Tax Payment System (EFTPS). If you're a new employer you need to enroll in the EFTPS, but the process of enrolling is fairly easy; go to www.eftps.gov and click on the button to open a new account. Enter your EIN (Employer Identification Number), the name of your business and your contact information. Then select your payment option – whether you want to have IRS debit your account directly (the "debit" or standard option) or if you want your financial institution to initiate the transfer (the "credit" option). If you want to use the credit option you will need to check with your financial institution to see if it offers this service (in most cases the debit option is the best choice). The next step is to set any payment limits you want (to avoid making a major overpayment by mistake) and then enter your bank account information. Once you've completed the setup process you should receive a packet from EFTPS within 15 days that will include your PIN (Personal Identification Number). At that point you can start making payments through EFTPS either by phone or over the internet.

Note: If your payroll taxes for the previous or current quarter are less than $2500 you can remit your federal withholding taxes with your quarterly federal tax return (Form 941) or your annual return (Form 944 for businesses that file annually) rather than make regular tax deposits, as long as your return is filed on time.

Q: **What payroll forms do I need to file and when do I send them?**
A: As an employer, there are a number of federal and state (and possibly city, county or other local) payroll reports that you are required to file. Federal forms include:

- Form 941 (Employer's Quarterly Federal Tax Return) – The 941 is basically a record of the employer's federal tax liability and tax deposits for a given quarter. It includes the gross taxable wages paid for the quarter, the employee and employer Social Security and Medicare tax amounts, and the federal income tax withheld during the quarter. For semiweekly depositors Form 941 must be accompanied by a Schedule B (Report of Tax Liability for Semiweekly Schedule Depositors), which lists the employer's tax liability by day for each day in the quarter. The due date for sending the 941 (and Schedule B) to IRS is the last day of the month following the end of the quarter (or the next business day if the last day of the month is on a weekend or holiday).
- Form 941-X (Supporting Statement to Correct Information) – Used to correct income and tax information previously reported on Forms 941, 943 or 945.
- Form 944 (Employer's Annual Federal Tax Return) – Form 944 includes the same information as the 941, but for the entire year. Businesses with $1,000 or less in taxes withheld for the year may use Form 944 instead of Form 941 – IRS will notify you if you are required to report payroll taxes annually on the 944 rather than quarterly with Form 941. Due date for filing the 944 is the end of January of the next year (or the next business day if January 31st falls on a weekend or holiday).
- Form 944-X (Adjusted Employer's Annual Federal Tax Return or Claim for Refund) – Used to correct income and tax information previously reported on Form 944.
- Form 943 (Employer's Annual Federal Tax Return for Agriculture Employees) – Form 943 is similar to the 941 but it's for employers who employ farm workers. Form 943 is filed annually for employers who have paid more than $2,500 in wages during the calendar year (for all employees).
- Form 945 (Annual Return of Withheld Federal Income Tax) – Used to report federal income tax withheld from non-payroll payments (including pensions, gambling winnings, and certain government payments). All federal income tax withholding reported on Forms 1099 or Form W-2G has to be reported on

Form 945 (do not use Form 945 to report federal income tax withholding from wages).

- Form 940 (Employer's Annual Federal Unemployment Tax Return) – Form 940 is a record of the FUTA taxable wages paid to all employees and the federal unemployment tax paid by the employer during the calendar year. Form 940 for a given year should be filed by the end of January of the following year.
- **Form W-2** – (Wage and Tax Statement) is an IRS tax form used to report wages paid to employees and the taxes withheld from them. The W-2 is used by employees to prepare their federal tax returns and to report FICA taxes to the Social Security Administration. Currently W-2 forms for a given year need to be provided to employees by January 31st of the following year. W-2 forms also need to be submitted to the Social Security Administration by January 31st of the following year, whether you submit paper forms or file electronically (if you have 250 or more W-2 forms you must file electronically).
- **Form W-2c** – (Corrected Wage and Tax Statement) is used to correct errors on W-2 forms previously filed with the Social Security Administration. W-2 corrections can be filed either on paper forms or online.
- Form 1099-MISC – You need to fill out a 1099-MISC form at the end of the year to send to any individual (non-employee) or company that you paid $600 or more to during the year in rents, royalties, commissions, fees, prizes and awards (you do not have to send a 1099-MISC to corporations – just individuals, independent contractors, partnerships, LLCs and other non-incorporated organizations). Enter rent payments in Box 1, royalties in Box 2, and other non-employee compensation in Box 7 and enter any federal or state income tax withheld in Box 4 and Box 16. Form 1099-MISC is a multi-part form with copies for the IRS, the payer, the recipient, and state or local tax departments. In addition, a Form 1096 (Annual Summary and Transmittal of U.S. Information Returns) must accompany copies of 1099-MISC forms that you mail to the IRS. 1099 forms can also be transmitted electronically using the FIRE system (http://fire.irs.gov). You can create a FIRE system account at: https://fire.test.irs.gov/Register.aspx. Recipients should have their copies by January 31st and the IRS copies are also due by January 31st of the next year.

Note: Employers are also required to report any federal tax withheld from non-payroll earnings (such as payments to independent contractors, pension payments, annuities, royalties and gambling winnings) on Form

945 which is filed annually. All federal income tax withholding (referred to as "backup withholding") that is included on Forms 1099 or W2-G must be reported on Form 945 which is due by the end of January for the preceding year (Note: if you made all deposits on time you may file by February 10th). The backup withholding rate is currently set at 24% of the amount paid. Do not report federal income tax (FIT) withheld on distributions to participants in non-qualified pension plans (such as 457(b) plans) – those amounts should be reported on the 941 or 944. Note: Payments to independent contractors are subject to mandatory "backup withholding" if the contractor has failed to provide a taxpayer identification number to the employer or has provided an incorrect taxpayer identification number.

Q: **What amounts are reported in Box 12 of Form W-2?**
A: Box 12 is used to report the following types of compensation and benefits:

- A – Uncollected Social Security or RRTA (RailRoad Tax Authority) tax on tips
- B – Uncollected Medicare tax on tips (but not Additional Medicare Tax)
- C – Taxable cost of group-term life insurance over $50,000 (included in the wages in boxes 1, 3 and 5)
- D – Elective deferrals to a section 401(k) cash or other deferred compensation plan (including a SIMPLE 401(k) arrangement)
- E – Elective deferrals under a section 403(b) salary reduction agreement
- F – Elective deferrals under a section 408(k)(6) salary reduction SEP
- G – Elective deferrals and employer contributions (including non-elective deferrals) to a section 457(b) deferred compensation plan
- H – Elective deferrals to a section 501(c)(18)(D) tax-exempt organization plan
- J – Nontaxable sick pay
- K – 20% excise tax on excess golden parachute payments
- L – Substantiated employee business expense reimbursements
- M – Uncollected Social Security or RRTA tax on taxable cost of group-term life insurance over $50,000 (former employees only)
- N – Uncollected Medicare tax on taxable cost of group-term life insurance over $50,000 (but not Additional Medicare Tax) (former employees only)
- P – Excludable moving expense reimbursements paid directly to employee

- Q – Nontaxable combat pay
- R – Employer contributions to an Archer MSA
- S – Employee salary reduction contributions under a section 408(p) SIMPLE plan
- T – Adoption benefits
- V – Income from exercise of non-statutory stock option(s)
- W – Employer contributions (including employee contributions through a cafeteria plan) to an employee's health savings account (HSA)
- Y – Deferrals under a section 409A non-qualified deferred compensation plan
- Z – Income under a non-qualified deferred compensation plan that fails to satisfy section 409A
- AA – Designated Roth contributions under a section 401(k) plan
- BB – Designated Roth contributions under a section 403(b) plan
- CC – HIRE exempt wages and tips (2010 only)
- DD – Cost of employer-sponsored health coverage
- EE – Designated Roth contributions under a governmental section 457(b) plan

Q: Can I file my Form 941, Form 944 and/or Form 940 online?
A: Yes, IRS provides an online filing option for Forms 941, 944 and 940. Business filers can apply to IRS for permission to transmit these forms electronically using a provider approved by IRS (that is, a third-party transmitter). Check the IRS website (www.irs.gov) for more information on how to file online and for a list of third-party providers.

Q: Can I file my W-2 forms electronically?
A: If you have 250 or more W-2 forms you must file electronically using the Social Security Administration's Business Services Online (BSO) web service (www.ssa.gov/employer). You also have the option to file electronically regardless of how many W-2s you have. To transmit your information online you must register with the Social Security Administration (for information on how to register with the SSA go to https://www.ssa.gov/employer/bsorahelp.htm. Once you've registered with SSA you can log in to the BSO system and send forms W-2 and W-2c (the form used to correct a previously submitted W-2) to SSA by uploading a specially formatted electronic file (or you can key the information directly into an online form).
For information on how to create a W-2 file to send to the SSA you can download Social Security Administration Publication No. 42-007 (Specifications for Filing Forms W-2 Electronically [EFW2]) at http://www.ssa.gov/employer/efw/10efw2.pdf. There are also

commercial programs available (such as W2 Mate, Tax Forms Helper, and others that allow you to key in or import W-2 (or 1099) information and create a file that can be transmitted to the Social Security Administration.

Note: All W-2, W-2c and W-3 forms are submitted to the Social Security Administration. Do not send W-2 information to the IRS. SSA forwards the information to the Internal Revenue Service.

Q: **Can I file my 1099 forms electronically?**
A: If you have 250 or more 1099 returns you must file your returns electronically, but the IRS encourages everyone to submit their 1099 data using its online service called the FIRE (Filing Information Returns Electronically) system (http://fire.irs.gov). Your 1099 information must be in a specially formatted file (see IRS Publication 1220) and you must have a Transmitter Control Code (TCC). To obtain a Transmitter Control Code go to http://www.irs.gov/pub/irs-pdf/f4419.pdf, fill in and submit Form 4419 to the IRS -- once your application is approved the TCC will be forwarded to you (be sure to submit Form 4419 at least 30 days before the due date of your 1099 returns).

Q: **What type of payroll reports do I need my payroll system to produce each pay period?**
A: Your payroll should provide at least the following types of reports:
- Payroll Register – Lists all employees who were paid, showing their gross pay, taxes withheld, voluntary or other deductions and net pay. If an employee is contributing to a retirement fund and the employer provides a matching contribution, the employer match amount should also be shown. In addition the payroll register often includes month-to-date and year-to-date amounts for each employee along with totals by department and overall totals for all employees.
- Payroll Tax Register – Shows all taxes withheld along with employer matching amounts for Social Security and Medicare taxes and the employer's total federal tax deposit for the period.
- Checks and/or Deposit Slips – Employees who are paid by check should receive a pay check which includes a stub showing gross earnings, deductions and net pay. Employees who are paid through direct deposit should receive a "deposit advice" of some type which shows the same information as on a payroll check stub.
- Payroll Ledger – A payroll ledger of some type should be kept for each employee and updated each payroll. The ledger should show each employee's accumulated earnings, taxes,

deductions and net pay.

- Additional reports may include a voluntary deduction register, department summary report, 401(k) listing, cafeteria plan report, vacation/sick leave/PTO leave reports and a bank reconciliation report.

Q: **What reports or forms do I need to produce at year-end?**
A: Each employee should receive a Form W-2 (Wage and Tax Statement) by the end of January for the previous year, showing taxable wages and income tax, Social Security, and Medicare taxes withheld for the year. In addition if you paid an individual (non-employee) or company $600 or more for services rendered during the year, you need to send that person or company a 1099-MISC form showing the total amount paid and any taxes withheld (Note: you do not need to send a 1099-MISC to corporations). You will also need to submit your W-2 information to the Social Security Administration and any 1099 data to the IRS. Currently, as part of the Affordable Care Act, you also need to produce 1095-C forms for all full-time employees (and copies for the IRS) if you employ 50 or more full-time (and full-time equivalent) employees.

Q: **Do I have to have Workers' Compensation Insurance?**
A: All businesses with employees are required to carry Workers' Compensation Insurance coverage either through a commercial carrier, on a self-insured basis, or through their state's Workers' Compensation Insurance program. The only exception is Texas; business owners in Texas are not required by law to carry workers' compensation insurance, although most employers do so. For further information on your state's insurance program check on the state agency links at:
www.nolo.com/legal-encyclopedia/workers-compensation-basics-employers-30333.html

Q: **What are Workers' Compensation insurance premiums based on?**
A: The premiums are based on your business classification, your employees' occupational classification codes and the total net amount of overtime premiums paid.

Q: **Are Workers' Compensation benefits taxable?**
A: No. Workers' Compensation benefits are not federal or state taxable and are not included on the W-2.

Q: **Is all Workers' Compensation insurance handled through state administered funds?**
A: No. Arizona, California, Colorado, Idaho, Maryland, Michigan,

Montana, New York, Oklahoma, Oregon, Pennsylvania and Utah allow employers to choose between the state administered fund and private insurers.

Q: **How do I record payroll information in the general ledger?**
A: Entries to the general ledger from payroll can become fairly complex, especially if you are allocating wages, taxes and other deductions between different cost centers in your company. The most basic case though would involve two entries. The first journal entry would debit a salaries and wages account for the total earnings paid and credit the appropriate accounts for deductions such as Social Security tax payable, Medicare tax payable, federal income tax payable, state income tax payable, United Way, Uniforms, and so on. This first entry would also include a credit to an account such as Cash in Bank or Accrued Payroll for the net amount of the payroll. A second journal entry would debit an account like "Payroll Tax Expense" and credit the appropriate accounts for the employer matching share of Social Security and Medicare taxes and the employer's state and federal unemployment taxes. When the withheld taxes or other payables (such as 401(k) amounts) are remitted another journal entry would be made debiting the taxes or other amounts payable and crediting an account such as "cash in bank".

Employees

Q: **Should I have an employee job application form?**
A: Every business should have an application form of some type. It can provide a complete record about an applicant's background including: name, address, phone number, social security number, educational background, previous employment and experience, references and special skills or qualifications.

Q: **What payroll information do I need from my employees?**
A: You need to have each of your employees fill out a Form W-4 (Employee's Withholding Allowance Certificate) so you can withhold the correct federal income tax. By filling out Form W-4 the employee provides the information you need in order to withhold the proper amount of federal income tax from the employee's paycheck. In addition, every new employee has to fill out a Form I-9 (https://www.uscis.gov/system/files_force/files/form/i-9-paper-version.pdf) before starting work and must produce documents verifying his or her identity and work eligibility (such as a valid driver's license, social security card, voter registration card or birth certificate). You can find additional information about Form I-9 in Appendix I. Other information you may need from your employees includes state withholding tax forms, bank account information (if the employee is going to be paid by direct deposit), and deduction/benefit enrollment forms.

Q: **What do I need to know about the new 2020 W-4 form?**
A: Beginning January 1, 2020 all new employees (and existing employees wanting to make changes to their federal withholding) will have to fill out the new W-4 form. Employers can request all employees to fill out the new form, but they can't make it mandatory. Actual changes to the W-4 include removal of the line for entering allowances (due to the elimination of personal and dependent exemptions under the Tax Cut and Jobs Act of 2017). The new version includes five sections or "steps":

- Section 1 – The employee's personal information – name, address, social security number, and marital status. This year there are 3 options for marital status: single or married filing separately, married filing jointly, or head of household (only if you're unmarried and pay more than half the cost of keeping up a household for yourself and a qualifying individual).
- Section 2 (optional) – This section has been added to try to help individuals working more than one job or couples where both work to come closer to the actual amount of income tax that needs to be withheld. If you fall into either category you can

follow the instructions to come up with an "adjustment" amount to your withholding that you can enter in Section 4.

- Section 3 (optional) – You can calculate another adjustment amount here based on the number of dependents you're claiming.
- Section 4 (optional) – Enter any adjustment amount from section 2 along with any additional amount if you plan on taking deductions on your tax return other than the standard deduction, and any extra tax you want to have withheld.
- Section 5 – Sign and date.

Because you may have some employees whose withholding information is on one form and some whose information is on the other form, the IRS has redesigned the federal withholding tax tables as well, to provide one set of tables with a section for those using the old W-4 and another section for those who have filed one of the new W-4s.

Note: You can the FAQ page concerning the new W-4 at: https://www.irs.gov/newsroom/faqs-on-the-draft-2020-form-w-4

Q: **What is E-Verify?**
A: E-Verify is an Internet-based system run by the Department of Homeland Security that allows employers to determine the eligibility of employees to work in the United States. E-Verify matches information from the person's Employment Eligibility Verification Form I-9 against U.S. Government records – if the information matches the person is eligible to work in the United States. If you have an employee who has applied for a Social Security number but hasn't received it, he or she may work while waiting for a number to be issued. The employer should complete a Form I-9, but wait to use E-Verify until the employee receives his or her SSN. You can register to use E-Verify at:
   https://www.e-verify.gov/

Q; **What is "New Hire reporting"?**
A: The Personal Responsibility and Work Opportunity Reconciliation Act of 1996 requires all employers to report newly hired or re-hired employees to the appropriate state agency within 20 days of the person's hire date (you can find links to state agencies that handle new hire reporting and information as to reporting requirements for each state at: https://www.acf.hhs.gov/css/resource/state-new-hire-reporting-websites).

Q: **Who is an Employee?**
A: Anyone who performs services for you is your employee if you can control both what will be done and how it will be done.

Q: **If I'm an owner can I also be an employee?**
A: If you're a sole proprietor or a member of a partnership you can't be an employee – you're considered to be self-employed and you have to pay self-employment taxes. If you're a member of an LLC (Limited Liability Corporation), the same thing applies – unless the LLC chooses to be treated as a corporation. Members of an LLC that elects to be treated as a corporation for tax purposes can classify themselves as employees. Similarly, owners in a sub-chapter S corporation who work for the company can be employees and so can owners in a "C-Corp" (a corporation that's taxed separately from its owners) who work for the corporation.

Q: **Who is an Independent Contractor?**
A: Basically, anyone who does work for you but isn't an employee. Employers can tell an independent contractor what to do and when the work should be completed, but not how to go about doing the job or what hours the contractor has to work.

Q: **What are "Statutory employees"?**
A: Statutory employees are somewhere between independent contractors and regular employees. They are workers in certain occupations who wouldn't usually be considered employees, but who have been declared employees under the federal tax laws so that their employer normally has to withhold FICA taxes (Social Security and Medicare tax) from their wages. Employers should not withhold federal income tax from statutory employees unless the employee is subject to backup withholding. Workers that may qualify as statutory employees include: full-time life insurance agents working primarily for a single company, certain types of salespeople, home workers and truck drivers. Statutory employees receive a W-2 form at the end of the year just like any other employee. You can find more information on statutory employees at:
https://www.irs.gov/Businesses/Small-Businesses-&-Self-Employed/Statutory-Employees

Q: **Who are "statutory non-employees"?**
A: Direct sellers, certain companion sitters and qualified real estate agents are considered non-employees and are usually treated as self-employed for federal tax purposes. Because they are considered non-employees no federal income tax, Social Security tax, Medicare tax or FUTA tax is withheld or reported.

Q: **What constitutes an "Independent contractor"?**

A: The general rule for defining someone doing work for you as an independent contractor (as opposed to a regular employee) is that you, the employer, have the right to control only the result of the work done by that person, not the means or method of accomplishing the work. If you can't decide whether a person or persons working for you should be classified as an employee or independent contractor, you can file Form SS-8, Determination of Worker Status for Purposes of Federal Employment Taxes and Income Tax Withholding with the IRS. They will review the information on the form and determine the worker's status. The drawback is that it can take at least six months to get a decision, but if you have a number of people whose status is in question it may be a good idea to go ahead and file an SS-8. Misclassification of an employee as an independent contractor can result in major penalties such as federal tax assessed at 1.5% of the wages that have been paid to the individual, 100% of the employer share of Social Security and Medicare taxes, plus 20% of the employee share of Social Security and Medicare taxes. Note: Certain workers are automatically considered employees, such as officers of corporations who provide services to the corporation, food and laundry drivers, full-time salespeople who sell goods for resale, full-time life insurance agents working for one company, and at-home workers who are supplied with material and given specifications for work to be performed.

Q: **Who is a "Common-Law employee"?**
A: Under common-law rules, anybody who performs services for you is your employee if you control both what will be done and how it will be done. Even if you let the employee accomplish the work in his own way, as long as you have the right to control the way the work is done that person is an employee and not an independent contractor.

Q: **What is the "Common Law Test"?**
A: The IRS uses a 20 question test to assess how much control an employer has over a worker in order to determine if that person is an employee or an independent contractor ("Yes" answers tend to indicate an employer-employee relationship):
1) Is the worker required to follow the employer's instructions in completing the job or accomplishing a task?
2) Does the employer provide the training necessary for completion of the job?
3) Are the worker's specific personal services required for successful completion of the job?
4) Are the worker's services crucial to the success or continued existence of the company?
5) Does the employer set work hours?

6) Does the worker have a continuing relationship with the company?
7) Does the employer hire, supervise or pay any of the worker's assistants?
8) Is the worker precluded from seeking assignments with other companies or from refusing assignments offered by the employer?
9) Does the employer specify the location where the work must be performed?
10) Does the employer direct the order or sequence of tasks to be performed?
11) Does the employer require regular progress reports?
12) Is the worker paid by the hour, week or month, rather than for completion (or stage of completion) of the project?
13) Does the worker work only for the employer?
14) Does the employer pay business overhead and incidental expenses?
15) Does the employer provide equipment, tools and materials?
16) Is the work performed on the employer's premises or using the employer's facilities?
17) Are the worker's services not available to the general public?
18) Does the employer provide a minimum "salary" and therefore shield the worker from the risk of profit or loss on the job.
19) Does the employer have the right to terminate the worker even if the job results are achieved?
20) Is the employer required to pay the worker for time spent even if the job is not completed?

Q: What is a W-2 contractor?
A: The term is sometimes used to refer to individuals who are employed by a temporary employment agency. Since they are paid by the temp agency but actually work for different companies as temporary help, they are basically contractors as far as the company they're working for is concerned, even though they receive a W-2 from the temp agency.

Q: What is IRS Section 530?
A: Section 530 specifies certain cases where an employee may be considered an independent contractor. Under Section 530, an individual will not be considered an employee if the employer treated him or her (and other workers performing similar tasks) as non-employees for all periods, had a reasonable basis for doing so, and filed the required information and other returns (such as Form 1099-MISC) on a consistent basis. Employees specifically excluded from 530 protection include technical service specialists such as engineers and computer

programmers.

Q: **Are sole proprietors and partners in a partnership employees?**
A: Sole proprietors and partners in a business are neither employees or independent contractors – they pay their own income tax and Social Security/Medicare self-employment tax. However shareholders in an incorporated business are legally an employee of the corporation in most cases (Officers/Shareholders in a corporation who don't perform any services – or only minor services – and are not entitled to compensation are not considered employees).

Q: **What's the difference between "exempt employees" and "non-exempt employees"?**
A: Under the FLSA (Fair Labor Standards Act) employees have to be paid at least the minimum hourly wage and must be paid overtime for hours worked over 40 hours a week. However the law provides for an exemption from these rules for employees working in an executive, administrative or professional capacity, outside salespeople, and certain employees in computer related positions. To be classified as "exempt" an employee has to fit into one of the classes listed above and has to be paid on a salary basis (meaning the employee has to receive the full salary each week regardless of the number of hours worked). Also, to qualify for the exemption an employee must be paid at least $455 per week (or $684 per week starting January 1, 2020). For further information check the Department of Labor web site at http://www.dol.gov.

Q: **What are the laws governing hiring of teenagers?**
A: There are both federal and state "child labor" laws. There are only a few jobs that youngsters under the age of 14 can be hired to do (such as newspaper carrier). For teenagers 14 or over but under age 18 there are certain occupations that are prohibited (such as meat cutter, jobs requiring the use of heavy machinery, hazardous material handling, etc.) and there are usually restrictions on working hours. In every case, an employer should make sure to have some proof of age for workers under 18 and the permission of a parent or guardian. Because of the number and complexity of many state child labor laws, you should also check with the Department of Labor in your particular state before hiring teenage employees.

Q: **What do I do in the case of an employee's death?**
A: If you're ever faced with the death of an employee, any unpaid wages (salary, vacation pay, sick leave, etc.) should be paid to the employee's beneficiary or to his or her estate. You will also need to send a Form

41

1099-Misc to the estate or beneficiary and report that final payment in box 3 ("Other income"). In addition, if the accrued wages are paid in the same year as the employee's death, the employer must withhold FICA (Social Security and Medicare) tax from those wages and include them on the deceased employee's W-2 as FICA taxable earnings. However, if the payment is made in a year following the employee's death, then no FICA withholding is required and the earnings do not have to be reported as FICA taxable. In either case the wages paid to a deceased employee are exempt from federal income tax withholding (and they are usually exempt from state withholding as well). Note: If the wages are paid in the same year as the employee's death they are normally subject to both FUTA and SUTA tax.

In the case where a paycheck has already been issued to the employee but the employee dies before cashing it, the check has to be reissued for the net amount, payable to the employee's beneficiary or a personal representative. The employer should make sure that the person receiving the check signs a statement that the money is being paid for a deceased employee's uncashed paycheck. The necessary taxes have already been withheld (on the original paycheck) so the wages and taxes will automatically be included in the employee's W-2 at the end of the year.

Example: John Doe, who worked for ABC Company passed away on August 14th. The company owed him a total of $1,980 in accumulated pay and vacation pay. A check was issued to his wife the next week for $1,828.53 ($1,980 less $122.76 in Social Security tax and $28.71 in Medicare tax) and a 1099-MISC form was also issued to his wife at the end of the year with $1,980 reported in Box 3 (Other Income) along with John's W-2.

Q: **Is there a way to verify an employee's social security number?**
A: Yes, you can go to http://www.ssa.gov/employer/ssnv.htm and check for valid social security numbers. You do have to register however in order to make use of Business Services Online.

42

Foreign Employees

Q: **Do I need to withhold any taxes on foreign employees working in their home country?**

A: If you have residents of a foreign country performing services for you in their own country, there is no U.S. withholding. There are no documents specifically required where payments are to foreigners outside this country -- however, it's a good idea to carefully document everything in situations like this in case the IRS has questions at some point.

Q: **What is a "resident alien"?**

A: You're a resident alien of the United States for tax purposes if you meet either the green card test or the substantial presence test for the calendar year.

Q: **What about foreign employees working in this country?**

A: The IRS has two separate tax systems: the resident alien tax system and the nonresident alien tax system. Resident aliens pay taxes on their worldwide income just the same as any U.S. citizen; non-resident aliens pay taxes only on their U.S.-source income. All foreign employees must complete Form UC W-8BEN (Certificate of Foreign Status for Federal Tax Withholding) -- this form is used to determine whether someone is a resident or nonresident alien for tax purposes. Resident aliens are subject to Social Security and Medicare tax and so are non-resident aliens (unless they hold an F-1 or J-1 visa). As for federal and state income tax withholding, aliens are subject to the same state withholding laws as U.S. citizens. Federal withholding is more complicated -- for example non-resident aliens from countries which have a tax treaty agreement with the United States may be able to exempt part or all of their income from federal withholding.

Q: **What about resident aliens working in foreign countries?**

A: Resident aliens are subject to U.S. taxes even if they're working in a foreign country. The rules for filing tax returns and paying estimated tax are generally the same whether you are in the United States or abroad.

Q: **Are foreign employees eligible for unemployment benefits?**

A: In general, foreign employees are not eligible for unemployment benefits (or for Medicare coverage).

Wages / Taxable Wages

Q: **What are gross wages?**
A: Gross pay is total wages before any deductions (taxes or other deductions). If you pay an employee 12 dollars per hour for 40 hours of work, the employee's gross pay is $480.

Q: **What types of compensation are considered taxable wages?**
A: Taxable wages include most types of compensation, such as wages and salaries, tips, vacation pay, bonuses, commissions, cash awards, and gift certificates. Meals and lodging furnished for the employee's convenience are also considered to be taxable. You can
refer to IRS Publication 525 (Taxable and Nontaxable Income) for more detailed information on what IRS classifies as taxable compensation. Also, IRS Publication 15-A contains additional information on wages and Publication 15-B provides information on many other forms of compensation including:
- Accident and health benefits
- Health Savings Accounts
- Group term life insurance coverage
- Lodging and meals
- De minimus (minimal) benefits
- Dependent care assistance
- Educational assistance
- Employee discounts
- Employee stock options

Q: **How do I calculate an employee's wages?**
A: Salaried employees are normally paid a fixed amount each pay period (usually their annual salary divided by the number of pay periods per year). To figure an hourly employee's pay, you multiply the individual's hourly rate of pay times the number of hours worked in the pay period. If an employee worked over 40 hours in a given one week period, you would pay him for 40 hours times his normal rate of pay plus the number of hours worked over 40 times his rate of pay times an overtime factor (usually 1.5). Employees may also be paid on a piece rate or on a commission basis.

Q: **Do I have to keep track of salaried employees' time?**
A: It's a good idea to keep a record of some type but it's up to the employer to decide whether to require salaried employees who are classified as exempt from overtime to track their hours worked. A record

of actual hours worked does need to be kept for non-exempt employees who are paid on a salaried basis since they are entitled to overtime pay for hours worked over 40 in a given workweek. Note: As of January 1, 2020, salaried employees who are paid less than $684 are considered non-exempt and are eligible for overtime pay).

Q: **How do I keep track of hourly employees' time?**
A: It can be as simple as having them fill out a time sheet each day or as sophisticated as a biometric time clock system or a web-based time accounting system. The important thing is to have as accurate a system as possible with as little hassle for your employees as possible.

Q: **What do I need to know about the minimum wage?**

A: The Fair Labor Standards Act contains mandatory standards for federal minimum wage rates. Non-exempt employees paid on an hourly basis must receive at least the federal minimum wage for each hour worked. For employees paid on some basis other than hourly (piece-rate, commission, etc.), their pay must be at least equivalent to the number of hours worked times the federal minimum wage. Many states, cities and counties also have minimum wage laws; in those states, cities and counties that do have a minimum wage law, the employee is entitled to whichever rate is higher. Every employer with employees subject to the Fair Labor Standards Act is required to post a notice explaining the Act in a conspicuous place so workers can read it. Note: The federal minimum wage for non-exempt employees was raised in May of 2007 increasing it from $5.15 per hour to:

    $5.85 per hour, effective July 24th 2007
    $6.55 per hour, effective July 24th 2008
    $7.25 per hour, effective July 24th 2009

NOTE: States with minimum wage levels greater than federal minimum in 2020:

- Alaska - $10.19 per hour
- Arkansas - $10.00
- Arizona - $12.00 per hour
- California - $13.00 per hour
  (some counties may have higher minimum wage amounts)
- Colorado - $12.00 per hour
- Connecticut - $11.00 per hour ($12.00 as of September 2020)
- Delaware - $9.25 per hour
- District of Columbia - $14.00 per hour ($15 per hour as of July 2020)

- Florida - $8.56 per hour
- Hawaii - $10.10 per hour
- Illinois - $9.25 per hour
- Maine - $12.00 per hour
- Maryland - $11.00 per hour
- Massachusetts - $12.75 per hour
- Michigan - $9.65 per hour
- Minnesota – $10.00 per hour ($8.15 per hour for employers with less than $500,000 in sales per year)
- Missouri - $9.45 per hour (Higher rates may apply in Kansas City and St. Louis)
- Montana - $8.65 per hour (if sales of $110,000 per year or more)
- Nebraska - $9.00 per hour
- Nevada - $8.25 per hour ($9.00 per hour as of July 2020)
- New Jersey - $11.00 per hour
- New York - $11.80 per hour (Higher rates may apply in New York City)
- New Mexico - $9.00 per hour
- Ohio - $8.70 per hour
- Oregon - $11.25 per hour ($12.00 per hour as of July 2020)
- Rhode Island - $10.50 per hour
- South Dakota - $9.30 per hour
- Vermont - $10.96 per hour
- Washington - $13.50 per hour
- West Virginia - $8.75 per hour

Q: **Is there a different minimum wage for young people?**
A: Workers under 20 years old can be paid at a rate below the federal minimum wage for the first 90 days of employment (but not less than $4.25 per hour).

Q: **If a salaried employee only works part of a day can I pay him just part of his daily salary?**
A: No, if a salaried employee works any part of a work day you have to pay him or her for a full day's work. However, if a salaried employee doesn't perform any work in a given week you don't have to pay him or her for that week.

Q: **Do I have to pay a salaried employee for vacation or sick days?**
A: Salaried employees are often entitled to a certain number of vacation and sick days each year. If one of your salaried people calls in sick or takes vacation days, he is paid for the full day or days if he has the leave time available; if he doesn't have any leave time hours left you do not

have to pay him for that time off.

Q: **Do I have to pay hourly employees for time off on holidays?**
A: No, you are not required to pay hourly employees for time off on a holiday.

Q: **Do I have to count paid time off as hours worked in determining overtime pay?**
A: No. An employee has to actually work over 40 hours in a week to qualify for overtime pay. Paid time off (vacation, sick leave, holidays, etc.) is not considered time worked (unless there is a collective bargaining agreement in place that states otherwise).

Q: **If an employee takes work home and does it there after normal working hours do I have to pay the employee for that time?**
A: In general, yes you do. Any time spent by an employee doing productive work for the employer is considered as "hours worked" under FLSA rules.

Q: **If employees are allowed to take two coffee breaks during the day does that time automatically count as hours worked?**
A: If a rest period or coffee break lasts 20 minutes or less that time should be counted as hours worked.

Q: **How can I calculate an hourly rate for a salaried employee?**
A: Divide the employee's annual salary by 2080 (52 weeks times 40 hours per week, the standard number of work hours per year).

Q: **Do I have to pay minimum wage to my employees who receive tips?**
A: Not necessarily. An employer can pay less than the federal minimum wage (or state minimum wage if higher than federal) if the employee's tip income plus his or her direct wages at least equal the minimum wage hourly rate times the hours worked.

Q: **Do I have to pay minimum wage to full-time students?**
A: Retail or service businesses and farms can hire full-time students (who are of working age) and pay them at 85% of minimum wage (subject to state laws).

Q: **My teenage son works for me – do I have to withhold taxes from his paycheck?**
A: If you have a son or daughter under 18 working for you, his or her wages are not subject to Social Security and Medicare taxes as long as

your business is a sole proprietorship or a partnership where each partner is one of the child's parents. Also, the child's earnings are not subject to federal unemployment tax until he or she turns 21. However, payments for the services of a child of any age who works in a parent's business are usually subject to income tax withholding.

Q: My husband is one of my employees – is his pay subject to withholding?
A: A person employed by his or her spouse in a sole proprietorship is subject to income tax withholding and Social Security and Medicare taxes, but not FUTA (federal unemployment) tax.

Q: Do I need to take out withholding tax on an employee advance?
A: No, just pay the employee the flat amount of the advance – but be sure to deduct that same amount from his or her next paycheck.

Q: What are "supplemental wages"?
A: Payments such as commissions or bonuses are considered by the IRS to be "supplemental" wages -- that is, money separate from an employee's regular income such as bonuses, commissions, severance pay, sick pay, retroactive pay increases and so forth. If you pay supplemental wages separately from an employee's regular wages the IRS requires that you withhold a flat 22% for federal withholding tax or use a formula to determine the withholding tax (see IRS Publication 15 for details). If you combine the supplemental and regular wages as a lump sum, then you withhold tax as if the total amount was a single payment for a regular pay period (note that this generally results in regular wages being more highly taxed than normal). For more information on types of supplemental pay and how to handle it, look at the appropriate section of your Circular E (IRS Pub 15).

Q: Are gifts to employees considered as part of their wages?
A: Yes, cash or cash equivalents such as watches, trips to Las Vegas, or a few shares of company stock are almost always considered taxable income, regardless of the amount. The only exception might be something like a company-wide drawing for a certain item, where the item is of relatively small value (in other words, not something like a new car).

Q: Are employee dependent care benefits considered wages?
A: Dependent care services you directly or indirectly pay for (or provide to an employee under a dependent care assistance program) to allow the employee to work may qualify as an excludable benefit. Generally, dependent care assistance up to a certain amount (currently $5,000 for

married couples or $2500 for married employees filing separate returns) is not taxable. At year end the total amount of dependent care benefits provided to an employee should be reported in box 10 of the employee's Form W-2 and any excess amount over the $5,000 or $2500 limit should be included in box 1, 3 and 5. For more information see IRS Publication 503 (Qualifying Person Test and Work-Related Expense Test).

Q: What is a "tipped" employee?
A: According to the Department of Labor, a tipped employee is one who "customarily and regularly" receives more than $30 in tips each month.

Q: How do I handle tips?
A: Tips are defined as payments made by customers of their own free will and in whatever amount they wish. If a restaurant includes a mandatory "gratuity" with each check, that gratuity is not considered a "tip" and is simply treated as normal taxable wages when it's distributed to the employee. Cash tips however, if voluntarily given, are not taxable wages for an employee if they run less than $20 in a month and are reported to the employer by the 10th of the following month (using Form 4070 and Form 4070A). Once the $20 limit is exceeded though, all cash tips for that employee (including the initial $20) become taxable income and should be reported to the employer on whatever form the employer provides (which can be paper or electronic) or on Form 4070 (Employee's Report of Tips to Employer) and Form 4070A (Employee's Daily Record of Tips). The employer is required to collect Social Security, Medicare and income tax withholding on taxable tips the same as on regular wages, and to pay the employer's share of the Social Security and Medicare taxes on the tips, along with with the appropriate FUTA tax.

Q: What is the minimum pay rate for a tipped employee?
A: You are only required to pay $2.13 an hour to tipped employees (employees who earn at least $30 a month in tips) if that amount plus the person's tip income at least equals the federal minimum wage (or state minimum wage if greater than federal). The difference between $2.13 an hour (or whatever hourly wage the tipped employee is paid) and the federal minimum wage hourly rate is generally referred to as a "tip credit".

Q: What if the taxes on an employee's tips are more than that person's wages?
A: Your obligation to withhold the employee's FICA and income taxes is limited to what can be withheld from the person's non-tip wages. If the non-tip wages aren't sufficient to cover all taxes, withhold taxes in the

following order: 1) Withholding taxes on regular wages, 2) Social Security and Medicare taxes on tips, 3) income tax on tips. If you still don't have enough money to cover the employee's FICA taxes, your responsibility to withhold the uncollected portion ends at that point (income tax shortages should be tracked and added to the income tax withholding on the next payroll though).

Q: **What if an employee doesn't report tips given directly to him or her?**
A: If the IRS determines that an employee has failed to report cash tips of over $20 a month to you, you can be held liable for the employer's share of FICA (Social Security and Medicare taxes) and the employee may be penalized the other 50 percent of the FICA tax due on the tips.

Q: **What are allocated tips?**
A: In general, food or beverage establishments that have ten or more tipped employees at work on a typical business day must allocate tip income to employees if the total amount of tips reported by all employees is less than a certain minimum percent (usually eight percent) of total sales. The amount of allocated tips is the difference between the minimum percent of total sales and the actual total of tips reported. The employer does not have to withhold any Social Security, Medicare or income tax on allocated tips, but he must file Form 8027 (Employer's Annual Information Return of Tips Income and Allocated Tips) each year and he must show the amount of allocated tips in box 8 (but not Box 1) of the W-2 for each employee who received allocated tips. Allocated tips can be split or "allocated" among tipped employees on the basis of hours worked, on the basis of each employee's actual gross receipts, or according to a "good faith" agreement between the restaurant and at least two thirds of its tipped employees. Once again, for further information refer to IRS Publication 15 (Circular E), the Employer's Tax Guide.

Q: **Are gratuities and auto-gratuities the same thing as tips?**
A: Although the word gratuity is often used as a synonym for tip, they are not really the same thing. Tips are discretionary amounts decided by the customer. Gratuities are fixed amounts (usually set by the employer) that the customer pays as part of his or her bill and a portion of which may or may not be given to the employees. The IRS has specified that in the case of actual gratuities, those amounts are to be treated as income to the employer and if some portion of the gratuities is distributed to employees, the gratuity amounts are to be included on the employees' paychecks as wages. In addition, since gratuities aren't the same as tips employers can't take a "tip credit" on those amounts even if the gratuities

are distributed to the employees. Common examples of auto-gratuities include:
- Per person cover charges at clubs and restaurants
- Room service surcharges at hotels
- Large party surcharges at restaurants

Q: **What is a "fringe benefit"?**
A: A fringe benefit is a form of pay (including services, property, cash or cash equivalent) in addition to normal pay. Fringe benefits include items such as meals, lodging and reimbursement of moving expenses. Non-monetary fringe benefits that are taxable are valued at their FMV (Fair Market Value); that is, the amount a buyer would be willing to pay for that item or service.

Q: **What fringe benefits are excludable from taxable wages?**
A: There are numerous items that may fall into this category such as employee educational assistance, moving expense reimbursements, and health savings plans. Rather than go over all of them individually you should send for (or download from www.irs.gov) a copy of IRS Publication 15-B, which covers each of these situations in detail.

Q: **Are health benefits excludable from an employee's taxable wages?**
A: Accident and health benefits are normally exempt from income tax withholding (except for long term benefits) and from Social Security and Medicare (except for S corporation employees who are at least 2% shareholders). These types of benefits are also exempt from federal unemployment taxes.

Q: **Is employee group term life insurance coverage taxable?**
A: Employee group term life insurance is exempt from federal income tax withholding and from federal unemployment taxes. It is also exempt from Social Security and Medicare withholding up to $50,000 of coverage - for coverage over $50,000 you have to calculate the cost of the additional coverage (see IRS Publication 15-B for details) and report that amount on the W-2 as wages in boxes 1, 3 and 5, and in box 12 with code "C". To calculate the taxable value of the amount of life insurance over $50,000:
1) Round the amount of life insurance to the nearest $100.
2) Subtract $50,000 from the total amount of coverage.
3) Multiply the number of thousands of dollars of insurance coverage remaining by the cost shown in the table below.
4) Calculate the insurance cost for each month during the year.
5) Multiply the monthly amount by 12 to get the annual cost.

6) Subtract any amounts paid by the employee.
7) Include the total amount on the employee's W-2 form.

Table:

Employee Age	Insurance Cost
Under 25	$0.05
25 through 29	$0.06
30 through 34	$0.08
35 through 39	$0.09
40 through 44	$0.10
45 through 49	$0.15
50 through 54	$0.23
55 through 59	$0.43
60 through 64	$0.66
65 through 69	$1.27
70 and over	$2.06

Q: **Does the actual cost of group term life insurance coverage matter when determining if the under $50,000 tax exclusion applies?**
A: No, the amount of the death benefit determines whether the $50,000 exclusion applies. If the total value of the death benefit for all employer-provided life insurance during a specific period of coverage (usually one month) exceeds $50,000 then the excess is taxable.

Q: **Are meals that are provided for employees taxable?**
A: No, if the meals are furnished on your business premises for your convenience then they are not taxable.

Q: **Is dependent care assistance taxable?**
A: As mentioned earlier, dependent care assistance is exempt from federal taxes up to certain limits. The services must be for a qualifying person's care and must be provided in order to allow the employee to work. Under those conditions, an employee can generally exclude up to $5,000 of benefits from gross income ($2,500 for married employees filing separate returns).

Q: **What's involved in providing educational assistance to an employee?**
A: Section 127 of the Internal Revenue Code allows employers to provide up to $5,250 per year of educational assistance (tuition, fees, books, supplies, etc.) to an employee, with that money being excluded from the employee's taxable income. Section 127 also applies to employer-provided job and non-job related courses of instruction. Employers who provide educational assistance to their employees can

deduct those costs as a business expense if the employer has a written qualified assistance program that is offered on a nondiscriminatory basis and meets all IRS requirements (see Section 127 of the IRC for details).

Q: **Are employee expense reimbursements subject to income tax withholding?**
A: Not if the reimbursement amounts are paid under an accountable plan. An "accountable" plan requires that the employee's expenses be business related, that they be accounted for within a reasonable time period (generally 60 days), and that the employee returns any money over and above the amounts on the expense report that are approved by the company.

Q: **Are employer reimbursed moving expenses taxable to the employee and deductible for the employer?**
A: Employers who pay moving expenses for an employee can pay for whatever expenses they choose to, but only those expenses that qualify as deductible can be excluded from the employee's income. All other expenses paid for by the employer are subject to withholding for federal income, social security, and medicare taxes. The employer is also responsible for FUTA taxes on those payments and, in most states, for state withholding tax. Moving expenses incurred within one year of when the employee started working for the company may be qualified expenses; however the move must have been required by the new job and the expenses must meet two other tests:
- Distance test – The new place of work must be at least 50 miles further from the employee's old residence than his old place of work was from his old residence (i.e. if his old place of work was 15 miles from his old home, his new place of work must be at least 65 miles (15 + 50) from his old residence.
- Time test – The employee must work full-time for at least 39 weeks during the first 12 months after arriving in the general location of his new job. However, the 39 weeks doesn't have to be all with your company and does not have to be all in a row.

The following expenses qualify as deductible moving expenses if the employee meets the tests above:
- Moving the employee's household goods and personal effects.
- Travel expenses for the employee and his/her family from the employee's old home to his or her new home, The expenses can include lodging but not meals. (Note: house-hunting trips do not qualify as deductible expenses).

For further information refer to IRS Publication 521.

Overtime

Q: **What is overtime?**
A: Overtime is simply the amount of time someone works over and beyond normal working hours. So what does that mean to an employer? In the U.S. the Fair Labor Standards Act of 1938 applies to all employees involved in or producing goods for interstate commerce. The FLSA dictates a standard work week of 40 hours for certain types of workers and calls for payment of hours over 40 at a rate of at least 1 and 1/2 times the worker's normal pay rate. FLSA rules do not mandate overtime pay for night work or work on weekends and holidays (although the 40 hours per week rule still applies). In addition, some types of workers (such as independent contractors, agricultural employees, outside salesmen, executives, truck drivers, railroad workers, administrative and professional people) are "exempt" from FLSA standards. Currently, somewhere around 40% of U.S. employees are considered "exempt".

Q: **Who is eligible for overtime pay?**
A: Generally, employees of organizations that have an annual gross volume of sales made or business done of $500,000 or more are covered by the FLSA. (Fair Labor Standards Act). In addition, employees of certain businesses are covered by the FLSA regardless of the amount of gross volume of sales or business done. Those businesses include: hospitals, businesses providing medical or nursing care for residents; schools (whether operated for profit or not for profit); and public agencies. Unless exempt, employees covered by the FLSA must receive overtime pay for hours worked over 40 in a workweek at a rate not less than time and one-half their regular rate of pay. The FLSA does not require overtime pay for work on Saturdays, Sundays, holidays, or regular days of rest, unless overtime is worked on such days. Also, even employees who would normally be classified as exempt are eligible for overtime pay if they earn less than $35,568 per year ($684 per week). Note: There is no limit on the number of hours employees aged 16 and older may work in any workweek.

Q: **What about hospital employees?**
A: Hospitals and their employees may agree to calculate overtime based on a 14-day period rather than a standard workweek.

Q: **What about employees who work on commission?**
A: Employees in retail or service industries who work primarily on commission are exempt from overtime regulations as long as their

weekly pay rate including commissions is at least one and a half times minimum wage and more than half their monthly pay comes from commissions.

Q: If an employee takes work home does that count as hours worked on the job?
A: In general the answer is "yes". Non-exempt employees (employees governed by the Fair Labor Standards Act or FLSA) have to be paid for all hours worked, even those outside the regular workplace, and that time counts toward the 40 hours per week used in determining overtime pay.

Q: If I pay an employee for sick time do those hours count in figuring overtime?
A: No, even if an employee is paid for sick time or other absences, those hours do not count toward the 40 hours a week for overtime pay purposes.

Q: What if an employee works at different rates for different jobs during the week?
A: Employers have three options for calculating overtime pay for an employee who worked at different rates during the week:
- Pay for all overtime hours at the higher rate
- Calculate the overtime by taking the employee's total earnings, divide by total hours worked, then take half of this average rate and multiply it by the overtime hours
- Use an overtime rate agreed on in advance with the employee

Q: How do I calculate overtime pay for employees who get paid by the piece?
A: If you have employees who are paid by the number of pieces produced, you have two options for calculating overtime pay. You can pay them, in addition to their piecework earnings, an amount equal to one-half of their hourly rate (calculated as their piecework earnings divided by the number of hours worked that week) multiplied by the number of hours in excess of 40 worked during the week. Alternatively you can (with the agreement of your employees) pay piece-work employees one and one-half times the piece rate for each piece produced during the overtime hours.

Q: Do I have to pay overtime to an employee who works more than 8 hours in a day?
A: Unless there is a state law or a collective bargaining agreement that requires you to pay overtime if someone works more than eight hours in a day, you only have to pay overtime if the employee works more than

forty hours during the work week.

Q: **How do I calculate overtime pay on commissions?**
A: Commissions are considered straight-time pay so you divide the amount of the commission by the total number of hours the employee worked during the week the commission was paid in order to get an hourly rate – then the overtime pay is calculated as one-half times that hourly rate times the number of hours worked over 40.

Q: **What else do I need to know about overtime?**
A: The FLSA rules apply to a "workweek" -- an employee's workweek is a fixed (and recurring) period of 168 hours – seven consecutive 24 hour periods. It doesn't have to correspond to a calendar week. It can begin on any day and at any hour. Hours cannot be averaged over two or more workweeks -- the 40 hour rule applies to each week individually. In determining the overtime rate for an employee, the employee's weekly earnings may be calculated on a piece-work, commission or other basis, but overtime pay must be based on the average pay rate for that week. Incidentally, a lump sum paid for work done during overtime hours without regard for the number of hours worked does not qualify as overtime pay (even if the amount exceeds the total of overtime hours times 1 1/2 times the employee's pay rate).

Q: **Do I pay workers' compensation premiums on overtime pay?**
A: In most states you pay workers' compensation premiums only on the "straight time" portion of overtime pay. In other words, your workers' compensation rate is calculated as if all hours are being paid at the employee's normal pay rate, not the time and a half (or double time, etc.) rate that the person receives for overtime.

Q: **Can overtime pay be paid in advance?**
A: Yes. If an employee works less than 40 hours in a week the employer can advance the employee the difference in pay between what he actually made and what he would have been paid if he had worked 40 hours. Then when the employee works over 40 hours in a week this "advance overtime pay" can be offset against the amount of overtime pay owed.

Sick Pay and Disability Insurance

Q: **What do I need to know about sick pay?**
A: Sick pay is income paid to an employee who is absent from work because of illness -- it can come from the employer, from a disability fund, from a welfare fund, or from an insurance company. If sick pay is paid directly by the employer it is generally treated as ordinary taxable wages (although if an employee is absent for an extended period of time, Social Security and Medicare withholding only apply for the first six months). If sick pay is provided by a third party such as an insurance company, income tax withholding doesn't apply unless the employee requests it; however, the insurance company is considered as the employer for FICA tax purposes and is responsible for withholding, depositing and reporting the employee's Social Security and Medicare taxes. However if the third party withholds and deposits the employee FICA taxes and notifies the actual employer of the amount of compensation paid, the responsibility for the employer portion of FICA taxes can be transferred back to the actual employer). Also, disability payments paid directly by the state or third party sick pay that comes from premiums paid by the employee are not taxable -- unless the premium contributions were made as part of a pre-tax cafeteria plan (where taxes were deferred). Sick pay does not include workers' compensation payments, disability retirement payments, medical expense payments or payments not related to absence from work. For further information about sick pay and sick pay plans, look at IRS Publication 15-A (Employer's Supplemental Tax Guide).

Note: Only the first six months of sick pay (following the employee's last day of work) are FICA taxable; however any return to work - even for a day - starts a new six-month period.

Note 2: Any portion of the sick pay attributable to after-tax deductions from the employee's pay are not subject to Social Security, Medicare or FUTA tax. For example if the employee paid for 20% of the plan cost through after-tax payroll deductions, then 20% of the sick pay benefits are non-taxable for Social Security, Medicare or FUTA purposes because those benefits have already been taxed.

Q: **What if an employee being paid sick pay by a 3rd party provider wants federal income tax withheld from those payments?**
A: An employee can fill out a Form W-4S (Request for Federal Income Tax Withholding From Sick Pay) to authorize the 3rd party payer to withhold federal income tax. If the 3rd party provider agrees to withhold

taxes the provider is liable for withholding the employee's share of Social Security and Medicare tax as well as the employee's federal income tax (the provider is also responsible for the employer share of FICA and FUTA tax unless an agreement has been made transferring that responsibility back to the employer).

Q: **What is the Federal Family and Medical Leave Act (FMLA)?**
A: Sick pay is strictly voluntary for employers; however under the terms of the Federal Family and Medical Leave Act of 1993, employees may be entitled to take leave to care for themselves or for certain family members without losing their job or benefits. The FMLA provides for up to 12 weeks of unpaid leave for employees with a family or medical emergency who work for a company with 50 or more employees within a 75 mile radius. The leave may be used all at one time or in separate days, weeks, or hours (however the leave must be taken within 12 months of the childbirth, adoption, illness or other qualifying event).

Q: **Can an employer dock an exempt, salaried employee's wages for sick days missed?**
A: An exempt salaried employee can't be docked for sick days missed unless the employer has a valid sick pay plan in place that offers at least five sick days per year. Even then, a person can only be docked for missing a full day -- not for a partial day. However, the employer is not required to pay full salary for weeks in which an exempt employee takes unpaid leave under the Federal Family and Medical Leave Act.

Q: **What is "disability insurance"?**
A: Disability insurance covers situations where an employee is injured on the job or suffers a job-related illness and needs at least a portion of their normal income while they're unable to work. Employers can choose to pay for short term and long term disability coverage, let the employee pay for the coverage, or share the cost of coverage with the employee. If you, the employer, pay the premiums, your employees aren't taxed on the premium amount (IRS Code Section 106). Under IRS Code Section 125, if you choose to make the employees pay the premiums, they pay the premiums on a pre-tax basis through payroll deductions. In turn, employees would be able to collect disability tax-free if they qualified for disability.

Q: **What is a "short term disability policy"?**
A: Short term disability insurance policies pay a percentage of an ill or injured employee's salary for a specified amount of time if he can't perform his duties on the job. Coverage usually starts within 14 days after the employee suffers the injury or illness. Short term disability plans

usually set out certain conditions that the employee has to meet to qualify for coverage, such as the employee needs to have worked for the company for a certain length of time prior to the injury or illness and the employee needs to work full-time (usually 30 hours or more a week). Benefits normally cover 50% to 70% of the person's weekly pay and last between 10 and 26 weeks (6 months). Some states such as New Jersey, New York, Rhode Island, and Hawaii mandate that short term disability benefits must be provided for up to 26 weeks.

Q: **What is "long term disability insurance"?**
A: Some employers provide long term disability insurance, which kicks in when short term disability payments end. Typically, long term benefits provide a percentage of the disabled employee's pay (50% of base salary for example) until the employee turns 65.

Paid Leave Time

Q: What are the different types of paid leave time?
A: Generally paid leave includes holidays, vacation and sick time, although PTO (Paid Time Off) has began to act as a catch-all in many companies, taking the place of the standard categories of time off.

Q: Are employers required to offer employees paid time off?
A: In general, employers are not required to offer paid time off to employees and even if they do, the leave time may be limited to just certain employees. However, the federal government does require employers to offer unpaid sick leave time to employees. The Family and Medical Leave Act (FMLA) provides for up to 12 weeks of unpaid leave for certain medical situations for either the employee or a member of the employee's immediate family. In general, employees are eligible to take FMLA leave if they have worked for their employer for at least 12 months and work at a location where at least 50 employees are employed by the employer within 75 miles.

In addition, a number of states and localities have adopted paid sick leave laws in recent years. Currently there are 11 states that have paid sick leave laws: Arizona, California, Connecticut, Maryland, Massachusetts, Michigan, New Jersey, Oregon, Rhode Island, Vermont and Washington (Washington D.C. also has a paid sick leave law). There are also a number of cities and counties with their own paid sick leave laws: Berkeley, Emeryville, Los Angeles, Oakland, San Diego, San Francisco, and Santa Monica in California, Chicago and Cook County in Illinois, Montgomery County in Maryland, Duluth and St. Paul in Minnesota, New York City and Westchester County in New York, Portland, Oregon, Philadelphia, Pennsylvania, Austin and San Antonio in Texas, and Seattle, Spokane and Tacoma in Washington.

Q: Can employers offer different types of paid leave to different groups of employees?
A: Yes, as long as long as the leave policy doesn't discriminate against a protected class of employees and it complies with federal and state laws. For example, employers often offer different amounts of paid leave time based on length of service, or they have different leave policies for full-time and part-time employees.

When an employee leaves, does the employer have to pay the person for his or her unused leave time?

There isn't any federal law that deals with this situation and state laws vary by state and by the type of leave time. For example:

- Unused vacation time – The following states require that employers pay terminated employees for unused vacation time: California (unless a collective bargaining agreement states otherwise), Louisiana, Massachusetts, Nebraska, and North Dakota (unless the employee quits and was notified in advance that unused vacation time wouldn't be paid).

  Other states require employers to pay terminated employees for unused vacation time IF the employer has promised to do so, has a policy to do so, or has included a promise to do so in the person's employment contract. The states that require employers to pay for unused vacation time on that basis are: Alabama, Alaska, Arizona, Arkansas, Colorado, Connecticut, the District of Columbia, Delaware, Hawaii, Idaho, Illinois, Indiana, Iowa, Kansas, Kentucky, Maine, Maryland, Michigan, Minnesota, Mississippi, Montana, Nevada, New Hampshire, New Jersey, New York, North Carolina, Ohio, Oklahoma, Oregon, Pennsylvania, Rhode Island, South Carolina, Tennessee, Texas, Utah, Vermont, Virginia, Washington, West Virginia, and Wyoming.

- Unused sick time – Currently there are no federal or state laws requiring employers to pay terminated employees for unused sick leave.

- Unused PTO time - Employment laws treat PTO days the same as vacation days, so the state laws listed above for unused vacation time also apply to unused PTO days.

Payment for unused leave time for employees who are fired differ considerably depending on provisions in state laws and company policies and are too varied to go into here.

Q: What is "PTO"?
A: PTO stands for "Paid Time Off" and can include vacation, sick and other types of leave time.

Q: How does PTO work?
A: PTO or Paid Time Off basically takes the place of paid holidays, vacation time and sick leave. Employees are usually given a certain amount of leave time to start each year and may accrue additional leave time each pay period. Typically, employers credit each employee with about 30 days of leave to start the year (the equivalent of 10 paid holidays, two weeks of vacation, 8 sick days and 2 personal days).

61

Q: What would be a typical system for determining how much vacation time an employee should receive each year?

A: Department of Labor statistics show an "average" vacation policy looks something like this:

- 5-10 paid vacation days after 1 to 5 years with the company.
- 10-14 paid vacation days after 5 to 10 years with the company.
- 15-19 paid vacation days after 10 to 20 years with the company.

Q: Does an employer have to pay a terminated employee for unused PTO?

A: There isn't a federal law requiring employers to pay for unused vacation time, but currently 24 states do require it including Alaska, Arizona, California, Colorado, Illinois, Indiana, Kentucky, Louisiana, Maine, Maryland, Massachusetts, Minnesota, Nebraska, New Hampshire, New York, North Carolina, North Dakota, Ohio, Oklahoma, Pennsylvania, Rhode Island (after one year of employment), Tennessee, West Virginia, and Wyoming, as well as Washington D.C.

Q: What is "bereavement leave"?

A: Some employers provide paid bereavement leave in the event of the death of an employee's immediate and extended family members or the death of a fellow employee. Company policy often specifies different amounts of paid leave depending on the relationship of the employee to the deceased.

Q: What's the difference between paid leave time and family leave time?

A: An employee can normally use company paid time off (PTO) for any purpose – vacation, sick time, or just personal time off. Family leave though, is specifically designated for providing care to others, including newborns, the elderly or close family members with an injury, serious illness or other emergency situation.

Earned Income Credit

Advance payments of the Earned Income Tax Credit can no longer be made through payroll after December 31, 2010. However employers are still required to notify employees who have no income tax withheld that they may be able to claim a refund because of the EIC. To do so, use IRS Notice 797 or an equivalent form.

Employee and Employer Taxes

Q: **What taxes does the employee pay?**
A: Generally, an employer withholds the following taxes from each employee's paycheck: Social Security, Medicare, federal income tax, and (depending on the state) state income tax and state disability tax. If you have employees in Alaska, New Jersey, or Pennsylvania, you will also have to withhold some state unemployment tax from your employees' wages and (in the case of New Jersey) Family Leave tax. In addition there may be local taxes that have to be withheld.

Q: **What are Social Security and Medicare taxes and how are they calculated?**
A: Social Security and Medicare taxes are components of the Federal Insurance Contributions Act (or FICA). Social Security tax provides funding for retirement income, survivor benefits and disability insurance. Medicare provides health insurance for people 65 and older (and some people under 65 with disabilities). Normally Social Security tax is calculated as 6.2% of the employee's FICA taxable wages and the employer pays an equal matching amount. For 2011 and 2012 the employee's Social Security tax rate was reduced to 4.2% but that rate returned to the normal 6.2% in 2013. Social Security withholding stops when FICA taxable wages reach the current year maximum wage limit ($132,900 for 2019 or $137,700 for 2020). Medicare is calculated as 1.45% of FICA taxable wages and, as with Social Security, is matched by an equal employer contribution. There is no wage limit on Medicare withholding, so it continues all year.

For 2013 and beyond there is also an additional Medicare withholding amount that kicks in when an employee's FICA taxable earnings exceed $200,000 – from that point on, the Medicare withholding rate goes up to 2.35% of FICA taxable wages (the law actually states that the Medicare rate goes up when a single person's wages exceeds $200,000 or a married person's wages exceeds $250,000 – however for payroll purposes all employees can be considered single in determining when to start the additional Medicare withholding and married individuals can recover the overpayment of Medicare tax on their annual tax return). The additional Medicare tax on wages over $200,000 applies only to the employee – there is no employer match.

Note: Wages that are deducted for certain pre-tax benefit plans (such as Section 125 Cafeteria plans) are (usually) not FICA taxable, which means that an employee's FICA taxable wages are not necessarily equal to his or her total wages.

Q: **How do I calculate FIT (Federal Income Tax)?**
A: If you do your payroll manually in-house, you will need a copy of the wage bracket tables issued by IRS. These tables are included in IRS Publication 15 (also known as the "Circular E"). You can download a copy from the IRS website at www.irs.gov. To figure the withholding tax for a given employee, you have to look at the marital status and number of allowances claimed on that person's W-4 -- then go the appropriate table for your pay period (weekly, bi-weekly, etc.) and for that employee's marital status (single or married). Then find the row in the table that includes the employee's gross pay and the column in that row for the number of allowances being claimed, and use the withholding tax shown there. If an employee's wages are greater than the last amount listed in the wage bracket table you will need to use the percentage withholding tables (also in Publication 15).

Q: **How do I calculate state withholding tax?**
A: Assuming you're not operating in one of the nine states that have no state income tax (Alaska, Florida, Nevada, New Hampshire, South Dakota, Tennessee, Texas, Washington, and Wyoming), the process of figuring state withholding is similar to calculating federal withholding. Most states have a set of tax tables which work the same way as the federal tables, although in some cases there may be an additional calculation or two, such as subtracting a "standard deduction" amount from gross pay along with the deduction for the number of exemptions claimed. Also, a few states have a different method of calculating withholding tax, such as simply multiplying federal withholding by a certain percentage. You can check on the exact method used in your state by contacting the appropriate state revenue agency. (Go to https://www.paycheckcity.com/payroll-resources#tax-rates for a clickable list of state revenue agencies).

Q: **What if I have employees who live in one state and work in a different state?**
A: Almost all states that have a personal income tax require that anyone working there, including non-residents, pay tax on the income earned in that state. In general non-resident employees who work in a state that has a personal income tax have state tax withheld in that state. At the end of the year those employees have to file a tax return with the state where they work and with the state where they reside. They get credit in their home state for the state tax paid where they work but if their home state has a higher income tax rate they have to pay the difference to their home state.

To avoid this double burden some states have reciprocal tax agreements with other states. If two states have a reciprocal agreement and an employee lives in one of those states and works in the other, he or she will only be subject to income tax in the state where he or she lives. Employers are not required to withhold tax for the state where the employee lives, but many employers will establish an account with a reciprocal state and withhold the tax for the employee's state of residence. Almost all states that have state tax reciprocal agreements have a form that an employee can complete that will make his income exempt from withholding tax in the state where he works.

Here is a list of states with reciprocal agreements, the reciprocating state or states, and the form the employee needs to fill out:
- District of Columbia – Any other state - Form D4-A
- Illinois – Iowa, Kentucky, Michigan, and Wisconsin - Form IL-W-5-NR
- Indiana – Kentucky, Michigan, Ohio, Pennsylvania, and Wisconsin - Form WH-47
- Iowa – Illinois - Form 44-016
- Kentucky – Illinois, Indiana, Michigan, Ohio, Virginia, West Virginia, and Wisconsin - Form 42A809
- Maryland – District of Columbia, Pennsylvania, Virginia, and West Virginia - Form MW 507
- Michigan – Illinois, Indiana, Kentucky, Minnesota, Ohio, and Wisconsin - Form MI-W4
- Minnesota – Michigan and North Dakota - Form MWR
- Montana – North Dakota – Form NR-2
- New Jersey – Pennsylvania – Form NJ-165
- North Dakota – Minnesota and Montana – Form NDW-R
- Ohio – Indiana, Kentucky, Michigan, Pennsylvania, and West Virginia – Form IT-4NR
- Pennsylvania – Indiana, Maryland, New Jersey, Ohio, Virginia, and West Virginia – Form REV-420
- Virginia – District of Columbia, Kentucky, Maryland, Pennsylvania, and West Virginia – Form VA-4
- West Virginia – Kentucky, Maryland, Ohio, Pennsylvania, and Virginia – Form WV/IT-104R
- Wisconsin – Illinois, Indiana, Kentucky, and Michigan – Form W-220.

Q: **As an employer do I have to pay taxes?**
A: Federal law levies certain payroll taxes on employers and you are

considered to be an employer if you paid wages of $1,500 or more during any calendar quarter in the current or previous calendar year or if you employed one or more persons on at least some portion of one day in each of 20 or more calendar weeks during the current or previous calendar year.

Q: **What taxes does the employer pay?**
A: An employer is required to match the Social Security and Medicare taxes withheld from employee paychecks (except for the additional employee Medicare withholding tax of .9% on FICA taxable wages over $200,000). You also have to pay federal unemployment (FUTA) taxes up to a maximum wage limit per employee of $7000 and state unemployment (SUTA) taxes up to whatever the SUI (state unemployment insurance) wage limit is in your state for the current year. There may also be additional taxes such as disability or family leave tax, depending on the state or states where you operate.

Q: **Which states have disability taxes?**
A: California, Hawaii, New Jersey, New York, Rhode Island (and Puerto Rico) all have disability insurance taxes,

Q: **Is a sole owner or a partner in a company subject to withholding taxes?**
A: In general an owner or partner is not considered an employee and is not subject to withholding taxes. However in some cases if a person has other partners who can control his wages and have the power to fire him, he may be considered an employee of the company.

Q: **At what point in the pay period do I become liable for the payroll taxes withheld?**
A: Your tax liability starts on the date you pay your employees, regardless of when they did the work being paid for on that paycheck. For example, if a pay period runs from September 16 through September 30 and you date the checks October 4, your tax liability begins on the 4th of October.

Q: **What is FUTA tax and how does it work?**
A: FUTA (the Federal Unemployment Tax Act) collects taxes from employers to administer the federal unemployment compensation program that provides payments to employees who have lost their jobs. The current FUTA tax rate is 6.0% and applies to the first $7000 in FUTA taxable earnings for each employee. Each state also has a State Unemployment Tax (SUTA) and employers who pay their state unemployment tax on a timely basis can take a 5.4% credit against their

FUTA rate, leaving a net FUTA rate of .6% (or 0.006). FUTA tax is calculated every quarter by multiplying .006 times each employee's wages for the quarter (but only on the first $7000 in FUTA taxable wages for each person). If the tax is $500 or less at the end of a quarter you are not required to make a deposit; however, you must add it to the tax for the next quarter. FUTA tax is due by the last day of the month following the end of the quarter (for example, first quarter deposits are due on April 30th -- unless that day is a holiday, in which case the tax is due on the next working day). Certain types of employees are exempt from FUTA tax, including:

- People who perform services outside of the United States
- Newspaper carriers under 18 years of age
- People working for 501(c)(3) non-profit organizations
- Children under 21 employed by parent(s)
- General or limited partners of a partnership
- Hospital interns

Note: If there are any states that borrowed money from the federal government during the year to pay unemployment benefits and failed to repay all the money they borrowed, they are designated by the Department of Labor as "credit reduction" states. Employers in those states must reduce their .054 credit on Form 940 by a specified "reduction rate". The exact amount of the credit reduction is computed by filling out Schedule A of Form 940 at the end of the year and any additional money owed for credit reduction must be included in the fourth quarter FUTA deposit. For 2019 there are no credit reduction states.

Q: Are U.S. citizens working in a foreign country subject to FUTA tax?

A: Yes, if the work they're doing would be subject to FUTA if it was being performed in the U.S.

Q: What is SUTA tax and how does it work?

A: Under SUTA (the State Unemployment Tax Act), each state has its own unemployment compensation program funded primarily by taxes on employers. With the exception of Alaska, New Jersey, and Pennsylvania, state unemployment taxes are collected from employers only and no taxes are withheld from employees. To calculate the amount of SUI (state unemployment insurance) taxes you owe for a given calendar quarter you simply multiply the total SUI wages paid to your employees in that quarter times the SUI rate assigned to you by the state. Each state sets a limit on the wages that you have to pay SUI tax on for each employee, so you only include the employee's wages up to that limit when you calculate the amount of SUI tax you owe.

Q: **If I hire someone in mid-year do I need to take into account his FUTA and SUTA contributions in his previous job?**
A: No, Federal Unemployment Tax (FUTA) and State Unemployment Tax (SUTA) start over again when someone takes a job with a new employer. The new employer is responsible for withholding FUTA up to the current $7,000 limit and state unemployment tax up to that state's current SUI (state unemployment insurance) wage limit.

Q: **What if a new employee has already met the Social Security limit with a previous employer?**
A: Regardless of how much the person has had withheld previously during the year, Social Security withholding starts from zero again with a new employer. If the employee is over-withheld at the end of the year he can get a refund on his individual tax return. The employer however is simply out the amount of the employer match on Social Security and isn't eligible for any type of refund.

Q: **If an employee is already receiving Social Security benefits do I still withhold FICA?**
A: Yes, employees are not exempted from FICA (Social Security and Medicare) taxes on the basis of age or the fact that they are receiving Social Security payments.

Q: **Do I have to withhold taxes on non-cash items given to employees, like food, lodging or equipment?**
A: Payments made in the form of food or lodging are generally taxable unless they are made in that form for the convenience of the employer and: (a) in the case of meals, they are provided on the business premises, and (b) in the case of lodging, the employee is required to accept lodging on the business premises as a condition of employment. Other forms of non-cash compensation are normally treated as taxable wages. Non-cash benefits should usually be valued at the "fair market value" for those items; i.e. the amount an individual would pay to an unrelated third party to obtain comparable benefits or property. The biggest problem with non-cash compensation is making sure you can collect the FICA and income taxes from the employee. If you also pay the employee cash wages, you can withhold all the required taxes from the cash portion of the compensation (provided there's enough money to cover all the taxes).

Q: **Are employees of a non-profit organization subject to FICA taxes?**
A: With the exception of ordained ministers, employees of non-profit

organizations are subject to FICA taxes if they earn $100 or more per year.

Q: **Are employees of a tax-exempt organization subject to federal taxes?**
A: Employees of tax-exempt organizations are subject to federal, state, and local taxes, including federal income tax withholding, FICA tax withholding, state income tax withholding, and federal and state unemployment taxes.

Q: **Do employees of a religious organization pay Social Security taxes?**
A: Some religious groups object to paying Social Security taxes and are allowed to choose not to participate in the Social Security program. They do not withhold those taxes from their employees' wages or pay the employer's matching share of Social Security taxes. Employees who work for religious organizations of this type must pay Social Security taxes if their earnings are more than $100 per year; in effect the employees are treated as if they were self-employed.

Q: **Do all states have a state income tax?**
A: No, there are currently nine states (Alaska, Florida, Nevada, South Dakota, Texas, Washington and Wyoming) that don't have an income tax. Accordingly, there is no state withholding tax for employees in those states.

Q: **What are "differential wages"?**
A: Differential wages are payments made by employers to employees who are on active military duty to make up the difference between their military pay and their normal pay. After 30 days the payments become subject to federal income tax withholding, but not FICA or FUTA withholding. In most cases federal withholding can simply be calculated as 22% of the wages paid.

Q: **Are there any special cases I should know about?**
A: If you're a sole proprietorship or a member of a partnership and you hire your own children under age 18, you're not required to withhold Social Security or Medicare from their paychecks. Also, if your child is under 21, you aren't required to pay FUTA tax on his or her wages.

Tax Saving Tips for Employers and Employees

Q: **What are some payroll-related tax-saving strategies for me and my employees?**

A: Here are a few suggestions:

- *401(k) Plans* - Employee contributions to 401(k) plans are tax-deferred so your employees pay federal and state withholding tax on the difference in pay after their 401(k) contribution is deducted.
- *IRS Section 125 plans* (also referred to as cafeteria or flex plans) allow employees to make tax-free contributions to an account which can be used to reimburse the employee for certain types of expenses. Since Section 125 plan contributions are exempt from Social Security and Medicare tax (as well as federal and state withholding), the employer also saves the cost of matching Social Security and Medicare taxes on those amounts.
  Note: Employees can select to make certain deductions under a IRS Section 125 plan after-tax deductions, so that FICA and income taxes are withheld on those particular deduction amounts.
- *Flex plans* can include options such as:
  - Flexible Spending Accounts – FSAs allow employees to contribute a portion of their pay (before taxes) to an account which can be used to pay for items such as over-the-counter medicines, eyeglasses or contacts, orthodontics, chiropractic care and other items not covered by another health plan. FSA funds can also be used to pay deductibles and co-payments, but not insurance premiums. Unused funds at the end of the year go to the employer, who can split it among the employees in the FSA plan or use it to offset the costs of administering benefits. The maximum contribution to an FSA for 2019 is $2,700.
  - Health Savings Accounts – HSAs allow employees to put part of their pay into a special account - either to save for future medical expenses or to pay for current expenses not covered by another health plan (employers may also contribute to HSAs). In order to contribute to an HSA the employee must be covered by an IRS qualified high-deductible health plan. Unlike FSAs unused funds in an HSA can be carried forward to a new year and can also be taken with the employee if he or she switches jobs.

- *Dependent Care Assistance* – Flex plans can include the option for employees to set aside part of their income (tax-free) to pay for day care expenses for children under age 13.
- *Premium Only Plans (POP)* - POP plans allow employees to elect to withhold a portion of their salary before taxes to pay their premium contribution for most employer-sponsored health and welfare benefit plans. Premiums may include the employee's share of employer-sponsored health, dental, accident, disability and group-term life insurance.

Employers save the cost of matching Social Security and Medicare taxes on the pre-tax amounts contributed to flex plans by employees. In addition, employer contributions to retirement plans and workers' comp insurance may also be reduced since they're based on lower taxable wages.

Timekeeping

Q: **What are the disadvantages of a manual timekeeping system?**
A; There are three main disadvantages of keeping time card data manually:
1) Time spent in preparing time cards by hand (including time spent in verifying the information and figuring shift and department totals).
2) Human error in collecting and posting the time card data.
3) Incorrect or missing time cards, as well as intentional "fudging" of time card information.

Q: **What type of features are included in automated timekeeping systems?**
A: Automated timekeeping systems offer features such as:
- Clock in/clock out by swiping a card through a card reader.
- Biometric scan capability to prevent "buddy punching".
- Automatically transferring time clock data to the payroll database.
- Clock in/clock out over a local network or over the Internet.
- Allowing employees to view their time card data online.
- Employee scheduling.
- Automatic lunch time deductions.
- Automatic overtime calculations.
- Holiday scheduling.
- The ability to see at a glance who is in and who is clocked out.
- Detail and summary time card reports and editing capability.

Q: **How do biometric time clocks work?**
A: Instead of using a code or key of some type biometric time clocks have each employee's hand print, finger print, retina pattern or some other physical feature scanned into the system and match that to the employee when a worker clocks in or out.

Q: **What if we want to install a PC based timeclock system but not all employees have access to a PC?**
A: Many time clock systems have the ability to add remote terminals or mobile devices that allow employees to clock in and clock out without using a PC.

Q: **I have an employee who clocks in early at 7 AM but his shift doesn't start until 8 AM – do I have to pay him for the extra hour?**

73

A: Yes, the Fair Labor Standards Act (FLSA) requires that an employer pay employees for all time on the job. Rather than not paying him for the extra hour, issue a written warning to all employees about clocking in early and if he continues to do so then fine him for violating company policy.

Q: **Can I require salaried employees to clock in and out?**
A: As long as the policy applies to all employees salaried workers can be required to clock in and out along with hourly employees. Note: Having salaried employees record their time in and out can help prevent lost time due to extra long lunch hours or other unaccounted for time away from the job.

Calculating Pay Checks

Q: **What if I need to convert weekly or bi-weekly pay to an hourly rate?**
A: To convert a per pay period rate to an hourly pay rate:
- For a weekly payroll divide the weekly pay rate by the number of hours in a standard work week (for example, if you pay someone $500 per week and the standard work week is 40 hours the hourly pay rate is $500 divided by 40 hours or $12.50 per hour).
- For a bi-weekly payroll divide the bi-weekly pay by 2, then divide the result by the number of hours in a standard workweek.
- For a semi-monthly payroll multiply the semi-monthly pay times 24 (the number of pay periods in a year), divide by 52 (the number of weeks in a year) and divide the result by the number of hours in a standard work week (40) to get the hourly pay rate.
- For a monthly payroll follow the same steps as for a semi-monthly payroll, but multiply the monthly pay rate by 12.

Q: **How do I figure an hourly rate for an employee who is paid according to the number of pieces he produced during the week?**
A: To calculate an hourly rate for a pieceworker add the total earnings from what was paid for the pieces produced plus any other pay and divide by the number of hours worked during the week.

Q: **How can I calculate federal income tax withholding by hand?**
A: Download a copy of IRS Publication 15-T and refer to the instructions and tables inside in order to calculate federal withholding tax for your employees. You will need to have the information from their W-4 forms in order to figure their withholding tax amounts.

Q: **How do I calculate state income tax withholding manually?**
A: Go to: https://www.paycheckcity.com/payroll-resources/#select-state, click the name of your state and use the tables or tax calculators on your state's web page to figure the state withholding for your employees.

Q: **Is there an easy, free way to figure paycheck amounts by hand?**
A: If you figure paychecks manually you may be able to use one of these free online calculators:
- http://www.paycheckcity.com – Offers standard (salary and hourly) calculators as well as specialized versions (gross up, 401(k), bonus-%, and bonus-aggregate).

- http://www.adp.com/tools-and-resources/calculators-and-tools.aspx – Includes several different types of pay calculators.
- http://www.paycycle.com/external/business/paycheckCalculators.jsp – Includes hourly, salary and gross-to-net calculators.
.

All of the above web-based calculators offer the ability to select the pay frequency, the state for which state taxes are to be withheld, and the option to enter multiple voluntary deductions any of which can be marked as exempt from FICA, federal, or state tax.

Q: **What if I want to print the paychecks I calculated?**
A: If you want to print actual paychecks one option is:
    http://www.paycheckmanager.com
Their free payroll calculator computes federal and state withholding, and provides for 401k, 125 plan, local taxes and other special deductions. You can also enter "year-to-date" information to ensure the accuracy of certain tax calculations (such as Social Security tax). You will also have to enter your bank information including the bank routing number and your account number. Once you have entered all the paycheck information you can download a PDF file containing the check images. To print the checks you have to open the PDF file in Adobe Reader and print it on a laser printer, using standard 3-part blank check stock. The MICR coding (the funny looking characters at the bottom of the check) contains the routing and account numbers - in order for the bank to be able to scan it properly you may also have to use a special MICR toner cartridge in your printer. **Note:** None of your information is saved after you leave the website so you have to enter your setup information each time you do payroll (to save your data you have to pay for their Payroll Manager service).

Payroll Tax Deposits

Q: **What payroll taxes do I need to deposit?**
A: You need to deposit the Social Security tax, Medicare tax and federal income tax withheld from your employees' wages plus your employer match amount (equal to the total of the Social Security and Medicare taxes). That amount makes up your 941 tax deposit and is deposited monthly or semiweekly. You also need to make a quarterly deposit of your 940 or FUTA (Federal Unemployment Tax Act) taxes, equal to 6.0% of the federal taxable wages (up to a limit of $7,000 of taxable wages) paid to your employees during the quarter. Normally you can take a 5.4% credit against your FUTA tax for SUTA (State Unemployment Tax Act) contributions made to the state, which reduces your FUTA deposit to 0.6% of the employees' taxable wages for the quarter (you may have to make an additional FUTA payment at the end of the year if any state where you do business is a "credit reduction" state – a state which has borrowed more in unemployment funds from the federal government than it has paid back). You also need to make quarterly SUI (state unemployment insurance) tax deposits to your state (contact your state unemployment agency for detailed information on making SUTA deposits). Note: A few states also have SDI (disability insurance) and/or workers compensation taxes that are collected through payroll.

Q: **How do I handle making tax deposits?**
A: It's a good idea to set up a separate bank account just for payroll transactions; then you simply make your tax deposits (Social Security, Medicare, federal/state income tax, FUTA and SUTA tax) from your payroll account. All employers are required to use the Electronic Federal Tax Payment System (EFTPS) to make their payroll tax deposits. You can initiate your deposit by calling the information in by phone or by entering it over the Internet at https://www.eftps.gov.

Q: **How often do I need to make payroll tax deposits?**
A: When you make your deposit depends on the total tax liability you've reported on your Form 941 (Employer's Quarterly Tax Return) during a four-quarter "lookback" period. The deposit schedule is based on your total taxes during those four quarters: if you reported more than $50,000 in total taxes during the period from July 1st of 2 years ago to June 30th of last year you must make tax deposits on a semi-weekly basis; if less than $50,000 you can make monthly deposits (all new employers make monthly deposits for the first calendar year). If you have a total tax liability of less than $2500 per quarter then you can simply send your tax payment in with your Form 941. For semi-weekly depositors, if your pay

date falls on Wednesday through Friday make your deposit by the following Wednesday; for pay dates that fall on Saturday through Tuesday, make your deposit by the following Friday.

Q: **Are there any exceptions to the above rules?**
A: Regardless of your normal payment schedule, if you accumulate a tax liability of $100,000 or more on any day during a deposit period, you have to deposit the tax by the next working day (this is the so-called "One Day" rule). Once you accumulate a deposit of $100,000 or more you automatically become a semi-weekly depositor for the remainder of the current year and for the following year. Also, if you write a manual check and date it in the middle of a pay period, the standard rules for depositing the taxes withheld still apply; if you're on a semiweekly schedule you need to deposit the taxes from the manual check based on the check date.

Q: **Can I be penalized for failure to follow the above rules?**
A: Yes. If you fail to make the required payments on time the IRS can impose penalties ranging from 2% of the amount due for payments one to five days late to 15% for amounts not paid within ten days after receiving a notice from IRS.

Q: **What is the "safe harbor" rule for payroll tax deposits?**
A: If you deposit a small amount less than your full tax deposit liability, IRS will forgo any penalties if:
- The amount of the shortfall isn't more than the greater of $100 or 2% of the entire amount due
- The deposit you made was made on time
- You deposit the shortfall amount by the appropriate make-up date (the make-up date for monthly depositors is the due date for the 941 quarterly return and the make-up date for semiweekly depositors is the first Wednesday or Friday, whichever is earlier, falling on or after the 15th day of the month following the month in which the deposit was due)

Q: **What if I need to make a deposit and don't have an EIN yet?**
A: If you have applied for an EIN (Employer Identification Number) but haven't received it yet and need to make a payroll tax deposit, make the check for the taxes payable to "United States Treasury" and mail it along with an explanation to the IRS office where you would normally send your Form 941 (Employer's Quarterly Tax Return). IRS addresses are on the Form 941 or you can find them at www.irs.gov. Be sure to use the "without a payment" mailing address.

Q: **What if I want to appoint an agent to make our tax deposits?**
A: You can file IRS form 2678 (Employer/Payer Appointment of Agent) to request to have an agent file information returns and make tax deposits for you.

Employee Benefits

Q: **What benefits are at the top of the list for employees and prospective employees?**
A: Job applicants want paid time off and health insurance above all, but retirement plans are a close second. Other "most wanted" benefits include overtime pay, paid medical leave, dental and vision coverage, and disability and life insurance. Flexible work schedules and the ability to work remotely are also becoming an important perk for employees.

Q: **Other than keeping employees happy, is there a financial upside for employers in providing employee benefits?**
A: In most cases, the cost of providing employee benefits can provide employers with a business deduction on their tax return, the same as the deduction they take for wages and salaries paid to employees. In addition, benefit packages can create employment tax savings for employers. If employee benefits were paid out as wages and salaries, the employer would have to pay matching Social Security and Medicare taxes on those amounts, as well as federal and state unemployment tax. For benefit plans such as Section 125 health care plans, employee contributions are exempt from both FICA and unemployment taxes, which means the employer doesn't have to pay matching FICA taxes or federal and state unemployment tax on those contributions.

Q: **Which government agency is primarily responsible for over-sight of employee benefits?**
A: The Employee Retirement Income Security Act ("ERISA") sets the standards for how employee benefits have to be administered, while the Department of Labor and the federal courts enforce those standards.

Q: **Which businesses fall under ERISA rules?**
A: Private sector businesses, whether for-profit or non-profit, which have at least one employee.

Q: **What type of benefit plan documents are required by ERISA?**
A: ERISA requires several types of written documents: a Plan Document (which describes the participants' rights, benefits, and obligations within the plan, along with the terms and conditions for administering the plan). a Summary Plan Document (SPD) to be distributed to participating employees, a Summary of Material Modifications (SMM) describing any significant changes to the plan, and a Summary Annual Report (SAR) to be submitted to the IRS.

Q: **Is there a financial advantage for employees who participate in employer-sponsored benefit plans?**
A: Employee contributions to employer provided benefit plans are often made as "pre-tax" deductions, which reduce the amount of the employee's pay that's subject to tax withholding.

Q: **What are "Pre-Tax Deductions"?**
A: Pre-tax deductions are subtracted from an employee's gross pay (and from his or her taxable gross) before any taxes are calculated, decreasing the amount of tax taken out of the paycheck. Cafeteria ("Section 125") plan deductions reduce the employee's taxable gross, which means less tax for the employee and less for the employer (because the Social Security and Medicare match is reduced as well). Other examples of pre-tax deductions are amounts withheld for Flexible-Spending Accounts, Health Savings Accounts, and Archer Medical Savings Accounts.

Q: **What are "Tax deferred deductions"?**
A: Tax deferred deductions (or "tax deferred benefits") are excluded from federal income tax (and normally from state income tax), although Social Security and Medicare taxes are still paid. Simple IRAs and 401(k) plans are examples of tax deferred deductions.

Q: **What are "defined benefit" and "defined contribution" pension plans?**
A: There are two general types of pension plans – defined benefit plans and defined contribution plans. A defined benefit plan promises participants a specified monthly benefit at retirement. The benefit may be stated as a flat dollar amount such as $500 per month or the benefit may be calculated through a formula that takes into account factors such as salary and years of service. A defined contribution plan doesn't promise a specified amount at retirement. In defined contribution plans the employer or the participant (or both) contribute to the employee's individual account and these contributions are invested on the participant's behalf. The participant will eventually receive whatever the balance is in their account. Defined contribution plans include 401(k) plans, 403(b) plans, employee stock ownership plans, and profit-sharing plans. The general rules of ERISA (the Employment Retirement Income Security Act) apply to all of these types of plans.

Note: Both types of plans described above are considered "qualified" compensation plans under IRS regulations and employer expenses associated with those plans can be deducted from the company's income. Employers may also set up "non-qualified" tax-deferred plans (which can include deferred compensation, executive bonuses, and split-dollar insurance) for key executives or other select employees. Expenses associated with non-qualified plans cannot be deducted from the company's income until the money is actually paid out to the individual participants but it can still provide tax-deferred income to the employees in the plan.

Q: **What is a 401(k) plan and how does it work?**
A: 401(k) plans are employer sponsored retirement plans which let an employee save for retirement while deferring income taxes on the money put into the plan until the funds are eventually withdrawn. As mentioned above, employee 401(k) plan contributions are exempt from federal income tax but not from FICA taxes (Social Security and Medicare). Each employee can elect to have a certain amount (or a percentage of earnings) paid into his or her 401(k) account. In most 401(k) plans the employee can select from a number of different investment options (mostly mutual funds) and divide his contribution amount among those options. In addition employers can contribute matching funds (usually a percentage of the employee contribution) and employer contributions are tax-free. Details concerning topics such as the amount of the employer match and whether 401(k) amounts are taken on bonus checks vary with the particular 401(k) plan involved. There is a maximum amount that an employee can elect to defer during the year. When an employee leaves, the 401(k) plan generally remains active for the rest of the employee's life (although funds have to begin to be drawn out by April 1st of the year following the date when the employee reaches the age of 72.

Q. **What are Roth 401(k) plans?**
A: Effective January 1, 2006, 401(k) participants have the option of allocating part or all of their contributions to a separate Roth account (generally known as a Roth 401(k)). In contrast to normal 401(k) contributions which are not taxed until the money is withdrawn, contributions to a Roth 401(k) are taxed when the contribution is made and distributions are tax-free.

Q: **When must an employer deposit withheld employee pension plan contributions into the plan?**
A: Employers must transmit employee contributions no later than the 15th business day of the month immediately after the month in which the contributions were withheld.

Q: **What is a 403(b) plan?**
A: 403(b) retirement plans are similar to a 401(k) plan, but are limited to

certain public school employees, employees of tax-exempt organizations, and ministers.

Q: **What is a Traditional Individual Retirement Account (IRA)?**
A: A traditional IRA is an individual account or annuity set up with a financial institution such as a bank or mutual fund company. Individuals can put personal savings in the account (up to a certain annual limit) and the money in the account grows, tax deferred. However, distributions from a traditional IRA are subject to federal and state taxes – and distributions prior to age 59 ½ are also subject to a 10% penalty. You may be able to avoid the early withdrawal penalty under the following circumstances:
- A first-time home purchase
- Death or disability
- Qualified educational expenses
- Unreimbursed medical expenses
- Health insurance if you're unemployed

After age 59 ½ distributions are penalty free – and starting at age 70 ½ traditional IRA owners must begin making withdrawals from their accounts or incur severe penalties.

Q: **What is a Roth Individual Retirement Account?**
A: A Roth IRA is basically the same as a traditional IRA except that it's not tax deferred – federal and state taxes are paid up front on the money placed in a Roth IRA. Contributions do not have to stop at age 70 ½ and qualified distributions for a Roth IRA are tax-free and penalty-free provided that five years have passed since the IRA was established and that one of the following conditions applies:
- Over age 59 ½
- Death or disability
- First-time home purchase

Q: **What are Simplified Employee Pension plans (SEPs)?**
A: Any employer may sponsor a simplified employee pension plan or SEP (generally referred to as an SEP IRA). Participating employees have to set up an individual retirement account or IRA - then the employer can make flat dollar amount contributions to the employee's IRA or percentage contributions of up to 25 percent of the person's annual compensation. Employees can also contribute to their SEP IRA if the plan allows non-SEP contributions (although the amount the employee can deduct on his or her tax return for IRA contributions may be reduced by the the employee's participation in the SEP plan). SEP plans have to be available to all employees who are at least 21 years old, have earned at least $600 for the year and who have worked for the

company for three of the preceding five years. Employers have the option of offering the plan to even more employees – those who have worked for the company for over a year for example. The employer can deduct all of the contributions made to the plan as a business expense and the money is not considered to be taxable income to the employees until they take withdrawals from their account (investment earnings are also tax-deferred).

Q: **Are employer contributions to an SEP taxable to the participating employees?**
A: No, employer contributions to SEP-IRAs are not included in their gross income (except for excess contributions).

Q: **Do contributions have to be made to an SEP every year?**
A: No, but if contributions are made to an SEP they have to be made to the SEP-IRAs of all participating employees.

Q: **How much of the contributions made to an SEP can be deducted on the business's tax return?**
A: A business can deduct the lesser of its contributions or 25% of employee compensation.

Q: **What is a Savings Incentive Match Plan for Employees (SIMPLE)?**
A: A SIMPLE plan (generally referred to as a Simple IRA) is a small business IRA-based retirement plan open to companies with 100 or fewer employees (and no other retirement plan in place). A SIMPLE IRA is particularly attractive to employers because it requires fewer administrative fees and less paperwork than a 401(k) plan. Employees can choose whether or not to make regular contributions and the employer has the option of matching employee deferrals up to 3% of the person's annual salary or making non-elective contributions of 2% or less to all eligible employees. In either case, for 2019 employees can defer up to $13,000 (with employees 50 or older able to make "catch-up" contributions up to $3,000 for a total contribution of $16,000 for the year).

Q; **When do pension plan participants receive distributions after terminating their employment?**
A: Generally the law requires plans to pay retirement benefits no later than the time a participant reaches normal retirement age. However many plans, including 401(k) plans, provide for earlier payments under certain circumstances – for example participants in a 401(k) plan may be eligible to receive payment of their proceeds once they have terminated employment.

Q: **What happens if a pension plan is terminated?**
A: If for some reason a pension plan has to be terminated the participants become 100 percent invested immediately upon plan termination, to whatever extent the plan is funded at that point.

Q: **What are "group health plans"?**
A: A group health plan is an employee benefit plan established or maintained by an employer (or an outside organization such as a union) that provides medical care for participants and their dependents through insurance or direct reimbursement.

Q: **What does it take to establish a group health care plan?**
A: ERISA (the Employee Retirement Income Security Act) requires employers to have a written "plan document" in order to establish a group health plan. The plan document has to provide for one or more fiduciaries who have the authority to manage the plan, and it has to include funding policies and procedures.

The plan document also has to describe what the procedures are for amending the plan and which individuals have the authority to make amendments. In addition, procedures have to be included detailing how payments are to be made to and from the plan and how participants can make a claim for a benefit from the plan.

Q: **What are the main types of employee health care plans?**
A: Health care plan options include:
- Health Management Organizations (HMOs).
- Preferred Provider Organization (PPOs).
- Point Of Service (POS) health plans.
- Exclusive Provider Organization (EPO) health plans.
- Traditional indemnity or "fee-for-service" plans.
- Health Savings Account (HSA) health plans.
- Health Reimbursement Arrangement (HRA)
- Major Medical plans.

Q: **Can employers get a tax credit for their group health plan contributions?**
A: Yes, contributions toward employees' health insurance coverage can be considered a tax credit if the employer has less than 25 full-time employees, the premiums are lower than the SHOP Marketplace and paid average annual wages are less than the amount prescribed by the IRS.

Q: **What are the basic reporting requirements for group health plans?**
A: Most group health plans are required to file a Form 5500 Annual Report with the Department of Labor within seven months of the end of the plan year, although they can apply for an automatic extension that gives them an additional 2 ½ months to file.

Q: **Are there state laws that affect group health care plans?**
A: Some states are mandating certain types of coverage that must be included in any employer sponsored group health care plan. If an employer in one of those states offers a group health care plan, the plan has to include the particular types of coverage specified by the state.

Q: **What is the Consolidated Omnibus Budget Reconciliation Act (COBRA)?**
A: The Consolidated Omnibus Budget Reconciliation Act requires employers with 20 or more employees who have a group health plan to provide participants and qualified beneficiaries the option to pay for continued coverage in cases where coverage would normally end. If an employee dies, becomes incapacitated, loses his or her job or suffers a reduction in work hours, health care coverage can be extended for up to 18 or 36 months, depending on circumstances.

The cost of health insurance provided under COBRA is usually high, because the recipient pays the entire premium including the portion that was being paid by the employer. In that sense, COBRA coverage is primarily a stop-gap until less expensive health insurance can be found.

To qualify for COBRA coverage, an employee has to have been enrolled in a company-sponsored group health insurance plan on the day before the qualifying event (loss of job, reduced hours, etc.) occurs and the insurance plan must have been in effect on more than 50% of the employer's typical business days during the previous calendar year. In addition, the employer must still be offering existing employees a group health plan; if the employer stops offering health coverage or goes out of business or drops below 20 employees the employee seeking COBRA coverage may no longer be eligible for extended insurance benefits..

Even small employers with less than 20 employees may be required to provide extended insurance coverage to employees who have suffered a qualifying event. Many states have laws similar to COBRA. These "mini-COBRA" laws generally apply to employers of all sizes, including those with fewer than 20 employees.

Q: **What are Cafeteria plans?**
A: Cafeteria plans (also known as "Section 125" plans) allow employees to obtain tax-free medical coverage and insurance. Generally, qualified benefits under a cafeteria plan are not subject to FUTA, Social Security, Medicare or income tax withholding. However, if an employee elects to receive cash instead of a qualified benefit, that money is treated as regular taxable wages. Most cafeteria plans offer a basic set of benefits including health, dental and life insurance, sick leave or disability benefits, plus a secondary group of optional benefits. Employees are allocated a certain number of dollars to split among the various options available, with the dollar amounts provided by the employer normally being supplemented by employee pre-tax deductions. That way each employee is able to use pre-tax dollars to pay his or her portion of any insurance premiums, deductibles and coinsurance amounts under health benefit plans, or to pay medical bills which may not be covered by the employer's plan.

Q: **Exactly what benefits can be offered as part of a Cafeteria (Section 125) plan?**
A: A cafeteria plan can offer insured benefits (accident and health insurance, dental insurance, vision insurance, disability insurance, and group term life insurance) and non-insured benefits (dependent care assistance programs and medical/dental reimbursement for non-insured medical and dental expenses).

Q: **What benefits cannot be offered as part of a Section 125 plan?**
A: Medical Savings Accounts, dependent group term life insurance, and educational assistance.

Q: **How does a Cafeteria plan benefit the employer?**
A: The employer benefits from a Cafeteria plan in several ways. First of course, you don't have to pay matching FICA (Social Security and Medicare) tax or FUTA (federal unemployment) tax on the gross amount of employee pay "redirected" into the plan as cafeteria plan deductions. Then too, the employer may also participate in the plan to help pay for uninsured medical expenses, dependent health premiums and dependent childcare. And, cafeteria plans can be a morale booster for your employees, removing some of the anxiety surrounding medical expense and health care issues.

Q: **Are there any drawbacks to participating in a Section 125 plan?**
A: Employees who select pre-tax benefits reduce their taxable income – but the fact that their taxable income is reduced also reduces benefits such as Social Security and retirement plans that are calculated based

on taxable income.

Q: **Can everyone in the company participate in a Cafeteria plan?**
A: Sole proprietors, partners in a partnership and owners who own more than 2% of a sub-chapter S corporation cannot take part in a cafeteria plan.

Q: **Can an employee change his mind during the year as to which Cafeteria plan benefits he wants?**
A: Not in most cases; normally participants can only change their electives at the beginning of the plan year. However there are some plans that allow the employee to make changes at any time and even give the employees the ability to make changes online.

Q: **What happens if there's money left in a participant's account at the end of the plan year?**
A: The employee loses that money, so it's important that each employee makes a careful estimate of how much he or she needs to contribute to the plan each year.

Q: **What is a health reimbursement account (HRA)?**
A: HRAs are IRS sanctioned programs that allow an employer to set aside funds to reimburse medical expenses paid by participating employees. Health Reimbursement Accounts are started by the employer and administered by a third party or plan service provider. The employer decides if a credit balance in an employee's account may be rolled over from year to year and if so, how much rolls over. An HRA must be funded entirely by the employer and contributions cannot be paid through a voluntary salary reduction agreement (i.e., a cafeteria plan). There is no limit on an employer's contributions, which are excluded from an employee's income. Employees are reimbursed tax-free for qualified medical expenses up to a maximum dollar amount for a given coverage period. HRAs reimburse only those items agreed to by the employer which are not covered by the company's standard insurance plan.

Q: **What are the different types of HRAs?**
A: There are a number of new types of HRAs that were introduced in 2020:
- The qualified small employer HRA (QSEHRA) – QSEHRAs are for businesses that employed less than 50 full-time employees (including full-time-equivalent employees) during the preceding year and that don't offer a group health care plan. These HRAs limit the amount of the expense reimbursement allowance

employers can provide - for 2020 the limits are $5,250 for an individual and $10,600 for a family. Additionally, employers must offer all employees (part-time as well as full-time) the same terms. With a QSEHRA, employers can reimburse employees tax-free for their medical expenses, including premiums for individual-market health insurance policies.

- The individual coverage HRA (ICHRA) - An ICHRA is very similar to a QSEHRA, but there are key differences:
  - There isn't any limit on employer allowances.
  - Employers can offer different terms to different classes of employees.
  - An ICHRA can be coordinated with an FSA.
  - An ICHRA can be offered stand-alone with no group health plan or as an option to an employer-sponsored group plan.
- The Excepted Benefit Health Reimbursement Arrangement (EBHRA) - EBHRAs allow employers to contribute up to $1,800 per year (for 2020) toward their employees' expenses that aren't covered by the company's group plan. This type of HRA can be used to reimburse employees for expenses such as short-term disability insurance, and dental and vision care.
- The Group Coverage HRA (GCHRA) - Group coverage HRAs are only available to businesses who also offer a group health insurance policy. With a group coverage HRA, businesses can offer employees monthly allowances to cover items that aren't eligible for coverage under the group policy, such as deductible amounts. Businesses of any size can offer a group coverage HRA, there isn't any maximum allowance amount, and different allowance amounts can be offered to different employees.
- The Dental/Vision HRA - Employers can use a dental/vision HRA solely for the purpose of reimbursing employees for dental and vision expenses.
- The Retiree HRA – This type of HRA is only available to a business's retired employees and employers of any size can offer it. There's no allowance limit or group health plan requirements and employers can permit funds to be rolled over into a new plan year.

Note: You can find a table listing the key items of information for each type of HRA at: https://vericred.com/insights/blog/health-reimbursement-arrangements-hra-changes-for-2020

Q: **What is an employee stock option plan (ESOP)?**
A: Employers may offer certain employees the right to buy a specific

number of shares of the company's stock during a time and at a price specified by the employer. The price the employer sets on the stock (called the "grant" or "strike" price) is discounted and is usually the current market price of the stock at the time the employee is given the options. If the company grows and performs well the price of the shares should go up and selling them will net the employees a profit, making stock options an incentive for employees to stay with the company.

Q: **What is a "safe harbor" 401(k) plan?**
A: Any size business can establish a safe harbor 401(k) plan, but they're especially popular with small businesses because there's no requirement for anti-discrimination testing. There are two other differences from a traditional 401(k) plan: 1) employers must make contributions to the plan, and 2) employer contributions are immediately vested when they're made (that is, the employee has immediate access to employer contributions).

Q: **What are QACA retirement plans?**
A: Qualified automatic contribution arrangements (QACAs) are a type of automatic enrollment retirement plan. QACAs are based on a rule in the Pension Protection Act of 2006 that's designed to increase employee participation in self-funded retirement plans. Self-funded retirement plans include 401(k)s, 403(b)s, and deferred compensation 457s.

Employers who use QACAs automatically enroll their workers in the company retirement plan with a deferral rate of 3% or greater, unless an employee elects to opt out. The default deferred contribution for a QACA also has to increase each year from at least 3% the first year to at least 6%, with a maximum of 15% in any year.

Q: **What is an Eligible Automatic Contribution Arrangement (EACA)?**
A: EACAs are basically the same as a QACA, but they have simpler requirements. Under an EACA, plan participants automatically contribute a set, uniform percent of their gross pay to the EACA. Employers using an EACA have to treat all employees who don't provide any definite enrollment instructions the same, enrolling them in the same plan at the same contribution rate. Also, unlike a QACA, employees in an EACA are immediately 100% vested in their automatic enrollment contributions.

Q: **How does the SECURE Act of 2019 affect retirement plans?**
A: The key provisions include:

- Provides a maximum tax credit of $500 per year to employers who create a 401(k) or SIMPLE IRA plan with automatic enrollment.
- Allows 401(k) plans to offer annuities as an investment option.
- Changes the age at which retirement plan participants have to start taking minimum distributions (RMDs), from 70½ to 72, and allows traditional IRA owners to keep making contributions indefinitely.
- Makes it easier for small business owners to set up "safe harbor" retirement plans that are less expensive and easier to administer.
- Increases the cap on qualified automatic contribution arrangement (QACA) 401(k) deferrals from 10 to 15 percent.
- Effective Dec. 20, 2019, qualified 401(k) plans aren't allowed to make participant loans through the use of credit cards or other similar arrangements.
- Makes it possible for employers with retirement plans to enroll part-time employees who work either 1,000 hours throughout the year or have three consecutive years with 500 hours of service. Plan sponsors aren't required to make contributions, matching or otherwise, and this class of participants isn't included in nondiscrimination and top-heavy testing.
- Effective for distributions made after Dec. 31, 2019, the SECURE act allows retirement plan participants to withdraw up to $5,000 for qualified adoption and/or birth expenses without paying an early withdrawal penalty. The distributions would be taxable to the participant, but they can repay the distributions into another qualified plan or IRA, in which case the distribution and repayment is treated as an indirect rollover.
- Requires most non-spouses who inherit IRAs to begin taking distributions that empty the account withing 10 years.

Q: What resources does the IRS provide to help with correcting plan errors?
A: Employers can contact the IRS directly or they can go to: https://www.irs.gov/retirement-plans/epcrs-overview, which includes links to IRS pages that address how to fix specific problems. The web page links cover the following types of benefit plans:
- 401(k) Plan Fix-It Guide
- SEP Fix-It Guide
- SIMPLE IRA Plan Fix-It Guide
- SARSEP Fix-It Guide

Q: What about dependent care assistance provided by employers?
A: An employer can pay for or provide dependent care assistance to employees, tax free, up to certain limits. However, the benefit can't discriminate in favor of highly compensated employees. The value of all payments must be reported in Box 10 of Form W-2, with any payments over the limit included in Boxes 1, 3 and 5.

Q: What about educational assistance provided by employers?
A: Employers can provide tax-free educational assistance to an employee. The assistance can include tuition, books, supplies and equipment, but to qualify as tax exempt the assistance must be provided according to an approved written plan. In addition, the benefit can't favor highly compensated employees.

Q: What about employee personal use of a company vehicle?
A: Personal use of a company-owned vehicle is considered part of an employee's taxable income and keeping accurate documentation is essential in determining what percentage of the vehicle's mileage constitutes personal use. If you can't determine business versus personal use, the value of the vehicle would be 100% taxable to the employee.

Normally, employers must withhold employment taxes (and pay their share of those taxes). However, for federal and state income taxes, employers can choose to withhold taxes or not, but only if they notify the employee of that decision beforehand and include the value of the employee's personal use of the company vehicle in Boxes 1, 3, 5 and 14 of his or her Form W-2.

How employers determine the value of company car usage is somewhat complicated. There are four methods available to value an employee's personal use of a company vehicle:
- General valuation rule. The value is based on fair market value (FMV), defined as the amount the employee would have to pay to a third party to lease the same or similar vehicle in the same geographic area where the employee used the vehicle.
- Commuting valuation rule. The value is equal to the cost of each trip from home to work or work to home multiplied by $1.50. There are very strict requirements for using this method of valuation, including a written policy limiting the employee's use almost entirely to commuting to work and back.

- Cents-per-mile. The most common method of valuation, this rule allows employers to multiply the business standard mileage rate (less up to 5.5 cents per mile if the employer doesn't provide fuel) by the total number of miles the employee drives the vehicle for personal use.
- Fleet average. Allows employers operating a fleet of 20 or more qualifying vehicles to use the annual lease value of the vehicle (as specified by an IRS table that bases annual lease value on a vehicle's fair market value) multiplied by the percentage of personal miles driven out of total miles driven by the employee. This amount also is subject to a fuel adjustment.

Q: **What about reimbursement of employees for business use of their own vehicles?**
A: In many cases, car allowances are paid to certain employees every payday to reimburse them for business use of their car. Those payments are taxable for both the employer and employee. To provide tax-free reimbursements, employers can make use of a Fixed and Variable Rate program (FAVR) that reimburses the employee for fixed costs like insurance, taxes, and registration and variable expenses such as gas and maintenance. These payments are tax-free for the employee if the program meets IRS expense-accounting requirements.

Employers can also use a cents-per-mile expense reimbursement to provide employees with tax-free payments. The employer does have to have a documented expense reimbursement policy in order to use this method.

Q: **What are "de minimus benefits"?**
A: de minimus or minimal benefits are items provided to employees that are of such little value that you can exclude them from the employee's wages. Cash and cash equivalents (such as use of a company credit card) can never be claimed as de minimus benefits, but there are numerous examples of items that do fit this classification: occasional use of a company copier, small inexpensive holiday gifts, occasional meals or movie tickets, etc. Group term life insurance benefits for the death of an employee's spouse or dependent also meet this requirement as long as the face amount of the policy is $2,000 or less. NOTE: IRS rules on de minimus items are not specific – in one case a $100 award was considered taxable, while in another case a $600 transfer of real estate proceeds was considered de minimus.

Q: **Are expense reimbursements subject to income tax withholding?**
A: Not if the expense reimbursement payments are made under an

accountable plan. To qualify as an accountable plan the expense reimbursement arrangement has to meet three conditions:

- Expenses have to be business connected.
- Employee expenses need to be reported within a reasonable time period (normally 60 days).
- Over-payment of expenses need to be returned within a reasonable period (normally 120 days).

Q: **What exactly is a "per diem" allowance?**
A: Per Diem is an allowance paid to an employee for lodging, meals and incidental expenses that occur when traveling. Employers can use either a per diem rate for lodging and meals or for meals alone. Per diem payments are not part of an employee's wages if the payment is less than or equal to the federal per diem rate (available in IRS Publication 1542) and the employer receives an expense report from the employee. The expense report must include the business purpose of the trip, the date and place of the trip, and must be filed with the employer with 60 days. Note: Employers can pay more than the federal per diem rate, but the excess will be taxable to the employee.

Q: **Is employer-provided parking taxable?**
A: No – up to a limit of $230 per month.

Q: **I want to give one of our employees a fixed "vehicle allowance" amount to cover expenses on his personal car – what are the tax consequences?**
A: The vehicle allowance is treated as additional income to the employee and is taxable. It's up to the employee to keep track of his auto expenses and to claim them on his 1040 form. Note: the vehicle allowance must be paid on a regular basis (at least once per quarter).

Q: **Are stock bonuses considered taxable wages?**
A: Yes, stock bonuses are considered the same as wages.

Q: **Can employers take the full value of a non-cash benefit as a business deduction?**
A: As a rule, no. Employers can only deduct the cost of the benefit, even though the actual value (usually the fair market value) of the benefit is normally higher. For employees, it's the benefit's actual value that has to be included in the employee's gross income.

Garnishments

Q: **What is a garnishment?**
A: A wage garnishment is a means of collecting a monetary judgment from a defendant by ordering a third party (the person's employer in this case) to pay a portion of the employee's earnings directly to the plaintiff. Title III of the Consumer Credit Protection Act (CCPA) limits the amount of an employee's earnings that may be garnished. Wage garnishments are normally limited to 25% of the employee's "disposable income" or whatever portion of the employee's wages are greater than thirty times the current federal minimum wage ($7.25 per hour), whichever is less. Garnishments can be taken for a number of reasons, but the most common ones are for child support or unpaid taxes. If an employee has multiple garnishments against his or her paycheck and there isn't enough money to satisfy all of them, the garnishments must be taken in order: federal first, then state or local, then any other judgments. If a state wage garnishment law differs from the federal law, the smaller garnishment must be used. Note that different states have varying laws concerning garnishments and you should check on the regulations in your particular state or states to make sure you are in compliance.

Note 1: In some cases involving child support or alimony, garnishments can be 50% or more of the employee's disposable income.
Note 2: In general, social security benefits, veteran's benefits, and railroad retirement benefits are not subject to garnishment.
Note 3: Garnishment restrictions do not apply to certain bankruptcy court orders or to amounts owed for federal or state taxes.
Note 4: Garnishment amounts are considered to be federal income taxable wages for the employee being garnished (that is, garnishments are taken after withholding taxes are calculated).

Q: **What are the restrictions on how wage garnishments are calculated?**
A: Garnishments are calculated based on the employee's "disposable earnings" which is the amount left over after all legally required deductions have been subtracted from earnings. Legally required deductions include Social Security and Medicare withholding taxes and federal, state and local income withholding taxes. They may also include withholding for an approved employee retirement plan. Once the disposable income has been determined multiply that amount by the garnishment rate to get the amount to be deducted.

Q: **Are tips considered to be wages when calculating a**

garnishment?
A: Tips aren't generally considered disposable earnings when figuring the amount of a garnishment.

Q: **What is a "voluntary wage assignment"?**
A: A garnishment is a form of involuntary wage assignment. There are also voluntary wage assignments, where an employee specifically asks to have a portion of his or her wages deducted and paid to a third party to take care of things like loans, child support, or back taxes. Some loans also stipulate that if the employee falls behind in making payments that the payments are to be deducted from the employee's paycheck.

Q: **Which type of garnishment has precedence – a child support order or a tax levy?**
A: Child support orders have priority over federal tax levies (if the child support order was received first).

Q: **What are the priorities of the different types of garnishments?**
A: Child support orders have the highest priority (except as noted above), followed by bankruptcy orders, administrative garnishments for federal agencies, federal tax levies, state tax levies, local tax levies and creditor garnishments. (Note: the dollar limits on wage garnishments as mentioned above apply regardless of how many garnishments are levied against a given employee's wages).

Q: **How do I know if an employee's wages are subject to a federal tax levy?**
A: IRS will send you a copy of Form 668-W (Notice of Levy on Wages, Salary and Other Income) when a federal tax levy is to be enforced. Form 668-W includes instructions to the employer on withholding and submitting the levy amount.

Q: **Can I fire an employee who has received a garnishment order?**
A: The Consumer Credit Protection Act prohibits an employer from firing an employee whose earnings are subject to garnishment for any one debt – however, the Act doesn't prohibit firing an employee who is being garnished for two or more separate debts.

Net Pay

Q: **How do I figure an employee's net pay?**
A: Take the employee's gross pay and subtract Social Security withholding tax, Medicare tax, federal income tax, state income tax, and any local withholding tax (and any other federal, state or local taxes). Then subtract any voluntary deductions (uniforms, health insurance, United Way, 401(k), etc.). That should give you the person's net pay. Keep in mind that certain other items can also affect net pay -- for example, if you pay auto allowances that add to a person's paycheck or if the employee has a garnishment.

Q: **What if an employee's deductions are more than his gross pay?**
A: If a worker's net pay ends up being negative, you have to start removing deductions (voluntary deductions first, then local withholding, state withholding, federal withholding, and finally FICA taxes) until you reach zero net pay. Then you simply issue a voided, zero amount paycheck to that person.

Methods of Payment

Q: **Why should I consider paying my employees by direct deposit?**
A: There are a number of advantages (to both employer and employee) in using direct deposit. It saves the employer the cost of buying and printing checks, cuts down on paper handling, and - for companies with workers in different locations - eliminates the hassle of getting the paychecks to each location safely and on time. For the employee, it removes the worry of lost or stolen checks and the need to physically take your paycheck to the bank to get it deposited (especially if you're on vacation or out sick on payday).

Q: **How does direct deposit work?**

A: Direct deposit is a method of transferring your employees' net pay directly into their bank accounts without the need for issuing paychecks. You, the employer, contract with your bank for the bank to automatically transfer your employees' net pay into their accounts each payday. There is normally a set charge by the bank for this service (say $1 for each payroll transaction). Once your company has been approved for direct deposit you will need to supply the bank with the routing and account numbers for each of your employees who signs up for direct deposit. Then, when you run your payroll, there's something you need to be aware of -- normally there is a 1 or 2-day lead time for direct deposit (although same day processing is becoming more common). For instance, you need to have your ACH (direct deposit) file submitted to your bank on Wednesday or Thursday to be sure that the employees pay will be in their bank accounts on Friday.

Q: **What's a transit number or routing number? And where can I find it?**
A: Each bank or similar financial institution has an identifying number (its ABA number) usually referred to as a "routing transit number" or just "routing number". If you look at a person's check you'll find both his bank's routing number and his bank account number printed in the MICR coding at the bottom of the check. The routing number should come first (reading from left to right), then the account number, and (usually) the check number on the far right.

Q: **What if an employee changes bank accounts?**
A: The employee needs to submit a new Direct Deposit Authorization so that his routing and/or account number can be changed before the next payday.

Q: Can I require my employees to use direct deposit?
A: It depends on the laws in your state -- most states require you to get written consent from the employee and make it clear that participation should be voluntary. However, there are a number of states that do not have laws that specifically prohibit mandatory direct deposit programs, including Alabama, Illinois, Indiana, Iowa, Louisiana, Missouri, Tennessee, and Texas.

Q: What are paycards?
A: Paycards (or "Payroll debit cards") work a lot like regular direct deposit. Pay cards came into being primarily for those employees who don't have a bank account. Payroll debit cards offer the same type of advantages as direct deposit, except that the employee's pay is transferred to a special employer-created account that allows the employee to use his or her pay card in much the same way as you would a regular credit card. The money is secured and employees with pay cards can withdraw cash from any ATM even if they don't have a bank account. However, one difference from a regular debit card is that there's no way to add money to the card other than through payroll.

Q: Are there any drawbacks to paycards?
A: Make sure that the paycard company you select allows employees to withdraw the full amount of their pay each pay period in multiple withdrawals without fees.

Q: What do I give to employees using direct deposit or pay cards in place of a check stub?
A: You can print a "direct deposit advice" or "remittance advice" for each employee (or – with your employees' permission – you can email the remittance advice to them).

Q: Any new pay options I should know about?
A: There's a movement that's gaining some traction to allow employees to get paid for whatever amount they earn during the day at the end of that day. Some employers are using third party services to make daily payments possible (and Gusto payroll service has added this option just recently). The way it works is that employees get a notification on their smartphones when they're done working for the day and at that point they can decide if they want to collect their pay for that day. If they do, the money is either transferred to a pre-paid debit card or deposited directly into the employees' bank accounts.

Self Employment Tax

Q: **What is "self-employment tax"?**
A: People who are in business but are not subject to withholding taxes (such as sole proprietors, members of a partnership, or independent contractors) are required to pay self-employment tax if they have an annual income of $400 or more. Self-employment taxes are basically the same as FICA taxes and, like FICA taxes, they consist of a Social Security tax and a Medicare tax. The total rate is normally 15.3 percent (12.4 percent for Social Security and 2.9 percent for Medicare). In other words the total self-employment tax is the same as if you added together the employee and employer portions of FICA tax for a normal employee. Just as for a regular employee, the maximum amount of income subject to Social Security tax is $132,900 for 2019 ($137,700 for 2020).

For sole proprietorships, partnerships, and limited-liability companies the self-employment taxes are imposed on your net self-employment income, which basically is just your business income minus your business deductions. In other words, self-employment tax gets charged on your business profit, but the IRS lets you count the employer half of the self-employment tax, or 7.65%, as a business deduction for purposes of calculating the tax. The 15.3% multiplier is actually applied to 92.35% of the business's net earnings rather than 100% - the difference, 7.65%, is the amount that an employer would normally pay for you and would take as a business expense. To compute your self employment tax you can use the formula:
12.4% x (.9235 x self-employment income) **or** 12.4% x $137,700 (whichever is less) + 2.9% x self-employment income

Q: **How do I report my self employment tax?**
A: You report self-employment taxes on your annual federal income tax return (on Schedule SE).

Q: **Do I need to make tax payments during the year?**
A: You are required to make quarterly estimated tax payments during the year (with each payment roughly equal to one fourth of the amount you expect to owe at the end of the year). Your quarterly payments are due on on the 15th of the month following the end of the quarter (or on the next business day if the 15th is a holiday or weekend). The simplest way to make your quarterly payments is through EFTPS (the Electronic Federal Tax Payment System).

Note: You are only required to make quarterly payments if you expect to owe $1,000 or more in federal income tax at the end of the year over and above any withheld tax and tax credits.

Q: **What if I am self-employed and also an employee?**
A: If you are self-employed and also an employee of someone else, both incomes are included in order to determine the total amount of Social Security and Medicare tax that you need to pay. For example:

- You earned a salary of $38,100 from a job and have a net profit from Schedule C of $73,000.
- Your net earnings on Line 6 of Long Schedule SE are $67,416 ($73,000 x .9235).
- Subtract your salary of $38,100 from the maximum social security wage base of $137,700 and the result is $99,600. Of the two amounts, $67,416 and $99,600, multiply the social security rate of 12.4% (employee 6.2% and employer 6.2%) by the lower amount, $67,416.
- Your self employment tax is $10,314.64: 12.4% x $67,416 (social security tax) plus 2.9% x $67,416 (medicare tax).

Note: The net profit reported on Schedule C is carried to Schedule SE where it is reduced by 7.65% (the Schedule C net profit times .9235).

Q: **What if, at the end of the year, I've underpaid my estimated taxes?**
A: If you didn't pay enough tax during the year, either through withholding or by making estimated tax payments, you may have to pay a penalty. Generally, most taxpayers will avoid this penalty if they owe less than $1,000 in tax after subtracting any withholding and credits, or if they paid at least 90% of the tax for the current year, or 100% of the tax for the previous year, whichever is smaller.

Payroll Tax Reports and Record-Keeping

Q: **What reports do I need to file and when do I file them?**
A: At the end of every quarter most employers must file a Form 941 (Employer's Quarterly Tax Return) to report payroll withholding tax liabilities and payments. Semi-weekly depositors must also fill out and attach a Schedule B showing tax liability by date. In addition employers must submit whatever state reports are required (usually a summary of taxes withheld and a report covering state unemployment tax payments). Agricultural employers must file Form 943 quarterly instead of Form 941, while employers whose annual liability for social security, Medicare and federal income tax withheld is $1000 or less file Form 944 annually rather than submitting a Form 941 each quarter. Seasonal employers file Form 941 but don't have to file a report in quarters when they have no income. At the end of the year all employers have to file Forms W-3 and W-2 to report employee earnings, taxes and other information for the year, and Form 940 to report federal unemployment liability and payments. In addition employers should prepare a Form 1099-MISC for any non-employee (other than corporations) that you paid over $600 to during the year in rents, royalties, commissions, fees, prizes, or awards. Gross royalty payments of $10 or more must also be reported at year-end on a 1099-MISC.

Q: **What information goes on the Form 941 and Schedule B?**
A: Form 941 is used to report your quarterly withholding tax liability and tax payments for Social Security, Medicare, and federal income tax withholding, along with your employer matching payments for Social Security and Medicare. If your quarterly taxes are more than $2500 and you're a monthly depositor the tax total on line 10 should agree with the tax liability total on Part 2, line 15. If you're a semi-weekly depositor, you need to fill out Schedule B (a detailed listing of deposit liabilities by date) and the tax total on line 10 should agree with the total tax liability shown at the bottom of the Schedule B.
Note: Forms 941 and Schedule B can be downloaded from the IRS website at www.irs.gov.

Q: **What if I get a notice from IRS that there's a problem with my 941 and I want my payroll service to talk directly with IRS?**
A: If you want to have a third party (such as a payroll service or accountant) receive and discuss your tax information directly with IRS you can file IRS form 8821 (Tax Information Authorization). Form 8821 simply allows an employer to authorize an employee or 3rd party to receive tax information from the IRS. If you want to designate someone

to actually represent your company in front of the IRS you will need to file Form 2848 (Power of Attorney and Declaration of Representative). If filing Form 8821 you simply designate the tax period for which you are authorizing a third party to send and receive information from the IRS and the name of the third party. After the form is processed the IRS will add the name of the third party designee to your account and that person will be authorized to discuss your tax account information. If you want to revoke a previously filed form 8821, write "Revoke" across the top of a copy of the previously filed form, sign your name and mail it to the same IRS office where you originally filed the form. You can also simply write a letter to IRS requesting to revoke the form 8821, listing the periods for which it is revoked and the tax matters for which it is revoked.
Note: You can also fax a Form 8821 to the IRS:

If you are west of the Mississippi River, use (855) 214-7522
If you are east of the Mississippi River, use (855) 214-7519

Q: **What if my company has a more serious problem and we want to appoint an agent to appear before IRS in our behalf?**
A: You can file Form 2848 (Power of Attorney and Declaration of Representative) to appoint an individual (someone knowledgeable about IRS regulations and someone you trust with your company's financial affairs) as your agent.

Q: **What is Form 944?**
A: Businesses with an annual payroll tax liability of $1,000 or less can file form 944 (Employer's Annual Federal Tax Return) at the end of the year rather than filing form 941 (Employer's Quarterly Federal Tax Return) each quarter. NOTE: If you file Form 944, you may NOT file Form 941. Normally IRS will notify you if you must file Form 944, but small businesses can also file a request with IRS to be allowed to file Form 944 instead of Form 941.

Q: **What information goes on the Form 940?**
A: Form 940 is the Employer's Annual Federal Unemployment Tax Act (FUTA) Tax Return. It lists the state where you pay unemployment (you'll need Form 940 Schedule A if you pay in more than one state), total payments to all employees, any payments that were exempt from FUTA tax (such as dependent care and group term life insurance), total of payments over and above the current $7000 FUTA wage limit, your FUTA tax liability (by quarter) and your FUTA tax deposited during the year. If you pay wages in a "credit reduction" state during 2018 you may also have to pay some additional FUTA tax by January 31, 2019. If your total tax liability for the year is under $100 you can simply send a check along with the form. Form 940 is normally due at the end of January --

however, if you made all of your deposits on time you have an additional 10 days to file your 940.

Q: **When do I have to have W-2 forms to my employees?**
A: Form W-2 is used to report wages paid to employees and the taxes withheld from them. You need to furnish a W-2 to each of your employees (including anyone who worked for you during the calendar year) by the end of January of the following year. You also need to submit a W-3 and Copy A of your W-2 forms or a properly formatted electronic file to Social Security by the end of January. You can transmit electronic W-2 files by using the Social Security Administration's Business Services Online system (requires registration).

Q: **Do I have to send copies of the W-2 forms to the state?**
A: The nine states that do not currently collect individual income tax (Alaska, Florida, Nevada, New Hampshire, South Dakota, Tennessee, Texas, Washington, and Wyoming) do not require employers to send copies of their W-2 forms. For all other states check with your state tax agency – some states require you to submit paper copies or file electronically, some states allow electronic filing only, and some states no longer require employers to submit W-2 copies at all.

Q: **Shouldn't the gross wages on a W-2 equal the employee's total wages for the year?**
A: Not necessarily. The wages shown in box 1 of the W-2 form are federal taxable wages only; so if an employee has pre-tax benefits (such as cafeteria plan deductions or a 401(k) deduction) the person's annual wages in Box 1 will be reduced by the amount of those benefits.

Q: **What if I discover a wrong Social Security number on a W-2 and the W-2s have already been filed with the SSA?**
A: Fill out a W-2C form (available for download from www.irs.gov) – provide a copy to the employee and to the Social Security Administration. Ir you have signed up to use the Social Security Administration's BSO (Business Services Online) system you can also go to www.ssa.gov/employer and fill out and file W-2C forms electronically.

Q: **If I find out I have a wrong address on a W-2 what do I need to do?**
A: Issue the employee a new W-2 with the corrected address and mark it as a "Reissued W-2 Form" (do not send the revised copy A to the Social Security Administration).

Q: **What about reporting payments to independent contractors?**

A: If you pay an independent contractor more than $600 in a calendar year you're required to issue that contractor (other than corporations) a Form 1099-Misc so that IRS can track tax payments by the contractor on that income.

Q: **What is Form 945?**
A: Form 945 (Annual Return of Withheld Federal Income Tax) is used to report withheld federal income tax from non-payroll payments, including: pensions and backup withholding. The form can be downloaded directly from the IRS website.

Q: **How long do I need to keep payroll records?**
A: There are a number of (sometimes conflicting) guidelines on retention of payroll and human resource records. Generally speaking, records relating to a particular employee should be kept while the employee is with the company and for three years after he or she leaves. You're generally safe if you retain other payroll records for six years; beyond that you should probably consider shredding those records to dispose of them in a secure manner. Note: Most federal forms (such as 941, 940, W-3, W-2, and I-9 forms) can be disposed of after 4 years).
Note: With the availability of inexpensive storage devices and secure cloud storage, scanning and storing important records indefinitely is becoming a more common option.

Q: **What is a "Certified Payroll" Report and why would I need one?**
A: If you are a contractor or subcontractor on a government-funded construction project you are required to submit weekly certified payroll reports to make sure you are complying with the terms of your government contract. The details of certified payroll reporting and what is required by different states is a complicated topic which is outside the scope of this book. For further information on exactly what reports you need to submit, you need to contact the appropriate state agency.

Basic Accounting Entries for Payroll

Q: What general journal entries do I make after a payroll has been run?

A: The first set of entries may look something like this:

	Debit	Credit
Hourly Wage expense	xxx	
Salaries expense	xxx	
Payroll tax expense	xxx	
Cash in Bank (Net Pay)		xxx
Federal withholding taxes payable		xxx
Social security taxes payable		xxx
Medicare taxes payable		xxx
Federal unemployment taxes payable		xxx
State withholding taxes payable		xxx
State unemployment taxes payable		xxx
Garnishments payable		xxx

Plus any voluntary deduction expenses:

	Credit
401(k) contributions payable	xxx
Health insurance payable	xxx

When the taxes and other liabilities are paid a second set of entries is made to relieve those payables:

	Debit	Credit
Cash in Bank		xxx
Federal withholding taxes payable	xxx	
Social security taxes payable	xxx	
Medicare taxes payable	xxx	
Federal unemployment taxes payable	xxx	
State withholding taxes payable	xxx	
State unemployment taxes payable	xxx	
Garnishments payable	xxx	
401(k) contributions payable	xxx	
Health insurance payable	xxx	

Payroll Audits

Q: What types of payroll audits are there?

A: There are three main categories of payroll audits: internal compliance audits, external audits and government audit. Audits can be held on-site or at a third party's establishment. They are carried out to ensure that organizations satisfy their obligations related to the employment of workers, payment of salaries and wages, the collection and remittance of statutory withholdings and the accuracy of annual returns. Internal audits are usually a "catch-all" audit, looking at everything from hiring practices to tax compliance to records security. External audits tend to focus on one or more specific areas, such as workers compensation or 401(k) plan management, while government audits are normally carried out by a particular agency, such as IRS tax audits, FLSA compliance audits or state unemployment insurance audits.

Q: Why conduct internal audits?

A: Employers are required to comply with federal,state and local tax laws, wage and hour regulations, and additional laws concerning everything from fair employment practices to proper handling of pension plan funds. Conducting periodic internal audits can help ensure that you are staying in compliance in all these areas and can also point out issues that need to be addressed in order to keep you prepared in case of an external audit.

Q: How can I check for fraud risks?

A: You need to watch for situations such as::

- Employee updates, payroll approval, payroll processing, recording of payroll, and/or reconciliation of the payroll account being handled by just one person (payroll preparation, processing and reconciliation duties should be divided among different individuals).
- The same employee receiving more than one check on a given payroll.
- The existence of duplicate or missing checks (make sure all payroll records are stored in a secure location).
- More than one direct deposit payment being made to the same bank account but with different employee names.
- Payroll checks or direct deposit payments being made to terminated (or non-existent) employees (run an employee census report occasionally and review it for inactive, terminated or fictitious employees).

- Exempt employees receiving overtime pay.
- Employees or departments with excessive overtime pay (periodically compare time sheet input with regular and overtime earnings).
- Direct deposit payments to an employee with the same bank account number as a vendor in your vendor file (periodically compare voluntary deduction amounts such as health insurance and retirement contributions to amounts paid to vendors for a given payroll).
- Differences between time card or time clock data and actual paycheck data.
- Unverified changes in salary or hourly pay rate.
- False or duplicate Social Security numbers.
- Federal, state or local quarterly tax reports that don't agree with payroll totals for the quarter (if possible, generate quarterly tax reports at times during the quarter and compare them to payroll totals to make sure you're in balance).
- Multiple records in the employee file with the same employee name and address, but with different bank accounts.
- Employee checks or direct deposit payments with no taxes or voluntary deductions taken out.

Q: In general, what documents should I make sure are available and up-to-date in case of an external audit of some type?
A: Documents that you need to have available include:
- Current employee census report.
- Employee listing show job title and duties.
- Payroll register (that can be run for one or more pay periods) showing earnings by type, taxes withheld, voluntary and involuntary deductions, and net pay by employee and pay date.
- Federal (Form 940) and state unemployment tax returns.
- Form 1040 Schedule C (if sole proprietor).
- General ledger and (if applicable) subcontractor ledgers and journal.
- Certificates of insurance for any subcontractors.
- Workers' Compensation insurance policy and workers compensation report showing regular and overtime earnings by state, by employee, by classification code.
- Corporate officer information.

Q: What about Human Resources audits?
A: The different types of Human Resource audits include:
- Recruitment and Hiring audit

- Do you have job descriptions for all openings and are they ADA compliant?
- If there is a "ban the box" law in your area that affects your company, are you in compliance with all the requirements of that law?
- Is everyone in your company who conducts hiring interviews aware of permissible interview questions and acceptable reasons for hiring or not hiring a particular applicant?
- Are benefits offered to all full-time employees?
- Is there a procedure for notifying rejected candidates?
- Are references routinely checked before hiring?
- Fair Labor Standards Act (FLSA) audit
  - Do you have written job descriptions?
  - Are all required federal, state and local labor law posters current and prominently displayed?
  - Are employees being properly classified as exempt or non-exempt?
  - Are overtime wages being properly calculated and paid?
  - Are all employees being paid at least federal minimum wage?
  - Are employees being given legally required breaks?
  - If minors are employed are their hours and duties in accordance with federal laws?
- Americans with Disabilities Act (ADA) audit
  - Does your anti-discrimination policy include disability?
  - Do your discipline, termination and drug testing policies comply with the ADA?
  - Are employee medical information being protected from improper disclosure?
  - Do you have a policy for how to address requests for special accommodation under the ADA?
  - Are your managers trained on ADA requirements?
- Family and Medical Leave Act (FMLA) audit
  - Do you have a written policy that addresses all the requirements of the FMLA?
  - Do employee job descriptions define job duties?
  - How are FMLA leaves treated for purposes of payroll?
  - What are the procedures involved in handling an employee's request for FMLA leave?

Q: What do I need to do to be ready for an HR audit?
A: Review all your personnel records:

- Personnel records – make sure there is a current I-9 form on file for each employee, ensure that employee medical records are kept in a separate (secure) file, and check employee files for voluntary deduction and direct deposit authorizations, emergency contacts, job applications and employment contracts, confidentiality agreements and W-2 copies.
- Payroll – check to make sure federal and state minimum wage requirements are being met.
- Posters – posters regarding federal, state, or local laws should be current and posted where they can be seen by all employees.
- Employee handbook – each employee should have a copy of the company's employee handbook, outlining company policies and procedures. In particular there should be sections on how to submit complaints and on the company's "Safe Harbor" policy.

Q: What's involved in a DOL (Department of Labor) audit?
A: DOL audits (often referred to as Wage and Hour audits) are done to ensure that employers are complying with the regulations set out in the FLSA (Fair Labor Standards Act) – specifically, the minimum wage and overtime rules, and the exempt or non-exempt status of employees. The FLSA requires employers to pay at least minimum wage to employees and to pay non-exempt workers at least one and a half times their normal pay rate for hours worked over 40 in a given workweek. In addition, the auditor may explore the company's compliance with child labor laws or hazardous job duties if those areas apply to the company's operations.

Q: Does the DOL tend to audit certain types of businesses more than others?
A: In recent years the DOL has concentrated more on businesses in areas such as healthcare, day care, temporary staffing, restaurants and agriculture – basically companies that employee lower wage workers.

Q: How much time will I have to prepare for a DOL audit?
A: The Department of Labor can choose to audit you at any time, usually with little (or no) advance warning. You can request additional time to gather the records you'll need for the audit, but the additional time granted depends on the auditor.

Q: What time period does a DOL audit involve?
A: Usually the audit will cover the past two years. However, if the auditor suspects major violations of the FLSA he or she can go back three years.

Q: What records do I need to have available?
A: Contact the auditor for guidance on what the focus of the audit will be and what records you will need to have on hand (Note: make sure you have the records requested by the auditor but don't offer additional records that weren't requested). Be prepared to provide documentation on company compensation policies and procedures.

What else do I need to do to get ready for the audit?
A: In addition to reviewing the payroll records for the last three years you should:

- Be prepared to explain exactly which job categories are being considered as exempt from overtime and the reasons for those exemptions.
- Be able to explain how employee time is recorded, how overtime is paid, and whether rounding is used in recording employee hours.
- Know how employee wage garnishments are being calculated and paid.
- Make sure that all required labor law posters and notices are current, clearly visible and posted in a common area of the workplace.
- Be aware that the auditor will likely want to interview certain employees and make sure those people are available to be interviewed.
- The DOL does permit an employer's attorney to be present during interviews with management (but not employees), so notify your attorney if you want him or her available to sit in on those interviews.

Q: What types of things could I get penalized for?
A: There are a number of items that the DOL is looking at in particular:

- Salaried employees who have been classified as exempt from overtime pay without any proof that their job duties justify treating them as exempt.
- Inaccurate or missing records of overtime payments to non-exempt employees.
- Employees being paid less than federal minimum wage.
- Insufficient tips that don't make up the difference between what the employee is being paid and minimum wage.
- Deductions from an employee's pay without the agreement of the employee.

Q: What kind of penalties could I face if the DOL finds any violations of the FLSA?

A: If willful violations are found the DOL can file suit for back wages for each employee (and an equal amount in damages), along with civil penalties of up to $1,000 per person. Obviously, if multiple employees are involved the penalties can add up to a substantial amount.

Q: What's involved in a Workers' Compensation audit?

A: Workers' Compensation premium audits are normally conducted at the policy expiration date to determine the cost of your coverage going forward. The audits are performed to ensure that the premiums employers pay for workers' compensation insurance accurately reflect the insurance company's financial risk. Insurers check to make sure that employers are properly classified (that is, that they belong to the correct group of employers who run similar businesses) and that the payrolls used for rating purposes are accurate. If an employer's policy contains the wrong classifications or payrolls, the employer may be paying too much or too little relative to other employers. Basically, your premiums are based on three factors: the total remuneration (pay) for all employees for the year, the injury risk factor attached to the job duties of individual employees, and the amount of payments made to sub-contractors and independent contractors who have no workers compensation insurance.

Q: What types of workers comp audits are there?

A: There are two types of audits:
- Physical audit - This type of audit is performed at your place of business within 60 days after the expiration of your workers compensation policy. The auditor will notify you by mail and schedule the audit appointment.
- Voluntary audit - Within 30 days of the expiration of your policy you'll receive a voluntary audit form from the insurance company in the mail. This form should be completed and returned to the insurance company as soon as possible. The form usually shows the classifications as shown on your policy and asks for your actual payroll exposures for each class. These forms can be confusing so if you have any questions be sure to contact the insurance company and ask them how to complete the form.

Q: What types of pay (remuneration) are included in determining employee pay for workers compensation purposes?

A: Do include:
- Regular hourly pay and salaries (including retroactive pay).
- The straight time portion of overtime pay (for example, if you pay overtime at one and a half times normal pay rate, you can

subtract 33% of overtime wages - the "premium" portion of overtime pay).

- Commissions and draws against commissions
- Bonuses including stock bonuses
- Holiday, vacation, or sick pay
- Payments for salary reduction, retirement or cafeteria plans (IRS Section 125 plans) which are made through deductions from the employee's gross pay.
- Annuity plans.
- Expense reimbursements to employees to the extent that an employer's records do not substantiate that the expense was incurred as a valid business expense.
- Payment by an employer of amounts otherwise required by law to be paid by employees to statutory insurance or pension plans, such as FICA taxes.
- Payment to employees on any basis other than time worked, such as piecework, profit sharing, or incentive plans.
- The rental value of an apartment, house or other lodging provided for an employee, based on comparable accommodations.
- The value of meals received by employees as part of their pay.
- Davis-Bacon wages paid to employees or placed by an employer into third-party pension trusts.

Q: What types of remuneration are excluded in determining employee pay for workers compensation purposes?
A: Don't include:

- Tips or other gratuities.
- Employer payments to group insurance plans.
- Employer contributions to Cafeteria (Section 125) plans.
- Employer contributions to 401(k) or other salary reduction retirement plans.
- Employer contributions to employee savings plans.
- Severance pay except for hours worked or unused vacation time.
- Expense reimbursements to employees (as long as the expense was determined to be a valid business expense).
- Payments to employees on active military duty.
- Allowances for employee work uniforms.
- Employee discounts on items purchased from the company.
- Use of company provided vehicles.
- Club memberships.
- Sick pay paid by a third party.

- Airline travel.

Q: How is my workers comp insurance premium calculated?

A: Workers' comp insurance premiums are calculated according to the job classifications codes assigned to your employees by the insurance company t(and there are usually different classification codes for different groups of employees – such as clerical workers and machine shop workers). The premium amount for each group with the same classification code is calculated as the rate for that classification times the total annual payroll for that group (minus any excluded amounts), divided by 100. The premium rate itself expressed as dollars and cents per $100 dollars of payroll for each class code.

Q: What records will I need to provide for a workers compensation audit?

A: Check with the auditor and make sure you have whatever records he or she requests ready on the day of the audit. Don't provide any other documentation though, just the specific records asked for by the auditor. In general the auditor will want:

- A payroll journal or earnings report for the year, showing all pay (remuneration) for each employee, broken down by regular pay, overtime pay, salaries, commissions, bonuses and any other special types of pay.
- Your federal 941 form for each quarter of the year.
- State unemployment insurance reports for each quarter.
- An annual workers compensation report that breaks down each employee's regular and overtime pay by state and classification code (if an employee works in more than one class code his or her totals should be split out under the appropriate codes).
- A detailed listing of the job duties for each of your employees.
- A cash disbursements journal showing all payments to sub-contractors and independent contractors.
- Certificates of insurance for all sub-contractors and independent contractors.

Q: What if I don't agree to an audit or the audit doesn't get completed?

A: If the audit isn't completed, or if the auditor feels that you were uncooperative in completing the audit, the insurance company is allowed to use estimated audit figures – and they get to calculate the estimated figures.

Q: If my company has a 401(k) plan will I be audited?

114

A: Federal law requires that "large" 401(k) plans undergo an annual audit from an independent CPA firm. Basically, an external audit is required if:

- You have 100 eligible plan participants or more on the first day of the plan year (or 120 if your plan has never had an external audit before).
- You have assets held in trust (as required by law).

Q: Who qualifies as an "eligible" participant in a 401(k) plan?
A: Eligible participants include:

- Active employees who are participating in the plan.
- Active employees who are eligible to participate but aren't currently doing so.
- Terminated, resigned or retired employees who still have a balance in the plan on the first day of the plan year.
- Beneficiaries of deceased employees who are receiving (or are entitled to receive) benefits from the plan.

Q: Can I avoid an external audit even if I have over 100 eligible employees?
A: Yes. If your plan was filed in the previous year as a "small plan" (that is, a plan with under 100 eligible participants) and you still have less than 120 participants, you can continue to file as a "small plan" and avoid the external audit requirement.

Q: What documents will I need for a 401(k) audit?
A: The documents you need will normally include:

- Current year employee census.
- Copy of the Form 5500 (Annual Return/Report of Employee Benefit Plan).
- Executed plan documents (including executed amendments).
- Participant statements and trust reports.
- Plan sponsor financial statements.
- Loan documents for all participant loans.
- Certification report from the plan custodian.
- Schedule of deposits to the plan by pay period.
- IRS Determination Letter.
- ERISA fidelity bond.
- Form W-2s or annual payroll register by employee.
- Form 1099 for plan distributions.

Payroll Software

Note: You can find detailed information on most of the in-house payroll software packages that are currently available in the author's book: *The Employer's Guide to In-House Payroll Software.*

Q: Why use payroll software rather than doing payroll manually, letting an accountant do it, or using a payroll service bureau?
A: In many cases one of the alternatives to in-house software may work fine for your company. Some reasons to consider using payroll software to process payroll in-house are:

- An automated system can make entering and maintaining payroll data easier and may include edit checking to help eliminate keying and calculation errors.
- In-house payroll software allows you to protect employee personal information along with wage and salary information and it makes it easier to deal with last-minute payroll changes.
- Having your accountant handle your payroll along with your other accounting can be convenient – but your accountant may not be a payroll expert and today's payroll regulations are much more complicated than they were even a few years ago.
- Payroll service bureaus can be a very good choice, allowing you to spend more time on business operations – but they can also be somewhat expensive, you forfeit some control of your business, and you're dependent on the payroll service preparing your checks, direct deposits, federal, state, local and other reports on time, as well as making the correct tax deposits when they're due.

Q: What general features should I look for in a payroll software package?
A: A comprehensive payroll package should include the ability to:

- Process payroll for employees in multiple states including state and local withholding tax calculations.
- Handle at least weekly, bi-weekly, semi-monthly and monthly pay frequencies.
- Pay salaried, hourly and piece-work employees.
- Handle multiple pay rates and shift differentials.
- Allow many different types of compensation such as regular pay, overtime, vacation, sick pay, commissions, bonuses, retro pay, dock (negative) pay, meals and tips.

- Accept data from time clock systems or provide an integrated time clock system.
- Provide for expense reimbursements.
- Do direct deposit payments (including pay cards) as well as checks.
- Print checks and deposit slips on blank laser stock and print signatures on checks.
- Handle various special types of deductions and benefits such as 401(k) contributions (pre-tax and Roth post-tax), 401(k) employer matching amounts, cafeteria plans, group term life insurance, IRAs, vehicle allowances and health savings accounts (HSAs).
- Create direct deposit files in standard NACHA (National Automated Clearing House Association) file format if necessary.
- Create either reports or electronic files needed to make federal payroll tax deposits through the Electronic Federal Tax Payment System (EFTPS), as well as state withholding tax and unemployment insurance tax deposits.
- Accrue and report various types of employee leave time (sick time, vacation, or paid time off).
- Provide reporting by cost center (department, store, property, etc.).
- Implement security features to protect your payroll data.
- Maintain detailed payroll history files.

Q: What are some desirable features to have in a payroll package?
A: Some features that would be nice to have include the ability for employees to have more direct access to their payroll information through web-based technology and direct entry of some data such as employee personal information by the employees.

Q: What's the best way to evaluate payroll software?
A: Look for software vendors who have been around for a while (as an indication that they have a relatively error-free package and that they will still be around in the future). And if at all possible arrange to get a live demo and a trial version of the software so that you can set up a few employees and run through some of your typical payrolls. That way you get a feel for how user-friendly the package is, how complete it is, and whether it can do everything you need it to do. Even if a package has the features you want, that doesn't mean that you'll like the way those features work – for example, you may be able to reverse and re-run a payroll but if it takes six steps and a half-hour to accomplish that you might want to consider some other software.

Q: **What about an interface to my financial accounting package – or our time clock system?**
A: Payroll software can be limited to processing payrolls and producing payroll forms and reports – or it can include a variety of additional products. If it's important to you to have your software interfaced with existing programs, make sure that any payroll package you're considering can be easily "connected" to your other accounting software.

Q: **What if I need a custom program?**
A: Even if the software handles your usual payroll processing, you may run into a situation where you need something the software doesn't do. So you need to know when you buy a payroll package whether or not the vendor is willing and able to do some customization if necessary and what the general time frame and cost is for program modifications.

Q: **What about training?**
A: Ideally a payroll software package should include (in addition to a good help file) an overview of the system, some simple text-based tutorials, videos showing exactly how the software works and covering all the basic features of the system, and an online forum where users can discuss any problems or questions they have about the software.

Q: **What if I run a payroll and then notice an error?**
A: Payroll software should allow you to back up, correct and re-run a payroll if you find that you've made an error or need to add, change or delete some information.

Q: **What if I need payroll information for a workers' compensation audit or a report of an employee's earnings for a previous year?**
A: Your payroll software should maintain a history of previous payroll data and allow you to generate various payment history reports.

Q: **Where can I find in-house payroll software packages?**
A: There are a number of software packages on the market that you can choose from, including Intuit's QuickBooks payroll, Sage Systems Abra payroll, Cougar Mountain payroll, Pensoft Payroll Plus, CheckMark Software's Payroll for Windows, and Red Wing payroll. You can find descriptions and ratings for these packages at various sites on the Internet (www.cpatechnologyadvisor.com for example) and in the author's book *The Employer's Guide to In-House Payroll Software*.

Outsourcing (Payroll Services)

Q: **We're spending too much time on payroll -- what can we do about it?**
A: Payroll and Human Resource functions can eat up a good deal of time -- time that you, as an employer, would much rather spend doing whatever it is you're in business to do. Not only that, IRS has reported that 40% of small businesses that handle their own payrolls are fined for inaccurate returns. If you can cost justify it, outsourcing your payroll can be a real time saver as well as reducing the number of things you have to worry about. Professional payroll processing companies have a variety of services available for employers. You can let them handle everything from payroll input to tax deposits to filing of forms or you can do the input, employee updates, tax deposits and quarterly/annual reports in-house if you want greater control over the payroll process. In either case, look for a company that does payroll as its main function, find out if they have clients with businesses similar to yours, be sure to check out the references they give you, and make certain you have a firm quote as to what you're going to be charged and what you get for that price.

NOTE: The vast majority of payroll processing services are competent and reliable – but you should always keep in mind that you, the client, are ultimately responsible for any errors made by your payroll processor. That fact was driven home by the collapse of MyPayrollHR, and the arrest of its owner, Michael Mann, which left more than 1,000 businesses across the country affected by the shutdown.

Q: **How can I check to make sure my payroll service is making my company's federal tax payments?**
A: You can verify your federal withholding tax payments are being made by logging onto the EFTPS website. To view payments made on your behalf you need to have registered with EFTPS and received your PIN (Personal Identification Number). Once you've registered with EFTPS you'll have access to view the federal payments being made by your payroll company. Note: It can take a couple of days after the payment date for the payment to post to your account.

Q: **What about doing my own input?**
A: Many payroll services provide software packages that you can install and run on your own PC as a front-end to their system. Some payroll processors also offer an online option that allows you to do almost everything on the internet, using just your browser.

Professional Employer Organizations

Q: **What is a Professional Employer Organization (PEO)?**
A: Professional Employer Organizations work with businesses of all sizes
to provide support for payroll, human resources, workers compensation,
and other functions. They actually enter into a legal partnership with their
clients, becoming the client's co-employer.

Q: **What can a PEO do for me?**
A: A PEO can relieve you of a good deal of the burden of payroll,
employee administration, and risk management concerns, giving you
more time to focus on growing your business. Because PEOs act as your
"co-employer", they can pool your employees with the employees of the
other companies that have partnered with them. By having such a large
employee base PEOs can usually offer workers' compensation insurance
and comprehensive benefit programs to you at very reasonable rates. A
PEO can also take on the majority of the risks involved in maintaining
compliance with the various payroll and employment laws and
regulations – not just tax compliance, but hiring and employment
management regulations as well.

Q: **What exactly is a "co-employer"?**
A: According to the National Association of PEOs, co-employment is "a
contractual allocation and sharing of certain employer responsibilities
between the PEO and the client.". The contract between your business
and a PEO divides the employer responsibilities. As the "employer of
record" the PEO handles payroll administration and associated tax filing,
provides human resources support, provides access to benefit packages
and workers' compensation insurance, and shares the burden of liability
for payroll and HR matters. You, as the client, retain control over day-to-
day operations and employee management.

Q: **Do I have to share control of the company with a PEO?**
You're still in full control of your company when you partner with a PEO.
The only change is that the PEO becomes the "employer of record"
which means it's legally responsible for everything to do with your
payroll, payroll taxes, benefit programs and insurance.

Q: **Do PEOs only partner with large companies?**
A: A recent survey by the National Association of Professional Employer
Organizations (NAPEO) indicates that about 15 percent of businesses in
the United States that employ between 10 and 100 people make use of a
PEO. PEOs may be able to benefit small employers even more than

120

larger ones because they can provide smaller companies with access to resources that they wouldn't have otherwise. Plus, as the employer of record, they may be able to offer your company a lower unemployment tax rate and lower workers compensation premiums.

Q: **What types of services do PEOs provide?**
A: Typically, a PEO will:
- Handle your payroll processing, including making payroll tax payments and filing federal, state and local tax reports.
- Maintain your I-9 forms and make sure they're up-to-date.
- Offer medical, dental and vision coverage to your employees at reasonable rates.
- Assist with benefit on-boarding and claims.
- Offer other options which may include:
  - New hire reporting.
  - Workers' compensation insurance coverage.
  - Life insurance.
  - 401(k) plans.
  - Employment practices liability insurance.
  - Employee recruiting and training.

In some cases a PEO may also provide life insurance, disability insurance, flexible spending accounts (FSAs), access to 401(k) plans, and other services.

Q: **What are the drawbacks of partnering with a PEO?**
A: Working with a PEO is somewhat like any other relationship. It can be great or there can be conflicts, such as whether or not the PEO's system fits well with your own established practices, or whether or not you have problems with the vendors the PEO picks to manage your benefits and workers compensation insurance. Probably the biggest drawback is the fact that you're not establishing a track record of your own if you're working with a PEO – which can be a significant problem if you have to suddenly part ways with your PEO and go out on your own.

Q: **How much does a PEO charge for their services?**
A: Generally a PEO charges in one of two ways:
1) A set amount per employee per month (generally between $40 and $160 per month depending on what services the PEO is going to provide).
2) A percentage of your total gross pay, ranging anywhere from 2% to about 12%. Obviously, if you have a lot of employees with very few highly compensated people, option 1 may be preferable

while option 2 may be better if you have a large number of highly compensated employees.

Q: **Where can I find out more about Professional Employer Organizations?**
A: You can take a look at the author's book: *Professional Employer Organizations: Can They Help You Grow Your Business?* Plus there are some good sources online including:
- *10 Tough Questions to Ask Your Future PEO* – https://www.peocompare.com/10-tough-questions-to-ask-your-future-peo/.
- *All You Need to Know About PEOs* - https://www.priorityhr.com/blog/entry/all-you-need-to-know-about-professional-employer-organizations-peos
- *Understanding a PEO: The Basics* - https://www.peocompare.com/understanding-a-peo/

Q: **Where do I go to find a PEO in my area?**
A: NAPEO (the National Association of Professional Employer Organizations) maintains a database of PEOs by state. To find one in your area go to:
https://www.napeo.org/what-is-a-peo/selecting-a-peo/find-a-peo

Human Resources

Q: **What does a "human resources system" include?**
A: Human resource management systems usually include:
- Job Openings and Applicant tracking.
- Benefits information.
- Tracking employee vacation, sick leave and personal time accrual.
- Training information.
- Performance, pay rate and promotion history.
- Employee review and reminder reports.
- Employee skills and education information.
- Affirmative action tracking.
- New hire reports.
- Wellness and emergency information reports.
- EEO reports.
- OSHA compliance and workers' compensation reports.

Q: **What is "SHRM"?**
A: The Society for Human Resource Management (SHRM) is the world's largest organization devoted to human resource management. The website at www.shrm.org includes information on employment law and other legal issues, sample job descriptions, guidelines for creating company policy manuals, human resource education and certification training, HR publications and community forums.

Q: **What is included in an HR audit?**
A: Typical areas covered in a Human Resources audit include:
- Recruitment and job applicant selection processes.
- Employee record keeping (especially to insure compliance with federal and state record-keeping regulations).
- Compensation and benefits information.
- Safety procedures and risk management practices.
- Employee training and career development programs and policies.
- Employee relations procedures and history.

Q: **What is "strategic HR management"?**
A: Traditionally human resource departments have been concerning with hiring people with the right skill set for specific jobs and dealing with the core functions associated with managing employees – hiring, employee

pay, benefits, and training, as well as generating all required reports. The idea behind strategic HR management is to determine how best to use the human resources department to contribute to the overall goals of the organization – improving individual performance, increasing profits, and providing the organizational flexibility needed to introduce and support new products and services.

Q: **What is a "SWOT" analysis?**
A: A SWOT (Strengths, Weaknesses, Opportunities and Threats) analysis involves defining an organization's goals and identifying those factors that are favorable or unfavorable to achieving those goals. In terms of Human Resources, strengths may include a compensation plan that's competitive with similar companies in the same industry, well-thought out and implemented workplace safety measures, and low employee turn-over. Weaknesses might include an employee benefit plan that is lacking a number of key features or a sub-standard training program. Opportunities may involve the prospective use of new technologies, while threats might include more restrictive employment laws or possible lawsuits from ex-employees.

Q: **What is normally included in an applicant tracking system?**
A: Applicant tracking systems include features such as:
- Posting job openings to the most popular online job boards.
- Collecting applicant information on a web page describing current job openings.
- Qualifying applicants according to pre-screening criteria.
- Automatic parsing and import of resumes to your company's database system.
- Tracking the progress of each job applicant during the hiring process.
- Sending automatic emails to selected job candidates.
- Ensuring that hiring procedures follow federal and state anti-discrimination rules.

Q: **What considerations go into creating an effective job description?**
A: Effective job descriptions should include:
- Basic information such as job title, responsibilities, necessary skills and experience required.
- Any required degrees, licenses, or certifications.
- Tasks that are compatible – for example you wouldn't ordinarily ask an employee to perform both complex analytical tasks and also work as a part-time salesperson.

- Sufficiently detailed information about the job so applicants have a clear idea of what to expect if hired.
- Enough detail so that the job description can be used as a reference tool when interviewing and evaluating applicants.
- At least some indication of what are the possibilities for advancement.

Q: **What are some important points to consider in setting up a recruitment program?**
A: Some things to consider in developing a recruiting program:
- Have a plan. Know what sources you're going to rely to locate applicants and know how you intend to process applications, resumes and cover letters.
- Decide how much effort you're going to put into researching an applicant's background on social media such as Facebook, LinkedIn and Twitter.
- Be flexible – the best applicant may not necessarily be the person who fits the job description the closest. {Author's note: the best hire I ever made was a young man with a high school diploma who was working as an orderly in a hospital emergency room – for a position where we were looking for a college degree and at least 3 years of experience in the field].
- Constantly evaluate the effectiveness of any ads placed in newspapers or on the web – and be sure to look inside your organization for qualified individuals.

Q: **Why should you continue recruiting even if you have no current job openings?**
A: It's always a good idea to have a few people identified and on file that you feel would be a good fit for certain jobs in your organization. Job openings in critical areas can occur suddenly – illness, injury or someone leaving abruptly with little or no notice – all those things can make it important to be able to find a qualified replacement in a hurry.

Q: **What goes into a policy manual?**
A: A company policy manual should cover items such as:
- Recruitment and employment policies
- Employee record keeping
- Employee benefits
- Payroll
- Workplace guidelines
- Employee conduct

Q: **What type of information goes into benefits reporting?**
A: A benefits management system maintains data on the various benefits offered by your company (such as health insurance, 401(k) plans and group term life insurance) and tracks employee eligibility, enrollment and withdrawal dates, along with employee and employer contributions and other pertinent information such as investment options, beneficiaries, and dependents.

Q: **Where can I find information and advice about employee benefit programs?**
A: One good source of benefit facts and figures is the Employee Benefit Research Institute (www.ebri.org). You can find FAQs about benefits, special reports, news briefs, and a variety of other information on benefits at the EBRI website.

Q: **What features are included in employee time off accrual reporting?**
A: Employee accrual systems usually keep track of sick days, vacation days and personal days accrued, used, and scheduled. An accrual system may also calculate days earned based on how long an employee has worked for the company, his or her seniority level and other factors.

Q: **What type of training information should a company keep?**
A: Most companies have training sessions for new employees, "continuing education" type training and/or training to familiarize employees with new equipment or new procedures. Information to keep on file might include: title, date, location, cost, instructor name, attendees and number of hours for each training session. If the training involves multiple sessions the data may also include the scheduled training dates and which sessions each employee has attended.

Q: **What type of items go into an employee review?**
A: Performance reviews can take different forms (text-based, numerical, comparison-based) but they generally include evaluations such as:
- Skill and proficiency in carrying out job assignments
- Ability to plan and organize workload
- Assumes accountability for assigned responsibilities
- Communicates effectively with peers and supervisors
- Capable of working independently or in groups
- Willing to take on additional responsibilities
- Delegates responsibility when appropriate
- Manages subordinates effectively and fairly
- Shows proficiency at improving work methods and procedures

Q: **What about "exit interviews"?**
A: It's a good idea to conduct exit interviews with employees who are leaving – it's an opportunity to get their viewpoint on everything from your company's work environment to your training and supervisors. Typical questions that could be asked during an exit interview include:
- Why are you leaving?
- What do think of working conditions here?
- Do you think you were adequately trained?
- How would you rate your supervisor(s)?
- Do you think the pay rate was fair?
- What do think about the employee benefits?
- Are there other benefits that you feel should be provided?
- Do you feel there was an adequate chance for advancement?
- How would you rate the general morale here?
- What did you like the most and the least about your job?

Q: **In HR terms, what is a "data warehouse"?**
A: A data warehouse is a large database of employee information, particularly "employee metrics" - measurements that attempt to quantify each employee's productivity, efficiency, and other items that contribute to the employee's overall "performance" rating.

Q: **What is Form I-9?**
A: Form I-9 is a U.S. Citizenship and Immigration Services form used by an employer to verify a new employee's identity and eligibility to be hired for employment in the United States. The job applicant must produce documents establishing his or her identity and employment authorization. Employers must keep the completed I-9 on file for three years from the start date of employment or for one year following the employee's termination, whichever is later.

Q: **How soon after hiring does a company have to complete a Form I-9 for the new employee?**
A: A form I-9 (Employment Eligibility Form) must be completed within 72 hours after the individual is hired.

Q: **What document is considered to be the definitive guideline covering the legality of employee selection procedures?**
A: The UGESP (Uniform Guidelines on Employee Selection Procedures).

Q: **When dealing with human resources, what are "protected groups"?**

A: "Protected groups" are those whose members are covered by federal or state anti-discrimination laws. The protected categories are: race, color, religion, age, sex, national origin, and disability handicaps.

Q: **What is "adverse impact" in regards to human resources?**
A: Adverse impact (also referred to as "disparate impact") refers to employment practices that have a discriminatory effect on a protected group, even if the effect is unintentional. Statistically, adverse impact occurs if the rate of selection of new employees from a protected class is less than 80% of the rate for the class with the highest selection rate. At that point the employer should either adjust hiring procedures or compile proof of the procedures as a business necessity.

Q: **What are EAPs?**
A: Employee Assistance Programs (EAPs) originated in the 1970s as a way to provide assistance for employees with various types of personal problems and are often handled by the HR department. Areas in which EAP providers can assist employees include:
- Alcohol and substance abuse.
- Legal aid sources for employees with legal problems.
- Marriage counseling.
- Financial counseling.
- Mental health evaluation and referral.
- Preretirement planning.

Q: **Is seniority a factor in determining equal pay for men and women under the Equal Pay Act of 1963?**
A: No. For men and women working at essentially the same job, skill and effort are factors in determining pay level, but not seniority.

Q: **If an employee, Tom Jones, is out on leave under the FMLA (Family Medical Leave Act) when bonuses are paid to all full-time employees, is the employer required to pay Tom's bonus when he returns to work?**
A: Yes – under the FMLA employees out on leave are to be treated the same as all currently working employees.

Q: **What is the "fellow servant rule"?**
A: Under the "fellow servant" rule, an employee who is injured because of the actions of a co-worker cannot bring a personal injury action against his or her employer. The fellow servant rule doesn't apply to cases involving workers' compensation – the injured employee can recover workers' compensation benefits even if the injury was caused by a co-worker.

Q: **What is the EEOC?**
A: The Equal Employment Opportunity Commission (EEOC) is the federal agency that enforces federal anti-discrimination laws in regard to employment practices.

Q: **What happens if someone files a complaint with the EEOC charging you with unfair employment practices?**
A: In general, these are the steps in an EEOC investigation:
1) The EEOC will notify you that a complaint has been filed and will supply you with a copy of the charges.
2) You can accept mediation and an EEOC member will meet with someone from your company and the person filing the complaint to try to resolve the issue.
3) If you refuse mediation or mediation doesn't resolve the issue the EEOC will conduct an investigation which generally involves interviews with members of your company and a review of any pertinent company documents.
4) Once the investigation is completed the EEOC will render a decision. If the EEOC finds against the person filing the complaint it will also issue that individual a "right-to-sue" notice. If the EEOC finds valid grounds for the complaint it will attempt to get you to participate in a conciliation process. If you refuse conciliation or conciliation fails the EEOC will either take you to court or issue a "right-to-sue" notice to the complainant.

Q: **What is an EEO-1 report and who has to file it?**
A: The EEO-1 report is a report of an organization's employees categorized by race/ethnicity, gender and job category. Most companies with over 100 employees are required to file an EEO-1 report annually. The employment data on the report has to taken from one pay period in July, August or September of the current year and the filing deadline is September 30th. Multi-location companies are required to file a report for the headquarters location and for each of the other physical business locations (even for those with less than 50 employees).

Q: **How should I submit my EEO-1 report?**
A: The preferred method of submitting EEO-1 reports is through the EEO-1 Online Filing Application or as an electronically transmitted ASCII text file. EEO-1 reports can also be submitted as computer printouts. Specifications for creating an EEO-1 data file as available at:
http://www.eeoc.gov/eeo1survey

Q: Which businesses have to keep records for OSHA (Occupational Safety and Health Administration)?

A: Businesses in certain industries with more than 10 employees are required to display OSHA safety and health information (OSHA 3165 or state equivalent) in their workplace and to record any occupational injuries or illnesses as they occur using OSHA form 300, Log of Work-Related Injuries and Illnesses. However, OSHA record-keeping is not required for most employers in retail trade, finance, insurance, real estate, and service industries.

Q: If a business has to keep OSHA records, is that business subject to inspection?

A: Yes, every business covered by the OSH Act has to comply with federal and state safety standards and is subject to inspection by federal or state officials.

Q: Who should I contact to find out if a substance we're using in a manufacturing or other process is toxic?

A: Contact NIOSH, the National Institute for Occupational Safety and Health (http://www.cdc.gov/niosh/).

Q: What is OFCCP compliance?

A: Contractors and sub-contractors working on federal government contracts worth over ten thousand dollars are required to comply with OFCCP (Office of Federal Contract Compliance Programs) regulations. Basically OFCCP compliance means you as an employer have to abide by basic affirmative action and equal opportunity (EEO) requirements that have to do with eliminating discrimination in hiring due to gender, race or ethnicity of applicants.

Q: What is the "Portal-to-Portal Act"?

A: The Portal-to-Portal Act of 1947 defines what employee non-work activities are subject to minimum wage and overtime rules. Generally speaking, activities that are outside of normal working hours and are not controlled by the employer (such as travel to and from the work site or arriving for work early and waiting for the start of the workday) are not subject to minimum wage or overtime regulations unless covered by a contract or by custom. Activities during the workday (such as coffee breaks or fire drills) normally are subject to wage and hour laws.

Q: What is the main requirement of the Employee Retirement Income Security Act?

A: ERISA makes it mandatory for the administrator of an employee benefit plan to furnish participating employees and beneficiaries with a summary plan description (SPD) describing the participants benefits, rights and responsibilities under the plan.

Q: **Is my company subject to Title VII of the Civil Rights Act of 1964?**
A: Title VII of the Civil Rights Act of 1964 prevents discrimination in employment because of race, color, religion or national origin. It applies to all employers with 15 or more employees.

Q: **Which federal agency enforces Affirmative Action?**
A: The Office of Federal Contract Compliance (OFCCP).

Q: **Can an employee be fired on the basis that he or she has been garnished for a single debt?**
A: The Consumer Credit Protection Act prevents an employee from being terminated solely due to the fact that his or her wages are being garnished for one debt.

Q: **What is OSHA?**
A: The Occupational Health and Safety Administration is the federal agency charged with issuing workplace health and safety regulations. OSHA conducts various training, compliance assistance and health and safety recognition programs.

Q: **What is the "Employee Right-to-Know law"?**
A: The Employee Right-to-Know law is an OSHA (Occupational Health and Safety Administration) standard that requires organizations handling hazardous materials to inform all employees about any chemical hazards to which they may be exposed.

Q: **If an employee requires first aid treatment does that incident have to be reported to OSHA?**
A: Generally minor injuries requiring first aid do not have to be reported to the Occupational Health and Safety Administration.

Q: **How quickly does OSHA Form 301 (injury and illness report) have to be submitted once the employer learns of a work-related injury?**
A: Form 301 has to be submitted to OSHA within 7 days.

Q: **If a union loses a representation election how quickly can they call another election?**
A: The union has to wait at least 12 months before they can call another election.

Q: **Where can I get more information about Human Resource Management?**
A: Workforce (www.workforce.com) offers newsletters, blogs, forums and articles on a wide variety of topics including employee compensation, benefits, HR administration, workplace safety, motivating employees, employee training and skills development, applicant interviewing and HR trends.

Federal Laws That Affect Payroll

Q: **What is the FLSA?**
A: The Federal Labor Standards Act of 1938 (usually referred to as the Federal Wage and Hour Law) covers federal minimum wage requirements, child labor, wage garnishments, and overtime pay requirements. There have been a number of amendments to the Act over the years, most of them dealing with increases in the federal minimum wage. Other amendments include the Equal Pay Act of 1963 (making it illegal to pay workers lower wages based strictly on their sex) and the Age Discrimination in Employment Act (ADEA) of 1967 (prohibiting discrimination based strictly on age). The FLSA **does not** require employers to pay extra wages for work on weekends or holidays, provide vacation or severance pay, or grant employees vacation time.

Q: **Are there employees who are exempt from the FLSA?**
A: There are a number of categories of employees who are exempt from the provisions of the FLSA including:
- Executives (must be paid a salary of at least $455 per week, must customarily and regularly direct the work of 2 or more other employees, must have the authority to hire and fire, and their primary duty must be managing the company or a sub-division of the company).
- Administrators (must be paid a salary of at least $455 per week and their primary duty must be office or non-manual work directly related to the management of the business).
- Professionals (must be paid a salary of at least $455 per week and their primary duties must be work requiring advanced knowledge for learned professionals or work requiring imagination or talent for creative professionals).
- Computer Employees (must be paid a salary of at least $455 per week, and must be a systems analyst, programmer, computer engineer, or someone holding a similar position).
- Outside Salespeople (primary duty must be sales and must be customarily and regularly working away from the employer's place or places of business).
- Agricultural workers.
- Police officers and firefighters.
- Hospital and nursing home workers.

Note: Exempt employees normally have to be paid on a salary basis – however administrative, professional and computer employees can also be paid on a "fee basis" (paid by job) as long as the time spent on the job

and the fee work out to at least $455 per week.
In addition there are certain employees who are exempt from just the overtime pay provisions of the FLSA, including:
- Employees covered by a collective bargaining agreement.
- Farm workers.
- Railroad and air carrier employees.
- Taxi drivers.
- Seamen on American vessels.

Q: **Does the FLSA require employers to pay holiday pay?**
A: FLSA regulations don't require employers to pay vacation, sick or holiday pay.

Q: **Do FLSA overtime rules apply to non-exempt employees time spent traveling to or from their place of work?**
A: FLSA overtime regulations don't apply to time spent traveling to and from work unless there is a contract or an established custom to the contrary. In additional employers aren't required to pay for time spent in activities before or after the normal work day unless those activities are essential to performing the employee's job.

Q: **Can I dock an employee's salary who is exempt from the FLSA?**
A: Normally, no. However you can dock an exempt employee's salary in certain cases:
- Full day absences under a sick or disability plan or for personal reasons.
- Unpaid leave under the Family and Medical Leave Act (FMLA).
- Disciplinary suspensions for one or more full days.
- Major safety violations.
- Weeks where the employee doesn't perform any work during the week.
- To offset money the employee receives for military or jury duty.

Q: **What is the Federal Insurance Contributions Act?**
A: The Federal Insurance Contributions Act (FICA) instituted a mandatory payroll tax on both employees and employers to fund Social Security and Medicare, the federal programs that provide benefits for retirees, disabled workers, and children of deceased workers. Social Security cover old-age, survivors and disability insurance (OASDI), while Medicare provides hospital insurance benefits.

Q: **What is the "small business health care credit"?**
A: The Patient Protection and Affordable Health Care Act of 2010

includes tax credits for small businesses that provide health care coverage to their employees. For tax years 2010 through 2013, the maximum credit was 35 percent for small business employers and 25 percent for small tax-exempt employers. In 2014 employers are eligible for up to a 50% credit of premiums (35% for tax exempt organizations). The tax credit can be carried back or forward to other tax years and, in addition, eligible businesses can also claim an expense deduction for the health insurance premiums in excess of the credit. To be eligible for the tax credit a business must cover at least 50 percent of the cost of single (not family) health care coverage for each employee, must have fewer than 25 full time equivalent employees (FTEs), and those employees must have average wages of less than $50,000 a year. Also, the amount of the credit works on a sliding scale; the smaller the business or charity, the larger the credit. For the full 50% credit, a business must have 10 or fewer FTEs who are paid less than $25,000 on average. You can use Form 8941 (www.irs.gov) to calculate the tax credit and you can also use the tax credit calculator at:
 http://www.nfib.com/issues-elections/healthcare/credit-calculator
to estimate your credit. "C" Corporations can use Form 8941 to report the credit; partnerships and S corporations report the credit on Schedule K and pass it through to the shareholders or partners. For more information go to:
http://www.irs.gov/newsroom/article/0,,id=223666,00.html

Q: **What are some other federal laws that affect employers?**
A: Federal laws that employers should know about include:

- **Title VII of the Civil Rights Act of 1964** - provides for fair employment practices and forbids employers to discriminate in hiring, firing, promoting, or compensating employees based on race, religion, gender or nationality. The act covers all employers who are involved in an industry "affecting commerce" and who employ 15 or more workers for each business day in each of 20 or more weeks in the current or preceding calendar year. Guidelines for enforcement of Title VII are established by the Equal Employment Opportunity Commission (EEOC).

- **Immigration Reform and Control Act of 1986** - makes it illegal for employers to hire aliens who aren't authorized to work in the United States and requires employers to verify an individual's employment eligibility by examining certain documents and having the prospective employee fill out a Form I-9 (Employment Eligibility Verification).

- **Federal Personal Responsibility and Work Opportunity**

Reconciliation Act of 1996 - PRWORA requires each state to establish a new-hire reporting program. Employers must report the name, address, and social security number of every new employee within 20 days of the hire date to the appropriate state agency. The state forwards the information to the federal Office of Child Support Enforcement (OCSE) to be entered into a national directory to help enforce child support obligations.

- **Employee Retirement Income Security Act of 1974** - ERISA covers employee pension plans set up or maintained by any employer or employee organization and regulates how pension funds are gathered and disbursed, who controls them and how to handle various situations that may arise. ERISA was established primarily to make sure workers who contribute to a pension fund over the years receive benefits from those funds in accordance with their years of service. If an employer maintains a pension plan, ERISA specifies when employees must be allowed to become participants, how long they have to work before they have a non-forfeitable interest in their pension, how long participants can be away from their job before it affects their benefits, and whether their spouses have a right to a part of their pension in the event of their death.

- **Age Discrimination in Employment Act (ADEA) of 1967** – This act prohibits employers, employment agencies and labor unions from discriminating on the basis of age in their employment practices and covers all employers with 20 or more workers. Employers subject to ADEA rules should keep a file of all employment applications (with notations as to their disposition) and all records relating to promotions, terminations, merit programs, incentive payment plans, etc.

- **Americans with Disabilities Act** – The 1990 Americans with Disabilities Act (ADA) prohibits employers with 15 or more employees, employment agencies and labor organizations from discriminating against qualified job applicants on the basis of their disability. In addition, accommodations such as wheelchair-accessible restrooms and ramps have to be provided for handicapped workers.

- **Family and Medical Leave Act of 1993** – The Family and Medical Leave Act (FMLA) requires employers with 50 or more employees within a 75-mile radius for at least 20 weeks in the current or preceding calendar year to provide workers unpaid leave for a family or medical emergency. Employers must offer workers up to 12 weeks of unpaid leave in cases of childbirth, adoption, or serious illness or injury to the employee, the employee's children, spouse, parent or a family member on active military duty. The leave can be taken all at once or spaced out in separate weeks, days or hours, although the entire amount of leave has to be taken within 12 months of the family or medical emergency. The employer must continue health coverage for the employee while the employee is on leave and must guarantee that the employee will return to the same job or an equivalent job. Employers can exempt the highest-paid ten percent of their workforce, as well as employees who haven't worked for them for at least one year or at least 1,250 hours in the past 12 months. Note: Some states (like New Jersey) have established *paid* family leave plans, funded by payroll deductions.

- **Consumer Credit Protection Act (CCPA)** - Protects employees from termination because their wages have been garnished for any one debt and limits the amount of an employee's earnings that may be garnished in any one week. All employers are covered by the Act, as are their employees who receive wages, bonuses, salaries, commissions or periodic payments from retirement or pension plans. Typically, tips income is not included in the Act.

- **Employee Polygraph Protection Act (EPPA)** - Prohibits employers from using lie detector tests, either for pre-employment screening or during the course of employment, with certain exceptions. In addition, employers may not discharge or discriminate against an employee or applicant for refusing to take the test or exercising other rights under the EPPA.

- **Employee Polygraph Protection Act (EPPA)** - Prohibits employers from using lie detector tests, either for pre-employment screening or during the course of employment, with certain exceptions. In addition, employers may not discharge or discriminate against an employee or applicant for refusing to take the test or exercising other rights under the EPPA.

- **Immigration Reform and Control Act (IRCA)** - Employers are prohibited from hiring and retaining employees who are not authorized to work in the United States. Once they're extended a job offer applicants are required to produce certain documents to prove their citizenship status and employers and employees must each complete a section of Form I-9 ("Employment Eligibility Verification Form"). Employers are required to retain the Form I-9 for each person hired and make it available for inspection by authorized government officers. Note: Employers may not specify which documents the applicant has to produce from the list of documents that are acceptable for proving citizenship status.

Note: Due to the COVID-19 pandemic, the Department of Homeland Security is not requiring employers to review new hires' identity and work eligibility documents in person. You can review the documents for Section 2 of the I-9 form by email, fax or videoconference instead. However, you should write "COVID-19" in the "Additional Information" field of Section 2 as the reason for the delay in physically inspecting the identity and eligibility documents. When your company resumes normal operations, you have three days to verify the new hires' documents in person. Once that's done, write "documents physically examined" and the date in the Additional Information field of Section 2.

- **Jury Systems Improvement Act (JSIA)** - Prohibits employers from discharging or taking other adverse employment action against employees who are summoned to jury duty in federal court. Most states also have similar employment laws regarding jury duty in state and local courts and, in many cases, protection has also been extended to employees who are summoned to testify in court.

The Affordable Care Act (Obamacare)

The Patient Protection and Affordable Care Act (also referred to as the "ACA" or "Obamacare" means big changes for employers and employees. The major provisions of the bill went into effect on January 1, 2015.

So, what does an employer need to know about complying with the law?

The health care bill requires nearly all Americans to obtain health insurance. The law expects that most workers will get that coverage through their employers and has created a system of subsidies and penalties to make this possible. If you're an employer, the size of your workforce is important, as the law has different requirements depending on the number of employees you have.

Here are the major aspects of the health care bill as it relates to employers:

Q: **Which businesses does the law affect?**
A: The ACA doesn't impose a straight-forward requirement that employers offer health insurance to workers but it does impose penalties on certain categories of employers who fail to do so.

Q: **What is a "small business"?**
A: Under the Act, a small business is not specifically defined, but a number of sections of the law apply only to organizations with fewer than 25 employees (for more detail see below.) However, under some sections of the law, the effective company size is 50 or 100 employees.

Q: **How does the Affordable Care Act determine the number of employees an organization employs?**
A: Determining then number of employees involves counting both full-time and part-time employees. An employer is required to count the number of regular full-time employees (those that work a minimum of 30 hours per week on the average) plus any "full-time equivalent" employees or "FTEs". To calculate the number of FTEs in a given month the employer must add up the hours (up to 120 hours per employee) of all part-time workers (those who worked an average of less than 30 hours per week) and divide by 120 hours. The result (rounded down) is the number of equivalent full-time employees. For example a company who has 9 full-time employees plus 5 part-time employees who worked a total of 380 hours during the month would have the equivalent of 12 full-

time employees (9 plus 380 divided by 120).

For salaried employees who are not paid by the hour there are 3 options for determining hours worked:
- The same method used for hourly employees (requires calculating hours worked for each salaried person during the pay period).
- A "days-worked" equivalency method (each salaried employee is credited with 8 hours for each day worked).
- A "weeks-worked" equivalency method (each salaried employee is credited with 40 hours for each week worked).

Although part-time employees count toward the 50 employee limit in determining "large" employers, employers are not required to offer health insurance to part-time employees. Because an employer may not be sure how many hours a particular employee (such as a seasonal worker) my work during a calendar year, the ACA allows the employer to wait up to 12 months to retroactively determine the status of variable-hour employees. The employer has to choose a "measurement period" of between 3 and 12 months to calculate whether 30 or more hours per week are worked by that person and whether the employee is entitled to coverage for a certain period thereafter.

Q: What are "insurance exchanges"?
A: Beginning January 1, 2014, health insurance will be available to individuals and small businesses through state-run "exchanges." These will require insurance companies to compete for business in the marketplace. The objective is to make it it easier for individuals and small businesses to obtain health insurance at a lower price. The exchange program for small businesses, known as the Small Business Health Options Program (SHOP), will allow small businesses to pool together to increase their purchasing power. This will allow these businesses to offer health insurance to their employees at rates similar to those available to large corporations.

SHOP is available to small businesses with up to 100 employees, although states have the option to limit participation to businesses with 50 employees or less until 2016. If a business participating in SHOP grows to over 100 employees, it may continue to take advantage of the program. Beginning in 2017, states may choose to allow businesses with more than 100 employees to participate in SHOP as well.

The exchange program is also important because larger employers may be penalized if some of their employees choose to obtain insurance through an exchange and not through the company's insurance plan (for more detail see below.)

Q: Are employers required to provide health insurance to their employees?

A: Businesses with fewer than 50 employees are exempt from having to provide health insurance. However, as explained above, such smaller employers may choose to offer health insurance at a reasonable cost by participating in a SHOP exchange.

Larger businesses are subject to a number of requirements and potential penalties, depending on the number of employees they have and the type of coverage they provide:

- Companies with 50 or more full-time or full-time equivalent employees will be required to offer health insurance to their workers and the workers' dependent children beginning in 2015 (however coverage for workers' spouses will not be mandatory).

- Automatic enrollment: Employers with more than 200 employees are required to enroll new employees in their health care plan, subject to any normal waiting period. Employers must also provide notice of employees' right to opt out of automatic enrollment.

- Notice of coverage options: Employers must give employees notice about the availability of an insurance exchange..

- Beginning in 2015 employers are required to keep track of the full or part-time status of each employee and report that status to the IRS.

Q: What about new employers?
A: A new employer - an employer not in existence during the entire preceding year - may be considered a large employers if it is reasonably expected to employ at least 50 full-time employees (taking into account FTEs) on business days during the current calendar year and it actually employees 50 full-time employees during the calendar year.

Q: What is the "shared responsibility" (or "play or pay") portion of the ACA?
A: Large business (over 50 employees) come under the Employer Shared Responsibility Provisions of the ACA. These provisions include:

- A penalty for not providing insurance: Employers with over 50 employees that do not provide insurance must pay a penalty of $2,000 for every employee in the company if even one employee chooses to obtain insurance through an exchange. However, the first 30 employees are not counted in calculation of the penalty. Example: an employer with 75 employees would pay the penalty for 45 workers, or $90,000 (45 x $2.000).

- A penalty for providing insurance that isn't "affordable" or doesn't provide "minimum value". Coverage is considered affordable if an employee's required contribution toward the employer's lowest cost self-only coverage doesn't exceed 9.5 percent of his or her household income. Under the ACA an insurance plan fails to provide minimum value if the plan's share of the total cost of benefits provided under the plan is less than 60% of those costs. If the employer's plan fails to provide minimum value, employees may be eligible to receive a premium tax credit. Employers with more than 50 employees that do provide insurance must pay a penalty if any of their employees receive a premium tax credit to help pay for insurance. The penalty equals $3,000 per worker who uses the subsidy OR $750 for every employee at the company, whichever is less.

Note: The IRS is expected to provide a minimum value calculator which will allow an employer to enter information such as deductibles and co-pays in order to determine if their plan meets the minimum value requirement.

Q: What information do employers have to share with their employees?
A: Under the ACA employers with 50 or more full-time or full-time equivalent employees must:
- Provide written notice informing their employees about their state's insurance Exchange, including instructions as how to contact the Exchange.
- Notify employees if the plan offered by the employer doesn't meet the "minimum value" standard and must let employees know that they may be eligible for a premium tax credit and a cost-sharing reduction if they purchase a health care plan through the state's insurance Exchange.
- Notify employees that if they purchase a plan through the state's insurance Exchange, they may lose the employer's contribution to health benefits.

Q: Is there help for small businesses to provide insurance for their workers?
A: From 2010 through 2013, businesses which had fewer than 25 employees and paid average annual wages of $50,000 or less were eligible for a tax credit of up to 35% if they paid for at least 50% of their employees' health insurance costs.

Beginning in 2014, small businesses that purchase health insurance for their employees through SHOP can receive a two-year small business tax credit of up to 50% of the cost of the premiums. Employers with 10 or fewer employees with an annual average wage of $25,000 or less are eligible for the full tax credit. Note: The employee average annual wage limit of $50,000 will be indexed by the cost of living.

While small businesses are not required to obtain insurance for their employees through the exchanges, the available tax credits may spur many smaller employers to purchase coverage for their workforce.

Note: Business owners, partners and family members of small business owners do not generally count as employees for purposes of qualifying for the tax credit.

Q: Will there be special taxes to help pay for the Affordable Care Act?
A: Beginning in 2013 an additional 0.9% Medicare tax was applied to any employee whose FICA taxable earnings exceeds $200,000 for the calendar year. The additional 0.9% (making the total Medicare percentage 1.45% + 0.9% = 2.35%) will apply only to the wages in excess of $200,000. (Note: employers do not have to pay a matching amount for the additional Medicare tax).

Q: Where can I find additional information about the Affordable Care Act?
A: Here are two websites that may be helpful:

- http://www.sba.gov/healthcare
- www.irs.gov/uac (go to this URL and enter "affordable care act" in the search box on the upper right)

ACA Affordability and Minimum Value Calculations

Q: **What is "minimum value health insurance" under the ACA?**
A: Coverage meets minimum value standards if the plan pays at least 60% of the actuarial value of benefits covered under the plan.

Q: **What is the "actuarial value" of an insurance plan?**
A: The percentage of total average costs for covered benefits that a plan will cover. For example, if a plan has an actuarial value of 60%, the plan would cover 60% of the cost of all covered benefits and the employee would be responsible for the other 40% of the cost.

Q: **What is considered "affordable insurance" under the ACA?**
A: For 2019, coverage is considered "affordable" if no full-time employee is required to pay more than 9.86% of his or her "household income" for self-only coverage under the employer's lowest-cost option that provides minimum value. (Note: for 2020, that percentage decreases to 9.78%). For employers using the federal poverty level safe harbor to determine affordability, an employee's premium payment can't exceed $99.75 per month, up from $96.08 per month in 2018.

Q: **How does an employer calculate affordability?**
Since employers won't know their employees' household income, there are three methods (or "safe harbors") for calculating the affordability of the health insurance offered to employees. They are:
- W-2 income. As long as no employee is paying more than 9.86% of his or her W-2 Box 1 wages (9.78% for 2020), the coverage is "affordable". For employees who are not full time for an entire calendar year the Box 1 wages must be multiplied by a fraction (the number of months during which coverage was offered divided by the number of months the individual was employed during the calendar year). Also, for employees that have pre-tax deductions such as cafeteria or 401(k) plans, the Box 1 wages will be understated by those amounts which could mean the employer's "affordable" coverage is less than it really needs to be.
- Rate of pay. To calculate "affordability" for 2019 using this method, multiply 9.86% times the hourly rate of pay for the lowest paid hourly employee (as of the beginning of the plan year) times 130 hours. However, an employer can't use this method if any employee's wages are cut during the year. Also,

an employer can only multiply by 130 hours regardless of how many hours the employee actually works per month.

- Federal poverty limit. To determine affordability with this method make sure the employees' premiums are not more than 100 percent of the individual FPL ($12,140 for 2018) times 9.86%. This "safe harbor" is essentially fail-safe, although the employer may end up paying more per employee than with the other methods.

Q: **Does an employer have to use one of the three safe harbors listed above?**
A: No, an employer can apply a different method if the method is applied in a uniform and consistent basis for all employees in a particular category.

Affordable Care Act Reporting

Q: **What reports will employers have to file under the ACA?**
A: There are two forms for employers to file, Form 1095-B (and the transmittal form 1094-B) and Form 1095-C (and its transmittal form 1094-C). Which form an employer has to file depends on the employer's health plan and number of employees. Note: If an employer has less than 50 employees and does not offer an insurance plan there is no reporting requirement.

Q: **Which employers have to file Form 1095-B or Form 1095-C?**
A: For employers with less than 50 employees who sponsor a health insurance plan through an insurance company, there is no filing requirement – the insurer will file the From 1095-Bs for the employer. However, employers with fewer than 50 employees who are self-insured must file Transmittal Form 1094-B and the accompanying 1095-B forms for any employees covered under their insurance plan. Large employers (50 or more employees) and small employers (less than 50 employees) who are part of a group of companies that combined have more than 50 employees are treated as follows:
- Employers in this category who do not offer health insurance must file Transmittal Form 1094-C and the accompanying employee 1095-C forms.
- Employers in this category who sponsor an insurance plan through an insurance company must file Form 1094-C and the accompanying 1095-C forms for all full-time employees – however the insurance carrier will file Form 1094-B and the 1095-B forms.
- Employers in this category who are self-insured have to file Form 1094-C and 1095-C including Part III but do not have to file 1094-B or 1095-B.

Q: **What are IRS Forms 1094-C and 1095-C?**
A: As part of the ACA (Affordable Care Act) the IRS has to identify which Applicable Large Employers offered health insurance (and the right kind of insurance) to full-time employees during the year in order to assess penalties for employers who don't comply with the ACA. To accomplish that goal, the IRS requires all Applicable Large Employers to fill out a Form 1095-C for any worker who was a full-time employee for one or more months during the year. The 2019 1095-C forms must be supplied to employees by March 2, 2020. Forms have to be submitted to the IRS by February 28, 2020 if filing on paper or by March 31, 2020 if filing

electronically. The 1095-C forms sent to the IRS also have to be accompanied by a transmittal form, Form 1094-C (similar to Form W-3 which accompanies W-2 forms).

Q: **Who has to file 1095-C forms?**
A: Every Applicable Large Employer must file a 1095-C form for each worker who was a full-time employee for at least one month during the preceding calendar year.

Q: **Who is an "Applicable Large Employer"?**
A: An applicable large employer (ALE) is an employer who averages at least 50 full-time employees (including full-time equivalent employees) for the calendar year.

Q: **So, if I average less than 50 full-time employees for the year I'm not an ALE?**
A: It depends. Organizations that are under common ownership or control are combined in order to determine if they have 50 or more full-time employees. If you have 30 full-time employees and you have a sister company with 25 full-time employees, then you are considered an Applicable Large Employer Member and are required to file 1095-C forms for your company.

Q: **What is a "full-time employee"?**
A: Under the ACA, a full-time employee is an employee who averages at least 30 service hours a week or 130 hours a month.

Q: **What is a "full-time equivalent employee"?**
A: Full-time equivalent employees are determined by adding up the hours of your part-time employees (individuals who averaged less than 30 hours a week) and dividing that total by the number of part-time employees.

Q: **How do I determine how many full-time employees I have during a given month? And how many full-time employees do I have on the average for the year?**
A: Combine the hours of all part-time employees for a given month (up to 120 hours per employee) and divide the total by 120. Then add that total to the number of full-time employees (individuals who averaged 30 hours or more a week) to get the number of full-time and full-time equivalent employees for the month. To determine your average number of full-time employees for the year, add together the number of full-time and full-time equivalent employees for each month of the calendar year and divide by 12.

Q: Is there a specific method or time period that should be used to identify full-time employees for coverage purposes?
A: The ACA specifies two methods for identifying full-time employees. The standard method for identifying full-time employees is the "look-back measurement method". The look-back method involves 3 different periods:

- A "measurement period" for counting hours of service (also called a "standard measurement period" or an "initial measurement period"). The standard measurement period (which deals with ongoing employees) must be between 6 and 12 months in length.
- A "stability period" during which the employee is treated either as full-time or non-full-time for Plan eligibility purposes. The stability period must be at least 6 months and must be at least as long as the SMP (standard measurement period).
- An "administrative period" between the SMP and the stability period which allows for Plan enrollment and dis-enrollment and can last for up to 90 days.

Q: Are there any employees whose hours I don't have to include?
A: Yes – leased employees, employees working outside the United States, certain seasonal employees, sole proprietors, partners, 2-percent S corporation shareholders, certain sales people, and workers described in IRS regulations as real estate agents.

Q: Do I have to count employees who are eligible for other forms of health insurance, such as Medicare, Medicaid, or insurance through a spouse's employer?
A: Yes, outside of the exceptions noted above, all employees are counted.

Q: If an employee was full-time for one month but left before our normal 60 day waiting period before offering insurance was over, do we still have to provide a 1095-C form for that individual?
A: Yes, any employee who was considered full-time for at least one month during the year must receive a 1095-C form, regardless of whether or not coverage was offered.

Q: Can you give me an example of how to determine my ALE status if I have 40 full-time employees for each month in 2018 and 15 part-time employees each month, each of whom works 60 hours per month?

A: The combined monthly hours for your part-time employees is 60 hours x 15 or 900 hours. Divide that total by 120 (the maximum number of hours per part-time worker per month) and you get 7.5. The number 7.5 represents the number of "full-time equivalent employees" per month. Multiply 7.5 by 12 months and add the number of full-time workers (40) times 12 months. That total comes to 90 + 480 or 570 for the year. Then divide 570 by 12 months, which gives you an average of 47.5 "full-time" employees per month - which, under ACA rules, is rounded down to 47, the nearest whole number. In this case even though you have 55 employees you only have an average of 47 full-time and full-time equivalent employees per month so you are not an Applicable Large Employer.

Q: **My company has 55 full-time employees in 2018 (no part-time employees) but I don't offer health insurance – will I be subject to penalties?**
A: If you don't offer coverage, you will owe a penalty if any full time employee is eligible for and purchases subsidized coverage through a Marketplace exchange.

Q: **My company is not an ALE or member of an ALE group – do I have to provide health insurance to my employees? Can I be penalized for not providing insurance or for providing insurance that doesn't meet the standards of the ACA?**
A: No to both questions.

Q: **My company is self-insured but it's not an ALE – do I have to file any forms?**
A: Yes. You must file Form 1094-B (transmittal form) and a Form 1095-B for each employee.

Q: **If my company is not self-insured and is not an ALE, then I don't have to file any ACA forms?**
A: Correct.

Q: **What is a "QHP"?**
A: A Qualified Health Plan or "QHP" is one that is certified by the Health Insurance Marketplace, provides essential health benefits, follows established limits on cost-sharing (like deductibles, co-payments, and out-of-pocket maximum amounts), and meets other requirements.

Q: **What is a Minimum Essential Coverage (MEC) health insurance plan?**
A: An MEC plan is a more limited version of a QHP.

Q: **What is "Minimum Value"?**
A: Under the ACA a health insurance plan is considered to provide "minimum value" if it covers 60% of the total allowed cost of benefits that are expected to be incurred under the plan. Employers can use a minimum value calculator developed by HHS (the Department of Human Health Services) to determine if their insurance plan provides minimum value.

Q: **What health coverage is considered "affordable coverage" by the ACA?**
A: The ACA considers health insurance to be affordable if it meets any one of three IRS "safe harbors" for 2018:
- If the employee's required premium co-share of the lowest cost, self-only coverage Is not greater than 9.56% for 2018 (9.86% for 2019) of the employee's W-2 Box 1 taxable income.
- If the employee's required premium co-share of the lowest cost self-only coverage Is not greater than 9.56% (9.86% for 2019) of the employee's rate of pay on the first day of the coverage period (usually the first day of the plan period).
- If the employee's required premium co-share of the lowest cost self-only coverage Is not greater than 9.56% (9.86% for 2019) of the current year's US mainland Federal Poverty Level (FPL) for a single individual.

Q: **So what exactly can I be penalized for if I'm an Applicable Large Employer?**
A: You can be subject to penalties for several reasons under Section 4980H(a) and Section 4980H(b) of the ACA:
1) Failing to offer health coverage or offering health coverage to less than 95% of your full-time employees and their dependents - and at least one of the full-time employees receives a premium tax credit to help pay for coverage obtained on the Marketplace.
2) You offer health coverage to at least 95% of your full-time employees, but at least one full-time employee obtains a premium tax credit to help pay for coverage on a Marketplace because the coverage you offered was either not affordable or it didn't provide minimum value.

Q: **Can I be penalized for not providing coverage if an employee is terminated during the month when coverage would have been offered if the person had remained employed?**
A: No, in that case the employee is treated as having been offered coverage during that month.

Q: **I'm an ALE. If I offer affordable health care coverage that provides minimum value to my full-time employees and offer health coverage to their dependents, can I be subject to Employer Shared Responsibility penalties if some of my employees buy health insurance through a Marketplace?**
A: No.

Q: **What if the insurance I offer isn't affordable and one of my full-time employees purchases health insurance through a Marketplace – am I subject to a penalty?**
A: Not unless the employee who bought insurance from the Marketplace receives a premium tax credit.

Q: **Who does the ACA consider a dependent?**
A: The ACA defines a dependent as a "child" of the employee who hasn't reached age 26 (excluding foster children, stepchildren, and most children who aren't U.S. Citizens or nationals). Note: ACA regulations state that a child is a dependent for the full month in which he or she turns age 26.

Q: **Do the ACA Employer Shared Responsibility provisions only apply to applicable large employers that have for-profit businesses?**
A: No. All applicable large employers are subject to the ACA provisions, including for-profit, non-profit and government entity employers.

Q: **Are there periods of time when I'm not responsible for offering coverage to an employee?**
A: Yes, there are a number of "limited non-assessment periods" when an ALE (Applicable Large Employer) isn't required to offer health coverage to an employee:

- If an employer is in the first year as an applicable large employer, coverage doesn't have to be offered until April 1 of that year.
- Coverage doesn't have to be offered to a new worker (who is expected to be a full-time employee) for the first 3 months of employment if the employee is otherwise eligible for coverage under the employer's group health plan.
- If a variable-hour or seasonal employee changes status during his or her initial measurement period such that he or she can now be reasonably assumed to be a full-time employee, the employer has 3 calendar months from the date of change of status to provide coverage.

- If the employee's first day of employment is a day other than the first day of the calendar month, then the employee's first calendar month of employment is a Limited Non-Assessment Period.

Note: The situations above only count as limited non-assessment periods if the employee is offered at least minimum value coverage on the first day of the first month following the non-assessment period.

Affordable Care Act – Form 1094-C

Q: **What is Form 1094-C?**
A: As mentioned in the overview, 1094-C is the transmittal form that accompanies the 1095-C forms submitted to the IRS (similar to Form W-3, the transmittal form that accompanies W-2 forms submitted to the Social Security Administration).

Q: **In Part I, line 2 asks for my FEIN/EIN – can I use my Social Security number if I don't have an EIN?**
A: No, you must have a Federal Employer's Identification Number in order to file a 1094-C (and the accompanying 1095-C forms).

Q: **My company is a member of a controlled group under a parent company – which address should I enter on lines 3 through 6?**
A: You can enter your company's address or the parent company's address – just be sure that the address you use on the 1094-C is the same address you use on the 1095-C forms.

Q: **What do I enter on lines 9 through 16?**
A: Unless you're a government employer you can skip lines 9 through 16.

Q: **I understand that I'm supposed to enter the number of accompanying 1095-C forms on line 18, but what does box 19 mean about this being the "authoritative transmittal"?**
A: If you are sending all your 1095-C forms along with this 1094-C, check Box 19 to declare this as your "authoritative" transmittal and complete Parts II, III and IV as applicable. However, for example, if you have already submitted an "authoritative" 1094-C and accompanying 1095-C forms and discover that you left out one or more employees, then you need to fill out a second 1094-C to go with those additional 1095-C forms – and that second 1094-C will not be your "authoritative 1094-C". Leave Box 19 unchecked on the second 1094-C and skip Parts II, III, and IV.

Q: **What number do I enter on line 20?**
A: Normally, if you only submit one 1094-C for your ALE or ALE member, line 18 and line 20 should be the same number.

Q: **My company isn't part of a larger ALE – do I still need to fill out anything in Section (d) of Part III or Part IV?**
A: No, you can skip those sections.

Q: **My company is part of a controlled group or "Aggregated ALE Group" so I need to check "Yes" on line 21 – but what "Aggregated Group Indicator" do I use in Part III, column (d)?**
A: If you were a member of an aggregated group for the entire calendar year enter "X" in the "All 12 Months" box. If you were a member of an aggregated group for fewer than all 12 months, enter "X" in each month that you were a member of the aggregated group. In either case you also need to complete Part IV, listing the name and EIN of the other aggregated group members (up to a maximum of 30 members).

Q: **What is the purpose of line 22?**
A: Line 22 gives employers the chance to certify that they are eligible for one of two kinds of relief from ACA regulations. The two types of relief have different requirements and different benefits.

Q: **What does certification 22A deal with?**
A: 22A allows the employer to use simplified methods of reporting. Instead of filling out a Form 1095-C for each employee by January 31, the employer can give (at least some) employees a generic statement. Note: self-insured employers can't use this certification; also, even if an employer can use a generic statement to give to employees, standard 1095-C forms still have to be submitted to the IRS, so this option doesn't significantly reduce the employer's reporting burden.

Q: **What relief is offered under 22D?**
A: Certification 22D (98% Offer Method) requires the employer to have offered affordable health care coverage providing minimum value to at least 98% of the employees receiving 1095-C forms and minimum essential coverage to their dependents (taking into account all months during which the individuals were employees of the employer and not in a Non-Assessment Period). Employers who meet this requirement don't have to complete the "Full-Time Employee Count" in Part III, column (b) of the authoritative 1094-C form.

Q: **What do I enter in Part III?**
A: For column (a), if you offered minimum essential coverage to at least 95% of your full-time employees and their dependents in 2018, enter "X" in the "Yes" checkbox on line 23 for the months that you offered that coverage – or enter an "X" in the "Yes" checkbox for "All 12 Months" if you offered that coverage for each month in 2018. For any months that you did not offer minimum essential coverage to at least 95% of your full-time employees and their dependents, mark an "X" in the "No" checkbox

(or in the "No" checkbox for "All 12 Months" if you failed to offer that coverage in any month of 2018).

For column (b), enter the number of full-time employees for each month, but do not count any employee in a Limited Non-Assessment Period. If the number of full-time employees (excluding employees in a Limited Non-Assessment Period) for a month is zero, enter "0". An employee should be counted as a full-time employee for a month if the employee satisfied the definition of full-time employee under the monthly measurement method or the look-back measurement method (as applicable) on any day of the month

Note: An ALE Member that sponsors a self-insured health plan must furnish Form 1095-C with Part III completed for each employee and family member who enrolls in the self-insured health coverage, regardless of whether the employee is a full-time employee for any month of the calendar year.

Q: **What do I need to fill out on Part IV?**
A: If you are part of an "Aggregated ALE Group" (companies under a common ownership), you need to enter the name and EIN of the other companies in the aggregated group (up to a maximum of 30 companies).

Affordable Care Act - Form 1095-C

Q: **If an employer is an Applicable Large Employer (ALE) and offers health insurance through an insurance company, what parts of Form 1095-C does that employer have to complete?**
A: An ALE who provides insurance through an insurance company must complete a 1095-C form, Parts I and II, for each full-time employee.

Q: **I had some summer workers who weren't offered health insurance – do I need to send them 1095-C forms?**
A: You need to send a 1095-C to any employee who was considered full-time for at least one month, regardless of whether or not that person was offered health care coverage.

Q: **If an employer is an ALE and is self-insured, what parts of Form 1095-C does that employer complete?**
A: Self-insured ALEs must complete a 1095-C form (Parts I, II, and III) for each full-time employee and a 1095-C form (Part I, Line 14 of Part II, and Part III) for each non-full-time employee.

Q: **In Part I, it asks for the name and address of my company. My company is part of a controlled group – do I put the name and address of my company or the name and address of our parent company?**
A: Put the legal name and the address of your company, not the parent company's name and address.

Q: **I don't offer health insurance – what do I put in the box "Plan Start Month"?**
A: That box is optional for 2018 - you can leave it blank.

Q: **I'm confused – what codes do I use for line 14?**
A: Line 14 is asking what kind, if any, of medical benefits did you offer the particular employee listed on this 1095-C. Here's a list of the codes for line 14 and when to use them:

- 1A (often used) – Minimum essential coverage providing minimum value offered to a full-time employee (with the employee monthly contribution for the lowest cost self-only coverage equal to or less than 9.56% of the 2018 mainland federal poverty level for a single individual divided by 12) and at least minimum essential coverage offered to the spouse and dependent(s). Note: the 2018 federal poverty level for a single individual was $12,140.

- 1B (seldom used) - Minimum essential coverage providing minimum value offered to employee only.
- 1C (sometimes used) - Minimum essential coverage providing minimum value offered to employee and at least minimum essential coverage offered to dependent(s) (not spouse).
- 1D (seldom used) - Minimum essential coverage providing minimum value offered to employee and at least minimum essential coverage offered to spouse (not dependent(s)). [Note: 1D is rarely used – if coverage is offered to the employee and spouse, coverage is also normally offered to dependents].
- 1E (often used) - Minimum essential coverage providing minimum value offered to employee and at least minimum essential coverage offered to dependent(s) and spouse (use instead of code 1A if coverage doesn't meet the affordability standard).
- 1F (sometimes used) - Minimum essential coverage NOT providing minimum value offered to employee; employee and spouse or dependent(s); or employee, spouse and dependents.
- 1G (seldom used) - Offer of coverage to employee who was not a full-time employee for any month of the calendar year (which may include one or more months in which the individual was not an employee) and who enrolled in self-insured coverage for one or more months of the calendar year.
- 1H (often used) - No offer of coverage (employee not offered any health coverage or employee offered coverage that is not minimum essential coverage, which may include one or more months in which the individual was not an employee).
- 1I (sometimes used) - Qualifying Offer Transition Relief 2015: Employee (and spouse or dependents) received no offer of coverage; received an offer that is not a qualifying offer; or received a qualifying offer for less than 12 months.
- 1J (seldom used) - Minimum essential coverage providing minimum value offered to employee and at least minimum essential coverage conditionally offered to spouse; minimum essential coverage not offered to dependent(s).
- 1K (seldom used) - Minimum essential coverage providing minimum value offered to employee; at least minimum essential coverage offered to dependents; and at least minimum essential coverage conditionally offered to spouse.

Note: If one of the above codes applies to a particular employee for all 12 months of the year just enter the code once, in the "All 12 months" column.

Q: **I didn't offer one of my employees coverage in January or February because she didn't work for me until March – so what code do I use on line 14?**
A: You use code 1H. Regardless of the reason, you enter 1H for any month that you didn't offer medical benefits to someone you employed during the year.

Q: **What code do I use for months where the employee was in a lawful waiting period?**
A: Again, use code 1H. The reason why you didn't offer medical coverage doesn't matter. However, you can enter 2D on line 16 to indicate that the employee was in a limited non-assessment period and no penalty should be applied. Use the same codes (1H on line 14 and 2D on line 16) if an employee finishes the waiting period and enrolls in coverage in the middle of a month.

Q: **When do I use code 1A versus code 1E?**
A: If you offer a plan to full-time employees and their spouse and dependents that provides minimum value, then you meet the requirements for using code 1E. If, in addition, the insurance is "affordable" according to the ACA then you also meet the federal poverty level safe harbor and can use code 1A instead.

Q: **If I offer minimum value coverage to my full-time employees and their dependents and the employee's monthly contribution is $90, do I use code 1A on line 14?**
A: No, code 1A requires that you offer the coverage to the employee and his or her spouse, as well as dependents. In this case since coverage isn't being offered to the spouse, you would use code 1C.

Q: **Do employees in a waiting period (an initial measurement period or a limited non-assessment period) have to be counted in determining whether you offered coverage to 95% of your full-time employees during a given month?**
A: No, employees in a waiting period aren't counted in determining whether an employer offered coverage to at least 95% of full-time employees I

Q: **Do I have to enter the employee share of the lowest cost monthly premium for self-only coverage in every box on line 15?**

A: You only have to enter the employee cost in one of the boxes on line 15 if the line 14 code for that month is 1B, 1C, 1D, or 1E. In fact, if you enter code 1A or code 1I on line 14 be sure not to enter anything on line 15.

Q: **Do I have to fill out the individual boxes on lines 14 and 15 if the medical coverage code and the employee's share of the lowest cost monthly premium amount were the same for all 12 months?**
A: No. Just enter the appropriate code in the "All 12 Months" box on line 14 and the employee's monthly cost in the "All 12 Months" box on line 15.

Q: **We had to lay off an employee at the end of July and she opted for COBRA coverage beginning August 1st. What codes do we use on lines 14, 15 and 16?**
A: Use code 1H on line 14 for August through December (whether or not the terminated employee elects COBRA coverage), leave line 15 blank and enter 2A (not employed) on line 16.

Q: **Since it's not necessary to provide a 1095-C form to part-time employees, when would you use code 1G?**
A: It's not necessary to report an offer of coverage to a part-time employee if coverage was declined. However, it is necessary to provide a 1095-C for part-time employees actually covered under a self-funded plan. If coverage was offered and accepted than you would use code 1G on line 14 of Part II (leaving lines 15 and 16 blank) and you would complete Part III to indicate which months the individual was actually covered under the self-funded plan.

Q: **Exactly what am I supposed to enter on line 16?**
A: You aren't required to make any entry on line 16 – but you can use line 16 to explain why you didn't offer coverage to an eligible employee or what the employee did after you offered coverage (accepted it, rejected it, etc.).

Q: **What are the codes for line 16?**
A: Here are the codes and when to use them:
- 2A – The employee was not employed during any day of the month.
- 2B – This code is used for several cases:
  - The employee was not a full-time employee for the month and did not enroll in minimum essential coverage (if offered).
  - The employee was a full-time employee during the month but his or her coverage (or offer of coverage) ended before

159

the last day of the month solely because the employee
terminated employment during the month (in other words,
the coverage or offer of coverage would have continued if
the employee hadn't left).

- 2C – Use code 2C for any month in which the employee was
enrolled in the coverage offered for each day of the month,
regardless of what other codes might apply.
- 2D – Use 2D for any month in which the employee was in a
Limited Non-Assessment Period.
- 2E – Use code 2E for any month in which the employer offered
health coverage to the employee and was required by a
collective bargaining agreement to make contributions for that
employee to a multi-employer plan offering affordable, minimum
value self-only coverage as well as coverage for the employee's
dependents.
- 2F – Use 2F on line 16 for each month if you used the Form W-2
safe harbor to determine affordability for this employee.
- 2G – Use 2G on line 16 if you used the federal poverty limit safe
harbor to determine affordability for this employee for any
month(s).
- 2H – Use 2H on line 16 if you used the rate of pay safe harbor to
determine affordability for this employee for any month(s).
  - 2I – Reserved (not currently in use).

Note: Employers eligible for relief provided in the multi-employer interim
guidance for a given month for an employee should use code 2E rather
than 2F, 2G or 2H.

Q: **I'm not sure which code to enter on line 16 – what should I do?**
A: If you can't determine which code to use, leave line 16 blank rather
than risk using the wrong code.

Q: **What code do I use for an employee who was hired March 15th
with coverage offered June 1st after a waiting period of 60 days
(with coverage to be offered on the 1st of the month following the
60 days), and the employee waived coverage? (Note: self-only
minimum value coverage cost was less than 9.56% of the federal
poverty level)**
A: On line 14 use code 1H (no offer of coverage) for January through
May and code 1A (offer of coverage at less than 9.56% of FPL) for June
through December. No entry is needed on line 15 since the offer is less
than 9.56% of the FPL. On line 16, use code 2A for January and
February (since the person wasn't employed then), code 2D (employee
in waiting period) for March through May, and leave line 16 blank for
June through December since the employee declined coverage (if he or

160

she had accepted coverage you would have used code 2C for June through December).

Q: **What codes do I use on lines 14 and 16 for each month for a full-time employee who was enrolled in minimum essential coverage (employee only), left on April 13th, was re-hired on September 2nd and coverage was resumed on October 1st?**
A: Use 1B on line 14 and 2C on line 16 for January, February, and March, code 1H on line 14 and 2B on line 16 for April and code 1H on line 14 and 2A on line 16 for May, June, July, and August. Then use 1B on line 14 and 2C on line 16 for October, November and December.

Q: **If a full-time employee leaves and is re-hired within 13 weeks can I wait 90 days to offer health care coverage?**
A: Under ACA rules, rehires who have been gone less than 13 weeks have to be offered coverage no later than the first of the month following their rehire date. (Note: Your insurance provider may specify that the employee has to go through an entire waiting period again).

Q: **I've finished with line 16 – now what?**
A: If you buy insurance coverage from an insurance company you're done. However, if you're self-insured you need to go ahead and fill out Part III which asks for information on covered employees (name, Social Security number, date of birth, and months of coverage).

Reporting Health Care Costs on the W-2

If you are required to report the total value of certain employer-sponsored health benefits on your employees' W-2 forms there are three main methods that can be used to calculate the value of health care benefits:

1) Premium charged method: The amount that goes on the W-2 is simply the premium the insurer charges for the employee's health care coverage for the year (this method can only be used for an employee covered by the employer's group health plan).
2) COBRA premium method: This method must be used for self-insured health care plans. The employer calculates the applicable COBRA premiums, excluding the 2 percent COBRA administrative fee and uses the amount on the employee's W-2.
3) Modified COBRA premium method: Employers can use this method if they subsidize the cost of COBRA coverage. The amount used on the W-2 is calculated based on a reasonable estimate of the COBRA premium if the estimate is used to establish the subsidized COBRA premium.

Note: Employers are not required to include standalone dental and vision plans when calculating the reportable health care costs.

Getting Help

Q: **Where can I find help from IRS with payroll questions?**
A: Here are a few of the publications that IRS provides containing information on payroll taxes and reports:
- IRS Publication 15 (Circular E) – Employers Tax Guide (www.irs.gov/pub/irs-pdf/p15.pdf)
- IRS Publication 15a – Employers Supplemental Tax Guide (www.irs.gov/pub/irs-pdf/p15a.pdf)
- IRS Publication 15b – Employers Guide to Fringe Benefits (www.irs.gov/pub/irs-pdf/p15b.pdf)

Q: **What about information from the Social Security Administration?**
A: www.ssa.gov/employer/ provides information on W-2 filing and Social Security number verification.

Q: **Where can I get advice about federal employment laws?**
A: The Department of Labor has created a group of online "advisors" (or "elaws") to help employers understand their rights and responsibilities under federal employment laws. The "elaws" cover a number of subjects including pay and overtime, employee benefits, and safety and health issues. The elaws are interactive tools designed to provide the same sort of advice you would get from an employment law expert. You can access the elaws at http://www.dol.gov/elaws.

Q: **What about payroll guides?**
A: Aspen Publishers (www.aspenpublishers.com) offers a number of publications by Wolters & Kluwer dealing with payroll and human resources. Their products include:
- *American Payroll Association (APA) Basic Guide to Payroll, 2017 Edition*
- *Multistate Payroll Guide, 2017 Edition*
- *U.S. Master Payroll Guide*
- *Wage and Hour Answer Book, 2017 Edition*
- *Wage-Hour Compliance Handbook, 2017 Edition*
- *Payroll Manager's Newsletter*
- *Complete Guide to Federal & State Garnishment, 2017 Edition*
- *Payroll Answer Book*
- *Quick Reference to Payroll Compliance*

Q: **What about payroll forums?**
A: Payroll forums and discussion groups include:

- www.payrolltalk.com – Discussions on payroll and human resources topics.
- www.payroll-taxes.com – Help with federal and state tax questions.
- www.taxforums.us/f-payroll-tax-forum-23.html – Discussions about payroll taxes and tax forms.

Q: **What about payroll blogs?**
A: There are some helpful blogs although most of them are connected to a specific payroll or payroll provider:

- www.hrpayrollsystems.net/hrblog/ - Human resources information.
- https://www.patriotsoftware.com/payroll/training/blog/ - General payroll information.
- Www.apspayroll.com/aps-blog/ - General payroll information.
- www.gtm.com/home/blog/ - General payroll information.
- www.blog.adp.com/category/payroll/ - General payroll information.
- Https://cs.thomsonreuters.com/blogs?tag=the%20payroll%20report – General payroll & accounting information.

Security

Q: **What should I do about keeping our payroll information secure?**
A: There are some general guidelines of course: limit access to payroll data, keep payroll records under lock and key, possibly even move archived payroll information to an outside storage location. If you're using pre-printed checks be sure to audit your checks periodically to make sure that all the unused checks are accounted for and in sequence. Using computerized time clocks and direct deposit can also help keep your payroll information free from tampering. And outsourcing your payroll also offers some advantages in that your payroll provider normally has your payroll information backed up on their system, in case of fire, flood, or some other disaster that could destroy your in-house data.

Q: **What about protecting computerized payroll records?**
A: Securing payroll data kept on computers is becoming more complicated all the time, especially if the data is on computers that are connected to the internet. Any computer with internet access needs to have a firewall up and running as well as real-time virus and malware scanning software. If you are transmitting payroll data over the web, encrypt that information if at all possible. Also, if you send ACH (Automated Clearing House) files such as direct deposit files via the internet, be sure to set up a verification process with the financial institution receiving the files to make sure that when they receive a file it's actually one that you sent.

Closing Your Business

Q: What do I need to do if I'm closing my business?
A: There are a number of steps you need to take to close down your business properly:

- Collect any outstanding accounts receivable
- Notify your creditors
- Notify your customers/clients and fulfill any remaining contractual obligations
- Notify your employees and make plans to pay your employees on the last day of business (including accrued vacation time)
- Sell off inventory
- Terminate your lease(s)
- Liquidate your business assets
- Settle your debts (at least as much as possible)
- Cancel business credit cards
- Close your business bank account(s)
- Cancel state or county licenses and permits
- Run your final payroll, distribute employee copies of W-2s and make your final federal and state payroll tax deposits
- Distribute 1099-MISC forms to vendors/sub-contractors
- File your final quarterly and annual employment tax forms (940, 941, 943. 943-A, W-2s and 1099s, Form 8027 (Annual Return of Tip Income and Allocated Tips), and state and local reporting forms.
- Report capital gains and losses:
  - Form 1040 – Individual tax return
  - Form 1065 – U.S. Partnership Return of Income
  - Form 1120 Schedule D – Capital gains and losses.
- Report partner's/shareholder's shares:
  - Form 1065 (Schedule K-1)
  - Form 1120 (Schedule K-1)
- File final employee pension/benefit plan (Form 5500)
- Distribute any remaining assets to yourself and any other owners
- Formally dissolve your partnership, corporation or LLC, filing the required forms (Form 966 – Corporate Dissolution or Liquidation)
- Consider allowing S corporation election to terminate (Form 1120S instructions)
- Report business asset sales (Form 8594 – Asset Acquisition Statement

- Report the sale or exchange of property used in your trade or business (Form 4797 – Sales of Business Property)

Miscellaneous

Q: **What do I need to know about workers' comp insurance?**

A: Workers Compensation Insurance is a system to provide medical care and compensation to workers who become ill from work-related causes or are injured on the job. The system usually operates by means of mandatory insurance coverage imposed on employers. Policies include two separate coverages: workers' compensation and employers liability. The insurer (state agency or private company) will pay benefits to employees for sickness or injury incurred on the job and the liability portion of the coverage protects the employer for employee work-related bodily injury that doesn't fall under workers' compensation coverage. Before you go looking for workers' comp coverage (assuming you're in a state that allows employers to deal with private insurance companies) you need to know your estimated payroll for the coming year so the insurance agent can determine the amount of coverage your company needs. You will also need job descriptions for all your employees for classification purposes -- you'll pay a higher premium for a construction worker than you would for a secretary.

Q: **How are a company's workers' compensation insurance premiums calculated?**

A: Premiums are calculated according to the job classifications of the company's employees, the size of the organization's payroll and the company's experience modification factor or "MOD" (which is based on the organization's record of job-related accidents and illnesses). Different job classifications are assigned a dollar rate based on the risk factor involved in that job and the rates vary by state. In a typical state for example, the dollar rate for a clerical worker may be 20 cents per $100 of payroll, while the rate for a carpenter working in residential construction might be $8.21 per $100 of payroll. The amount of a company's insurance premium is equal to the total over all the company's job classifications of the wages paid to workers in each classification (divided by $100) times the rate for that classification times the company's experience modification factor.

Q: **What is the employer's responsibility for providing medical treatment for an employee's job-related injury?**

A: Employers are responsible for arranging immediate medical treatment as soon as the employee notifies them of the injury (Note: in most states the employee has to inform the employer of the illness or injury within a certain period of time – usually from 7 to 30 days). Once informed of the injury or illness the employer is also required to provide the employee with a claim form to fill out so the claim can be submitted to the workers' compensation insurance provider. Depending on the state, the injured employee may have to select from a network of physicians provided by the insurance company or, If the employee selected a personal physician in a written notice to the employer prior to any injury or illness, he or she may be able to go to that physician for treatment immediately after an injury.

Q: **If an employee leaves do I have to pay him severance pay?**
A: The Fair Labor Standards Act (FLSA) requires an employer to pay an employee who has been terminated his or her regular wages through the employee's termination date and for any time the person has accrued (accrued time usually includes vacation or personal days but not sick days). Severance pay however, unless specifically provided for in the employment contract, is up to the good will of the employer. If you do offer severance pay it may be a good idea to ask the employee to sign a release from any future claims in return for accepting the severance pay (Note: If the employee is 40 or older the "Older Workers' Benefits Protection Act" dictates what must be included in the release).

Q: **What is "Escheatment"?**
A: Escheatment has to do with unclaimed payroll checks. An employee never gives up his or her right to a wage payment, no matter how long that payment goes unclaimed. After a certain length of time -- in most states, one year -- uncollected wages are considered to be abandoned and the employer is obligated to turn them over to the state, which holds the money in custody for the payee (the actual transfer of funds to the state is the escheatment process). The state keeps these funds on behalf of the owner but can use the money however it wants to until the owner actually comes to collect it -- which means that state governments are often actively checking on employers to make sure that they are turning over all unclaimed funds in a timely manner.

Q: **What do I do about an unclaimed employee paycheck?**
A: See "escheatment" above.

Q: **What is "COBRA"?**
A: The Consolidated Omnibus Budget Reconciliation Act of 1985 requires employers who sponsor employee health plans to provide workers and their dependents and beneficiaries with the opportunity to keep continued group health coverage for a given period of time if their coverage is lost due to certain "qualifying events". The continuation coverage must be the same as that provided to workers still on the

payroll. Qualifying events include the death of an employee, termination of the employee or reduction of the employee's hours (other than for gross misconduct), divorces involving a covered dependent, and several other situations. The continuation period is usually either 18 or 36 months and the employer must provide the recipient an option to switch to individual coverage before the continuation period runs out.

Q: Are all employers with group health care plans subject to COBRA?
A: Only organizations with 20 or more employees on more than 50 percent of their typical business days in the previous calendar year are subject to COBRA. Note: Part-time employees count as a fraction of an employee with the fraction equal to the the number of hours the part-time employee worked divided by the number of hours a full-time employee would have worked.

Q: What is "COBRA Premium Assistance"?
Note: COBRA Premium Assistance expired as of February 2012.
A: The American Recovery and Reinvestment Act (ARRA) of 2009 provides for premium reductions for COBRA health benefits. Eligible individuals pay only 35% of their COBRA premiums and their insurance provider (you, the employer in this case) pays the other 65% which is reimbursed to you as a tax credit on the Form 941 (Employer's Quarterly Federal Tax Return) or Form 944 (Employer's Annual Federal Tax Return). The premium reduction applies to periods of health coverage that began after February 17, 2009 and lasts for 15 months. To qualify, individuals must have experienced one of the qualifying events listed above (under "What is COBRA") and the event must have taken place from September 1, 2008 through May 31, 2010.

Q: What does "Gross Up" mean?
A: If an employer wants to pay an employee's taxes for him (on a Christmas bonus check for example), then the net pay has to be "grossed up" to include the tax amounts the employer paid. For example, you would take the percentage of wages that goes for Social Security (.062) plus the percentage for Medicare (.0145) plus some reasonable percentage for federal income tax (.2500) plus a percentage for state income tax (.0800) and add those percentages together (.4065); then divide that percentage into 1.0000 and multiply the net pay by the result to get the correct gross pay. If the employer is taking FICA taxes only, you can divide the net pay by .9235 to get the "bumped up" gross pay.

Q: What is the normal length of a "pay period"?

A: Pay periods are usually weekly, bi-weekly (every two weeks), semi-monthly (twice a month), or monthly. In any case a pay period cannot be longer than 31 consecutive days.

What You Don't Know About Payroll Can Cost You

Q: I have an employee who works from 10 am to 5 pm, Monday through Friday and I pay him $2000 a month. That makes his regular rate of pay $11.54, right? ($24,000/year divided by 52 weeks times 40 hours/week).
A: Under the FLSA (the Fair Labor Standards Act) you also have to consider the number of hours worked per week. Since your employee actually works 7 hours a day five days a week, that's 35 hours per week – which makes his regular rate of pay $13.19 ($24,000/year divided by 52 weeks times 35 hours/week). That difference in rate can make a big difference in any overtime pay since you should be calculating overtime pay at one and a half times $13.19, rather than $11.54 per hour.

Q: What is "constructive receipt"? **
A: Technically, if you mail a paycheck to an employee with a check date of 12/30/2019 and the employee doesn't receive the check until January 1st, 2020, or later, then the withholding taxes should be calculated based on 2020 tables and should be included in the employee's 2020 W-2 instead of the 2019 W-2. Basically, that person's pay should be moved out of 2019 and into 2020. Note: The author has never heard of this actually being enforced by an auditor, but it is something to keep in mind.

Q: Is money provided to an employee for financial counseling considered taxable income?
A: Yes, if an employer pays for financial counseling for an employee who is chronically in debt, that amount is considered taxable income for the employee.

Q: I provide sandwiches and pizza for my employees from a lunch wagon that comes by at noon – saves them from having to go buy lunch somewhere. That doesn't have anything to do with payroll does it?
A: Technically, the cash value of meals provided for the convenience of your employees is considered "wages" under the Federal Insurance Contributions Act (FICA) and should be taxed. If you pay for their lunch for YOUR convenience, then the cash value would not be considered wages.

Q: I have an employee who works in our office here most of the time but also works out of a small office in another state for a week or

two at a time. Do I need to pay state unemployment tax in both states?
A: No,in this case your employee is "localized" in your main office and you should pay SUI tax for him or her to your state.

Q: Who is exempt from Social Security and Medicare tax withholding?
A:Exempt workers include:
- Children under 18 working for their parents.
- Students working for a school while attending classes there.
- Student nurses.
- Individuals working for a foreign government or an international organization.
- Temporary foreign agriculture workers.
- Workers holding certain types of visas.

Q: If I need to correct a 941 form I submit a 941-X form with the appropriate adjustments, right?
A: Yes – unless you're asking for a refund and reporting both over-reported and under-reported amounts. In that case you need to submit one 941-X with the over-reported amounts and another 941-X with the under-reported amounts.

Q: If you're paying an employee a bonus you only need to withhold Social Security and Medicare taxes (true or false)?
A: According to the IRS employers need to withhold federal income tax as well (although it's common practice on smaller bonuses up to $200 to $300 to withhold just FICA taxes). To calculate federal withholding on supplemental payments such as bonuses you can either:
- Withhold a straight 22% of the taxable gross.
- Add the bonus to the employee's regular earnings on the current and calculate the federal withholding tax on the combined total.
- There is a third method, which is considerably more complicated and seldom used. It won't be covered here due to the complexity of the steps involved.

Q: As long as I pay employees time and a half for any time over 40 hours worked in a given workweek I'm OK, since that's what's required by the FLSA (Fair Labor Standards Act) - correct?
A: Maybe or maybe not. It depends on your state regulations – some states have overtime requirements that are different than the FSLA. Colorado for example, requires overtime to be paid to any employee who works over 12 hours in a given workday. Be sure you know the overtime rules for each state where you have employees.

173

Q: How do I calculate overtime pay if I have a semi-monthly payroll and the pay period ends in the middle of a week?
A: You have to pay overtime for any hours worked over 40 in a full workweek. If the pay period ends during a week, you can wait till the next pay period to determine which employees (if any) qualify for overtime pay for that week. Any overtime pay for that workweek needs to be added to the person's pay for the next pay period.

Q: I just arranged to pay all my employees by direct deposit. I'll make the announcement Monday and get all their bank information so we can get started – that's all I need to do isn't it?
A: You could have a bit of a problem. Some states don't allow employers to require their employees to be paid by direct deposit. Depending on what state(s) you operate in, you may need to get a signed form from your employees agreeing to have their pay direct deposited before you do so.

Q: I have to pay my employees extra for working on a holiday, right?
A: Federal law considers holidays just another business day, so no – you aren't required to pay extra for having employees work on a holiday (although many companies do).

Q: Can I offer my employees compensatory time off in place of overtime pay?
A: Not unless you're a government agency – non-governmental organizations must pay their employees for any overtime hours worked.

Q: My employees have to change clothes and put on uniforms when they get here in the morning before they start work – I don't have to pay them for the time they spend changing clothes do I?
A: According to the U.S. Supreme Court, if an activity is integral to the employee's principal activity it's considered part of the person's work time and the employee must be compensated for that time. So yes, you may need to pay them for the time they spend getting dressed.

Q: John, one of my hourly employees, has come in late several times in the last two weeks because (according to him) he got held up in traffic. Is it OK to dock him for the missed time and to deduct an additional $25 for missing a departmental meeting?
A: It's OK to dock John for the missed worktime, but it's not alright to charge him the additional $25 – that could be considered an unlawful

deduction. Employees must agree to any deductions other than taxes (or special deductions such as garnishments).

Q: I promised Mary a salary increase but business has dropped off and I can't give her the increase at the moment. Now she's threatening to turn me in to Wage and Hour for failing to give her the raise I promised – can she do that?
A: Be careful about promising raises ahead of time. Technically, promising a raise and not following through might actually be considered as taking an unlawful deduction from the employee's paycheck. Not giving the raise amounts to reducing the pay the employee was promised without their permission.

Q: I have an employee in Accounting who also has some background in graphic design. Last month she helped the Marketing department work up an ad campaign and she wants to be paid for that work as an independent contractor. Is that possible? Can she be paid both as an employee and as an independent contractor?
A: According to an IRS ruling in 2012 it is possible (under very specific circumstances) for a person to be paid by the same company as both an employee and as an independent contractor. Since this case involves an individual working in two completely unrelated jobs in different departments, it seems to meet the IRS requirements for her to be paid as both employee and contractor.

Q: Do I have to pay overtime to salaried employees?
A: Salaried employees who are non-exempt (i.e., they don't meet the standards to be classified as exempt) are also entitled to overtime pay.

Q: What makes an employee exempt from overtime pay requirements?
A: Generally speaking to be exempt an employee has to:
- Be paid at least $23,000 per year ($455 per week). Note: Beginning January 1, 2020, that amount will change to $35,568 per year or $684 per week.
- Be paid on a salary basis.
- Perform exempt job duties as outlined in the FLSA regulations. Note: Employers often classify an employee as salaried and overtime exempt without making sure they meet the job requirements to be classified as exempt.

Q: If I realize I've misclassified a worker as an independent contractor instead of treating him as an employee, what's it going to cost me?
A: The Voluntary Classification Settlement Program (VCSP) allows employers to reclassify workers as employees and get back into compliance by paying 10 percent of the employment tax liability that would have been due on compensation paid to the worker during the most recent tax year.

Q: Do I have to treat a gift card given to an employee as wages?
A: Gift cards (at least those over $25 or so) are a form of monetary compensation and need to be added to the employee's compensation for payroll purposes. Note: If the gift card or similar item was a retirement or going away present and the employee is no longer with you, you can gross up the amount of the gift card so the net matches the actual value of the card, then run the entry through payroll (with a deduction such as "cash received" to bring the net pay back to zero). That will get the amount of the gift into the person's compensation for the year (however, the company will have to pay the employee's portion of the FICA tax since the person is no longer there).

Q: Would I ever have to include an employee's expense reimbursement in his or her taxable wages?
A: Not if the expense reimbursement is connected to business and is done under an "accountable" plan – that is, a plan where there is an adequate accounting of expenses and any excess reimbursement is returned to the employer.

Q: I pay a number of my employees the federal minimum wage (which is also the state minimum wage). Most of them don't have bank accounts so I also pay them with paycards. Any problem with that?
A: Maybe - there are fees associated with some paycards and those fees could reduce an employee's pay below minimum wage, leaving you open to penalties.

Q: Am I correct that all I have to do when hiring a new employee is to have them fill out a Form I-9, a W-4 form, and make sure they provide a valid Social Security number?
A: There's one other item you need to deal with. Most states require employers to report all new hires to the state in order for the state to locate individuals who owe child support.

Q: Our computers are protected by anti-virus, anti-malware, anti-keylogger and anti-rootkit software so we're covered against cyber attacks. Correct?

A: Not necessarily - no defense is perfect and something as simple as using an easily guessed password or clicking on an official-looking email can open your computers to a cyber attack. If your business suffers a loss of data or a monetary loss from having to pay to free your data from a ransomware attack, your only defense is to have cyber insurance. Types of cyber attacks include:

- Brute force (using software to acquire login information)
- Ransomware
- Denial-of-service
- Social engineering
- Insertion of malware
- Back-door attacks

It may be worthwhile to look into obtaining insurance to cover you against cyber risks. And cyber attacks aren't launched just against large companies – attackers gain experience by targeting individuals and small businesses.

Q: We just ran a regular payroll with $58,000 in federal withholding taxes and made the 941 payment due on the 2rd working day after the pay date. And we also ran a bonus payroll with $45,000 in federal withholding taxes (for the same pay date) and also made the 941 tax payment for it due on the 2nd working day after the pay date – so we're covered, right?

A: Unfortunately, no. Since both payrolls were run with the same pay date and the total 941 taxes for the two payrolls combined totaled over $100,000, the 941 tax payments should have been made on the next business day following the pay date under the $100,000 rule. Be careful when running multiple large payrolls with the same pay date.

Q: Mary's taxable earnings for the current payroll amounts to $3,500 which will increase her year-to-date FICA taxable earnings to $201,500 - how much will her Social Security and Medicare taxes be for this payroll? How much will I have to pay in matching FICA tax for Mary?

A: Mary's Social Security tax will be zero since her FICA taxable wages were already over the $137,700 wage limit for 2020. Since an employee's Medicare tax rate increases from 1.45% to 2.35% when the employee's taxable earnings reaches $200,000, Mary's Medicare tax will be $3500 x .0145 + $1500 (the amount of FICA taxable wages over $200,000) x .009 (the additional Medicare tax rate) which equals $50.75 + $13.50 or $64.25. Your matching FICA tax for Mary will be $50.75

($3500 x .0145) since the additional Medicare tax only applies to the employee.

Q: 57) Do "temp" workers count as "employees" of the business they're working for under the Affordable Care Act?
A: Workers hired through a temporary staffing agency for short-term assignments are presumed to be employees of the staffing agency. However, temporary workers who have more than a short-term assignment with an employer are generally considered employees of that business, not the staffing agency, and must be included in the monthly employee counts and offered appropriate healthcare coverage.

Q: We've started outsourcing our payroll to a payroll service and we're sending them the clock hours for our hourly employees. Is there anything we should watch our for?
A: Make sure the payroll provider knows that the hours you're sending to them are in clock time. If they're entering 7 hours and 45 minutes as 7.45 hours (in decimal format) you could end up having to make up for underpaying all your hourly employees.

Q: How exactly does the IRS distinguish between employees and independent contractors?
A: The IRS uses three main categories to determine if an individual is an employee or independent contractor:
1) Behavioral – how much control does the company have over how, when and where the individual works.
2) Financial – who pays for tools, supplies and other items necessary for the individual to do his or her job.
3) Relational – does the person receive benefits, and does he or she work on day-to-day tasks or on a project-by-project basis.

Q: We've got several paid interns – can I treat them as independent contractors since they're just observing, learning the job, not actually working as employees?
A: Paid interns are employees in training and should be classified as employees, not contractors. An intern's activities are normally controlled by the employer and once that relationship is established, the intern is effectively an employee.

Q: I employed a person from a temp agency and she's been working here for over six months - does that make her an employee of my company?

A: In general a temp worker who has been with you for more than a few weeks is normally treated as an employee of your company even though he or she is being paid by the temp agency.

Q: I run a small business (a sole proprietorship) and recently I hired my son and daughter to help out at the office. A friend of mine who has a subchapter S corporation and employs his 16 year old son and told me I have to withhold FICA taxes on my son and daughter just like other employees. Is that right?
A: If your son and daughter are under the age of 18 you don't have to withhold FICA taxes since you're a sole proprietor. However, under most conditions children of owners in a partnership or a corporation do have to withhold FICA.

Q: I just hired a couple of employees who are 18 years old, just out of high school. They're in training right now – do I have to pay them full minimum wage?
A: Employees who are 18 or over but under 20 years of age can be paid less than minimum wage (but not less than $4.25 per hour) for the first 90 days they're employed by you (or until they turn 20 years old).

Q: I filled out my Form 940 and filed it in January but I forgot to check the "multi-state employer" box (I have one employee in another state). Is that going to matter?
A: It could – if you're required to pay state unemployment tax in another state then you're required to fill out Form 940 Schedule A. And if your employee is in a "credit reduction" state (a state that has borrowed funds from the federal government to pay unemployment benefits and hasn't been able to repay all those funds) then you're also going to owe additional federal unemployment tax for the wages paid in the credit reduction state.

Q: I fill out my Form 940 by hand and I entered my taxable FUTA wages on lines 7 and 9. My FUTA tax came out to be 6% of the taxable wages – that's the correct rate isn't it?
A: Assuming you made all your state unemployment tax payments correctly your rate would be 6% minus a credit of 5.4% for your state payments for an effective rate of 0.6%. If you read line 9 carefully, you only make an entry on that line if none of your federal unemployment tax is subject to state unemployment tax. So in this case you overpaid your FUTA tax by 5.4%. (Note: This has actually happened to some employers who failed to read the instructions carefully – make sure you understand all instructions on federal or state forms).

Q: I accidentally paid one of our salespeople too much on her last commission payment so can I just subtract the over-payment from her next check?

A: Not without her permission – the employee has to agree that there was an over-payment and that she's OK with paying it back. If it's a large enough amount and the employee refuses to give back the over-payment you could take it to court (and if you wanted to take it that far, you would probably also have reasonable cause to fire the person).

Q: What do I do if I discover that the amounts on one of my employee's W-2 is wrong and the W-2 has already been sent to the Social Security Administration?

A: There are probably two things that need to be done. You need to file a W2-C correction form with the SSA (either on paper or online) and you need to fill out and file a 941-X (941 correction form) for the quarter in which the error occurred.

Q: If I'm late making a payroll tax payment to the IRS what kind of penalty can they charge me?

A: Failure to Deposit penalties are based on a percentage of the amount of tax due:

- 1 to 5 days late – 2% of the tax due.
- 6 to 15 days late – 5% of the tax due.
- 16 or more days late – 10% of the tax due.
- More than 10 days after the first IRS notification – 15% of the tax due.

In addition to the penalties above you will also have to pay interest and the interest rate (which is determined quarterly) ranges between 3% and 6%.

Q: How much of a penalty will the IRS charge me if I'm late filing my Form 941 and have unpaid tax due?

A: The IRS imposes a penalty of 5% of the unpaid tax due with your Form 941 for each month (or partial month) that your return is late, up to a maximum of 25% of the unpaid tax due. There is also a 0.5% penalty for each month or partial month that you pay the tax late.

Q: We're a small company with just five employees and we've all been taking minimal salaries while we built up our business, so we're a monthly depositor for payroll tax purposes. This month though we paid our normal payrolls on the 5th and 20th (with a total of $12,500 in payroll withholding tax due for each of those payrolls) but we're also going to finally pay out some large bonuses on the last day of the month (which will include $80,000 in payroll

withholding taxes). Do we just make a $105,000 payroll tax payment on the 15th of next month as usual?

A: You've accumulated over $100,000 in payroll taxes in one month. That means that you've just automatically become a semi-weekly depositor (and will be from now on) and that you need to make that $105,000 tax payment on the next business day following the last day of the current month. Waiting till the 15th of next month will result in some sizable penalties for late payment.

Q: We have a Section 125 cafeteria plan that our employees participate in. We also have a "cash-out" option for our senior employees if they opt out of coverage under the 125 plan. Any problem with that?

A: Offering a cash-out option to only certain employees (giving the employee a set dollar amount in lieu of coverage under the cafeteria plan) violates the non-discriminatory rules of Section 125 plans. A cash-out option (if offered) must be available to all employees participating in the plan.

Q: I just reimbursed an employee for travel expenses - $300 for meals, $1200 for hotels and $750 for airfare. How much can I claim as a business deduction?

A: You can only claim $2,100 as a deduction. Fifty percent of meal expense is generally assumed to be personal expense, not directly business related.

Q: We provide cars for several of our employees – what if they use those vehicles for personal activities?

A: Using employer provided vehicles for personal use can be classified as "imputed income". Imputed income should be added to the person's wages and is subject to social security and medicare taxes. The employer isn't required to withhold federal (or state or local) income tax, but the employee can elect to have the employer do so.

Q: How do I calculate an employee's imputed income on a company car provided to him?

A: Do the following:
- Determine the fair market value of the vehicle for the current year (you can use the cost of a comparable leased vehicle).
- Have the employee keep a log during the year of all trips in the company car and record the mileage driven for both business and personal trips.

- Divide the personal mileage by the total miles driven and multiply that percentage times the fair market value of the vehicle to get the imputed income amount.

Q: One of our employees passed away suddenly last week – what do I need to do about a final paycheck?
A: There are several situations to consider:
- If a paycheck has already been issued to the employee, but he or she dies before cashing it, the original check should be canceled and a new one issued for the net amount of the check, payable to the employee's beneficiary or personal representative (who should sign a statement that the check is for the employee's uncashed paycheck). Taxes have already been withheld from the original paycheck, so the gross wages and taxes will appear on the person's W2 at the end of the year.
- If you still owe unpaid wages to the deceased employee, have the beneficiary or personal representative fill out a Form W-9 (Request for Taxpayer Identification Number) so that you have that information on file. Once you have the W-9 make out a check to the estate or beneficiary and record the payment on a Form 1099-MISC in box 3.
- If the payment is made in the same calendar year as the employee's death you should withhold FICA taxes (and pay FUTA tax), but don't withhold federal income tax (you may or may not need to withhold state income tax depending on state regulations). You also need to do the following on the person's W-2: add the final wages to box 3 (Social Security wages) and to box 5 (Medicare wages), add the Social Security tax withheld to box (4) and add the Medicare tax withheld to box (6).
- If the final payment is made in the year following the employee's death, don't withhold any taxes and don't include the final payment on the person's W-2. Do fill out a 1099-MISC however, as noted above.

Q: Is imputed income (group term life insurance over $50,000, auto allowances, etc.) FICA taxable?
A: Yes, employers should withhold FICA taxes on imputed income amounts (the employer may or may not withhold federal, state or local taxes).

Q: When can I dock one of my exempt salaried employee's pay without violating the FLSA (Fair Labor Standards Act)?
A: Here are the situations where it's OK to dock an exempt employee's pay:

- If the employee performs zero hours of work during a workweek you can deduct any amount up to the entire week's pay. However, if the employee was idle simply because there wasn't any work available to be assigned to him, then deducting from his pay would be a violation of FLSA rules.
- The employee can have a day's pay deducted if he misses the entire day for personal reasons other than sickness or accident.
- If the company has a plan that compensates employees for "sick" days and an exempt employee has used up his allotment of sick time, then he can be docked for any additional time missed due to illness or disability.
- An exempt employee can have pay deducted for major violations of (posted) safety rules.
- An exempt employee can have his pay reduced in order to offset any amount he received for jury or military duty.
- A reduced amount can be paid to an exempt employee for his initial or final week of work if he only works a part of that week.

Q: Some of our hourly employees who are paid bi-weekly get a $50 bonus every pay day if they process a certain number of orders. If one of them works over 40 hours in a week and also qualifies for the $50 bonus for that pay period, do I have to take the bonus into account in calculating his or her overtime pay?

A: Since the bonus is non-discretionary (that is, it's paid automatically if the employee qualifies for it) then the answer is yes, you have to include the bonus in figuring overtime pay. In this case to figure the employee's earnings for the week in which he or she worked overtime you would add $25 (one week's portion of the bonus) to the person's earnings for the week (number of hours worked times rate of pay). Then you would divide that dollar total by the total number of hours worked for the week to get an adjusted hourly rate of pay. To calculate the overtime pay you would multiply the number of hours worked over 40 times the adjusted rate of pay times 1.5.

Q: Business has been slow lately and one of my salespeople who's on straight commission is threatening to complain to the wage and hour people because she's only made a couple of hundred dollars in the last month. Should I be concerned?

A: Non-exempt employees, including those on commission, have to make the equivalent of at least the federal minimum wage ($7.25 per hour). If your salesperson's commissions figure out to less than that per hour worked, then you could be in violation of FLSA regulations.

Q: Are our commission-only salespeople that work in the store entitled to overtime pay if they work more than 40 hours in a given workweek?

A: Yes – although, in general, you don't have to pay them for overtime if their regular rate of pay (total commissions divided by number of hours worked) is more than one and one half times the applicable minimum wage (federal or state, whichever is greater) for every hour worked.

Q: How do you calculate overtime pay for a commission-only employee?

A: As an example lets say you have a commission-only employee who worked 45 hours last week and made a total of $720 in commissions. To calculate the employee's total pay including overtime:

- Divide the person's earnings by the number of hours worked ($720 / 45) which equals the employee's regular rate of pay ($16 per hour in this case).
- Multiply the number of overtime hours worked times the regular rate of pay times one half (5 x $16 x .5 = $40). That gives you the premium portion of overtime pay.
- Add the commission amount for the 45 hours to the premium pay to get the total pay for the employee ($720 + $40 - $760).

Q: If I pay an employee for sick time do those hours count in figuring overtime?

A: No, even if an employee is paid for sick time or other absences, those hours do not count toward the 40 hours a week for overtime pay purposes.

Q: We've got a small sandwich shop that's only open on the weekend. My employees make maybe $20 to $25 a month in tips, but last month one of them made $50 – do I have to fill out tip reports for her?

A: No, you don't. An employee has to *regularly* make $30 or more a month in tips to be considered a "tipped" employee.

Q: What if an employee doesn't report tips given directly to him?

A: If the IRS determines that an employee has failed to report cash tips of over $20 a month to you, you can be held liable for the employer's share of FICA (Social Security and Medicare taxes) and the employee may be penalized the other 50 percent of the FICA tax due on the tips.

Q: I have a tipped employee who worked 50 hours last week. His base pay is $7.00 an hour (my state has a minimum wage of $10/hour, with a maximum tip credit of $3/hour) and I normally pay

him overtime at one and one half times his base rate. So that makes his total pay for last week 40 x $7 plus 10 x $7 x 1.5 or $385 – right?

A: Not quite. Overtime pay for tipped employees has to be based on either the federal minimum cash wage or your state minimum case wage if greater than the federal rate. In this case your employee's pay for last week would be:

- 40 x $7 = $280 (regular time)
- $10/hour (state min. wage) x 1.5 = $15.00/hour (overtime rate)
- $15.00/hour - $3.00/hour = $12.00 (adjusted overtime rate (overtime rate – max. tip credit)
- $12.00/hour x 10 hours = $120.00 (overtime pay)
- $280 + $120 = $400 (total pay)

Q: Last week one of my employees worked 10 hours at $12/hour and 35 hours at $15/hour. What should I be paying her?

A: Overtime pay for an employee who worked at two or more different rates of pay during the week is based on a weighted average. To figure the total pay for his employee you need to:

- Calculate the straight time wages (10 hours x $12/hour + 35 hours x $15/hour = $120 + $525 or $645.
- Calculate the regular rate of pay ($645 / 45 hours = $14.33/hour).
- Calculate the premium portion of overtime pay ($14.33/hours x .5 x 5 hours = $35.83).
- Total pay = $645 + $35.83 = $680.83.

Note: To keep things simple you can also pay all overtime hours at the higher rate of pay.

Q: I have someone who runs our payroll on a software package of his and prints out the Form 940 and 941 for use to sign and send in. Is he supposed to fill out the "paid preparer" section on the 941?

A: Not unless he's providing you with advice on how to fill out the 941 form. If all he does is run your payroll according to the information you give him and give you a printed copy of the 941 to look over then he isn't required to fill out the paid preparer section.

Q: Is employee group term life insurance coverage taxable?

A: Employee group term life insurance is exempt from federal income tax withholding and from federal unemployment taxes. It is also exempt from Social Security and Medicare withholding up to $50,000 of coverage - for coverage over $50,000 you have to calculate the cost of the additional coverage (see IRS Publication 15-B for details) and report that amount on the W-2 as wages in boxes 1, 3 and 5, and in box 12 with code "C".

185

To calculate the taxable value of the amount of life insurance over $50,000:
1) Round the amount of life insurance to the nearest $100.
2) Subtract $50,000 from the total amount of coverage.
3) Multiply the number of thousands of dollars of insurance coverage remaining by the cost shown in the table below (accurate for 2018).
4) Calculate the insurance cost for each month during the year.
5) Multiply the monthly amount by 12 to get the annual cost.
6) Subtract any amounts paid by the employee.
7) Include the total amount on the employee's W-2 form.

Table: Employee Age	Insurance Cost
Under 25	$0.05
25 through 29	$0.06
30 through 34	$0.08
35 through 39	$0.09
40 through 44	$0.10
45 through 49	$0.15
50 through 54	$0.23
55 through 59	$0.43
60 through 64	$0.66
65 through 69	$1.27
70 and over	$2.06

Q: Does the actual cost of group term life insurance coverage matter when determining if the under $50,000 tax exclusion applies?
A: No, the amount of the death benefit determines whether the $50,000 exclusion applies. If the total value of the death benefit for all employer-provided life insurance during a specific period of coverage (usually one month) exceeds $50,000 then the excess is taxable.

Q: What steps should I take if I have to terminate an employee?
A: There are several things you should do:
- Assemble a record of the details involved in the decision to terminate the employee (including performance reviews, warnings and disciplinary actions) and place a copy in the employee's personnel file. The employee should also be given a termination letter with the date of termination and detailing any pertinent information such as his benefit status.
- Reclaim any company property the employee has his possession (including documents, keys, tools, computers, and cell phones) as soon as possible.

- Change any log in and password information the employee used to access company records.
- Make sure that his final paycheck includes all money owed to him, including any unpaid expense reimbursements, commission payments, or payments for unused vacation, personal or sick time.
- Ask for his new contact information so his year-end W-2 can be sent to them (and so you can reach him if you need to for any other reason).

Q: I had 22 employees but I had to let four of them go in August since business slowed down. And I had to tell the people that I let go that I wasn't offering any COBRA health insurance coverage to replace our company insurance since I now have less than 20 employees and don't fall under the COBRA rules anymore.
A: Actually COBRA rules apply to any employer who had 20 of more employees during at least 50% of the year. Since you had over 20 employees for better than half the year, you're still obligated to provide COBRA coverage for the employees (and their families) who lost their jobs. Ignoring that obligation can be expensive: the tax penalty is $100 per qualified beneficiary, up to $200 per family. If it was an unintentional violation, the maximum penalty is the lesser of $500,000 or 10% of the amount the employer spent for group health care during the previous year.

Q: I had an employee who worked overtime one week last month and she also earned a $100 performance bonus that we offer to any employee who meets certain goals for the month. I paid her overtime wages at one and a half times her normal pay rate for the overtime hours she worked and paid her the performance bonus at the end of the month. Now my accountant says I didn't pay her correctly – what did I do wrong?
A: Actually you did exactly what the great majority of employers do. Technically though, you mishandled the overtime calculation according to IRS rules. Since the bonus applied to the entire month (let's say 4 weeks), the $100 should be pro-rated for that period so $25 applies to each week. To calculate the overtime pay for the week the employee worked more than 40 hours, $25 should be added to the employee's regular earnings for the week. That total should be divided by 40 hours to get an adjusted rate of pay and the adjusted rate (times 1.5) should be multiplied by the the number of overtime hours worked to determine the overtime pay.

Q: How do I calculate overtime pay for employees who get paid by the piece?

A: If you have employees who are paid by the number of pieces produced, you have two options for calculating overtime pay. You can pay them, in addition to their piecework earnings, an amount equal to one-half of their hourly rate (calculated as their piecework earnings divided by the number of hours worked that week) multiplied by the number of hours in excess of 40 worked during the week. Alternatively you can (with the agreement of your employees) pay piece-work employees one and one-half times the piece rate for each piece produced during the overtime hours.

Q: Do I have to pay overtime to an employee who works more than 8 hours in a day?

A: Unless there is a state law or a collective bargaining agreement that requires you to pay overtime if someone works more than eight hours in a day, you only have to pay overtime if the employee works more than forty hours during the work week.

Q: Can overtime pay be paid in advance?

A: Yes. If an employee works less than 40 hours in a week the employer can advance the employee the difference in pay between what he actually made and what he would have been paid if he had worked 40 hours. Then when the employee works over 40 hours in a week this "advance overtime pay" can be offset against the amount of overtime pay owed.

Q: If I give an employee a pay advance do I have to withhold taxes on that amount?

A: No, but have the employee pay back the advance on the next payroll if at all possible (even if it drops the employee's pay below minimum wage).

Q: We had an employee who quit and left a forwarding address. We sent his final paycheck to that address and it came back marked "undeliverable" - what do we do now with his paycheck?

A: The first thing to do is to send a certified letter to the address he left you. When the certified letter comes back you'll have a record that you tried to reach him at his last known address. Then you need to check the "escheat" laws in the state where he worked – at some point (usually 6 months to a year from the date of the check) you have to turn the check over to the state as unpaid wages.

Q: When it mentions "disposable income" on a garnishment order, it's talking about net pay, right?

A: No, the term "disposable income" refers to an employee's remaining pay after all taxes and mandatory deductions have been taken out.

Q: I have an employee with a garnishment who makes $1,000 a week. His only deduction is a pre-tax 401(k) contribution of $100 per week. To calculate his disposable income for garnishment purposes I subtract his pre-tax 401(k) deduction which leaves me with $900, then I figure his withholding taxes ($250) on the $900 taxable income and subtract that amount from his pay. His net pay then is $900 minus $250 or $650 and that's also his disposable earnings – correct?

A: Even though you had to subtract the 401(k) contribution from the employee's gross in order to calculate his federal and state withholding, you have to add any pre-tax deductions back in to determine his disposable earnings. In this case the disposable earnings would be $650 plus $100 or $750.

Q: Are employee dependent care benefits considered wages?

A: Dependent care services you directly or indirectly pay for (or provide to an employee under a dependent care assistance program) to allow the employee to work may qualify as an excludable benefit. Generally, dependent care assistance up to a certain amount (currently $5,000 for married couples or $2500 for married employees filing separate returns) is not taxable. At year end the total amount of dependent care benefits provided to an employee should be reported in box 10 of the employee's Form W-2 and any excess amount over the $5,000 or $2500 limit should be included in box 1, 3 and 5.

Q: How long do I need to keep payroll records?

A: There are a number of (sometimes conflicting) guidelines on retention of payroll and human resource records. Generally speaking, records relating to a particular employee should be kept while the employee is with the company and for three years after he or she leaves. You're generally safe if you retain other payroll records for six years; beyond that you should probably consider shredding those records to dispose of them in a secure manner.

Q: Is there a new version of Form I-9?

A: The U.S. Citizenship and Immigration Services (USCIS) issued a new version of the Employment Eligibility Verification, Form I-9. Employers may begin using the new Form I-9 (revision date 07/17/17) immediately, although the previous version (revision date 11/14/16) may also be used through September 17, 2017. Beginning on September 18, only the new version will be acceptable.

Q: I make all my SUI (state unemployment insurance tax) deposits on time but I got a notice after the first quarter of this year that I still owe SUI tax plus a late payment penalty – how could that happen?
A: It's common for states to send out notices to employers in the fall with their SUI tax rate for the coming year. If your rate goes up and you don't remember to change your rate at the beginning of the new year (or forget to send it to your payroll provider) you could end up owing additional tax because you calculated the current year's SUI tax using the previous year's rate.

The Future of Payroll

Q: What are some of the current trends in payroll?
A: Here are a few examples:
- An increase in cloud-based services with more firms offering downloadable applications that smaller firms with a lower budget can use to automate their payroll processing.
- Same day ACH payments which allow employers more leeway for last minute payroll changes and still get their employees paid on time.
- The use of mobile payments – payroll "checks" sent directly to the employee through a mobile app.
- An increased use of apps that allow employees to check their compensation history, ask questions about deductions and benefits, make changes to their W-4, and schedule leave time.
- The possibility of using AI (Artificial Intelligence) to catch potential problems such as an employee who is missing a worker's compensation code or an employee with an hourly rate that's too high for the department he or she is assigned to.
- Increased integration between payroll, human resources management, financial accounting and other systems.
- Increased cyber security – payroll data (particularly data stored in the cloud) should be protected by security software and advanced encryption techniques.
- The use of comprehensive payroll software that interacts with some human resource functions such as applicant tracking, employee training programs, and employee productivity tracking.

Q: What has been the single biggest change in recent years?
A: The biggest change has been the move from in-house payroll processing (either manually or with the use of desktop software) to online payroll processing, with vendors offering a complete range of services from direct deposit to workers' compensation coverage. In recent years online payroll services have progressed from running your payroll and producing the required reports to effectively becoming your payroll department – even paying your taxes and filing the tax reports for you automatically.

Now online providers are moving into the human resources area as well, offering software to do everything from applicant tracking to employee productivity analysis. The emergence of AI powered payroll software has also helped speed up this latest trend of a third party in effect becoming your HR department.

As the move to online payroll services has accelerated, the cost of signing up with one of these providers has decreased, making that option available even to very small companies. With some experts predicting that payroll departments will continue to shrink as their function is taken over by third party online vendors, the question may be how much control will employers retain over their payroll processing in the future – and will there even be a need for books like this one?

Payroll Quiz

1) What is the current federal minimum wage?
   A) $5.15 per hour
   B) $5.75 per hour
   C) $8.50 per hour
   D) $7.25 per hour
2) The tax paid by the employer that amounts to 0.6% of each employee's first $7,000 of annual wages is called ____ tax.
3) An employee is paid $12.50 per hour (time and a half for overtime) and during the past week the employee worked 52 hours. What are the employee's gross wages for the week?
4) Cafeteria plan contributions are generally federal income taxable (True/False)
5) According to IRS statutes, to qualify as part-time an employee should work no more than __ hours per week.
   A) 20
   B) 29
   C) 30
   D) 32
6) The combination of Social Security tax and Medicare tax is referred to as ____ tax
7) For 2021 the Social Security tax rate for employees is ____
8) The 2021 wage limit for Social Security withholding is:
   A) $128,400
   B) $137,700
   C) $132,900
   D) $142,800
   E) $127,200
9) What is the total amount of **employer and employee** FICA tax liability in 2021 for an employee with FICA taxable wages of $205,000?
10) ABC Company has a employee named Adam who makes $820 a week. For last week ABC made the following payroll calculations for Adam: $825 gross pay, $63.11 for FICA withholding, $76.00 for Federal Income Tax withholding, $37.00 for state income tax withholding, and $40 due for federal and state unemployment taxes
    .A) If Adam has no other deductions what is his net pay for the week?
    B) What is ABC's total expense for Adam for the week?
11) 401(k) contributions are:
    A) FICA taxable but not federal or state taxable

B) FICA, federal and state taxable
C) Exempt from FICA, federal and state withholding
D) FICA and federal taxable, but not state taxable

12) The 940 Federal Unemployment Tax Return is submitted:
A) Quarterly
B) Yearly
C) Monthly

13) What determines whether a person is an independent contractor or an employee?

14) ABC Company is using a person from a temporary help agency to fill in for an employee on maternity leave – does that person become an employee of ABC Company?

15) If ABC Company has an employee who works in one state and lives in another does ABC have to take out withholding tax for the employee's state of residence?

16) ABC Company wants to give each employee a $500 bonus – what amount should each person be paid so that the net after deducting FICA tax equals $500?

17) ABC's most recent payroll had a check date of Friday, February 18 – Monday the 21st is a federal holiday – ABC (a semi-weekly depositor) should make the federal tax deposit by what date?

18) How can ABC Company get reimbursed for COBRA premium assistance payments?

19) In March ABC Company transferred Mary Sanders from state X to state Y. At the end of the year she had been paid $4,600 in state X and $31,200 in state Y. ABC has an SUI rate in state Y of 3.5% and state Y has an SUI wage limit of $7000, while state X has an SUI wage limit of $9500. How much does ABC Company owe in SUTA tax to state Y for Mary Sanders?

20) What is the maximum amount Ron Norvil (age 49) can contribute to ABC Company's 401(k) plan in 2021?

21) What form is used to apply to IRS for an employer identification number?

22) Use the following information for questions 22 -24: An employee worked the entire year in 2020 and earned two weeks of vacation as specified in the company's policies manual. The policy manual also states that the amount paid will be 80 hours times the employee's rate of pay as of December 31, 2020. At that time the employee's pay rate was $15 per hour. Which financial statements are affected in 2020? (Balance Sheet only, Income Statement only, Balance Sheet and Income Statement, Neither the Balance Sheet or Income Statement)?

23) The amount that will be reported on the 2020 income statement as Vacation Expense for the vacation earned in 2019 is _____?

24) When the employer pays the employee for the vacation earned in 2019, what account will be debited (Cash, Vacation Expense, or Vacation Payable)?
25) In January an employer remits the state unemployment tax that pertains to its employees' wages for the final quarter of 2019. On which income statement will the state unemployment tax appear under accrual accounting?
26) If an employee who is paid weekly makes $14 an hour and is also being paid $500 a month for housing, how much should he be paid for working 45 hours last week?
27) ABC Company wants to pay each shop employee a bonus of $500 - each person will have FICA taxes taken out but no federal, state, or local withholding tax. What should the gross amount of each bonus be if the employees are to get exactly $500?
28) Do W-4 forms have to be submitted to the IRS?
29) Do you need to file a form 940 quarterly?
30) Can IRS penalize an employer for failing to obtain an employee's Social Security number?
31) If an employee is paid weekly and has disposable earnings (earnings after taxes) of $285 per week, what portion of the disposable earnings can be garnished?
32) If an employee regularly takes 30 minute coffee breaks do I have to count that half hour as hours worked?
33) Do I have to pay extra to employees who are working a night shift?
34) You have a non-exempt employee (i.e., an employee subject to overtime rules) who is being paid a salary of $550 per week. If that person worked 48 hours last week how much should he be paid?
35) A restaurant includes a charge on the tip line of its bills equal to 10% of the total charges for food and beverages. Does the server need to include that charge in his or her record of tips received?
36) Janice Doe's taxable earnings for the current payroll amounts to $3,500 which will increase her year-to-date FICA taxable earnings to $201,500 - how much will her Social Security and Medicare taxes be for this payroll? How much will her employer have to pay in matching FICA tax for Janice?
37) Mindy made $18 in tips this month – are those tips taxable and does she need to report them to her employer?
38) What does the Fair Labor Standards Act say about an employee's paid time off?
39) If IRS advises you that an employee's W-4 if invalid you should:

A) Take no action.
B) Have the employee fill out a new W-4 and send it to the IRS.
C) Withhold taxes for the employee based on the information provided by the IRS.

40) Karen is paid $12 per hour. During the past week she worked 24 hours on day shift and 24 hours on night shift (which pays an additional $1.00 per hour). How much should Karen's gross pay be for the week?

41) How long should an employer keep records about an employee who took leave based on the Family and Medical Leave Act?

42) True or False – An employee who is paid a salary is automatically exempt from minimum wage and overtime rules.

43) Jonathan is a nonexempt employee and is paid $525 per week for a 35 hour workweek. If he works 50 hours during a given week, what should his gross pay be for the week?

44) You want to pay Marion a net bonus of $2000 (YTD gross earnings are $22,000). Using the federal income tax current flat rate of 22% for supplemental wages and assuming that the only other taxes are for Social Security and Medicare, what should be the gross amount of Marion's bonus check?

45) Are workers compensation payments taxable?

46) Tim works for two employers and, as a result of taxes being taken out by each employer, has overpaid on social security tax. Can he ask for a refund from either or both employers?

47) Janice's gross pay for the (semi-monthly) pay period is $1,835 and she has a cafeteria plan deduction of $60 and a 401(k) deduction of $40. Assuming there is no state tax, that Janice claims married and zero deductions on her W-4, and that her YTD gross is $25,750, what should her net pay be for the pay period?

48) If you provide severance pay as a separate check for a terminated employee how should you calculate the amount of federal income tax to be withheld?

49) How much will Tom's employer have *remitted* in FICA taxes for Tom if Tom ends up with $50,000 in FICA taxable earnings for 2019? What if Tom's FICA taxable earnings for the year are $205,000?

50) If a new employee is in the United States on an H1-B visa, what taxes need to be taken out of his or her pay?

51) What is the total cost of my payroll?

52) An employee only needs to change his or her W-4 if there's a change in filing status or exemptions – True or False?

53) What form is used to apply for a Social Security number?

54) To qualify as an "exempt" employee for overtime purposes a workers must be paid on a salary basis at not less than _____ per week.

55) Can a temporary employee hired through a "temp" agency participate in the company's pension plan?

56) Do "temp" workers count as "employees" of the business they're working for under the Affordable Care Act?

57) Which federal taxes are an employee's final wages subject to after his or her death?

58) A salaried-exempt employee is unable to work for two days during the work week because the office is closed due to a water leak. The employee's weekly guaranteed salary is $800. Under FLSA rules what amount must the employee be paid for the work week?
   A) $600
   B) $750
   C) $800
   D) $400

60) Which of the following individuals would most likely be classified as an independent contractor: a salesman working from home, a repairman called in on a regular schedule to service the company's PCs, or a person who normally works in the shipping department but comes in after hours to clean the offices.

61) Can a Cafeteria (Section 125) plan offer a deferred pay benefit?

62) Which of the following has to be determined before overtime calculations can be done for an employee:
   a) the employee's marital status
   b) the company's workweek
   c) the employee's pay frequency

63) What is "imputed income" and is it taxable?

64) Can an employee select both a pre-tax and a post-tax item from the company's list of Section 125 cafeteria plan options?

65) Which worker would be considered a statutory employee: a) real estate agent, b) full-time life insurance salesperson, c) accountant

Payroll Quiz Answers

1) D - $7.25 per hour
2) Federal Unemployment Tax
3) $725 (40 hours at $12.50/hour + 12 hours of overtime at time and a half or $18.75/hour)
4) False (in general) – Cafeteria plan insurance is exempt from both FICA and federal income tax (and in most cases, state income tax) unless the employee chooses to have the deduction treated as post-tax (after taxes have been taken).
5) B – Employees who work 30 or more hours a week are generally considered to be full time.
6) FICA (Federal Insurance Contributions Act) tax
7) 6.2 %
8) D - $142,800
9) $23,724,70 (142,800 x .062 + 200,000 x .0145 + 5,000 x .0235 for the employee + 142,800 x .062 + 205,000 x .0145 for the employer share)
10) A - Adam's net pay = $648.89 ($825.00 – $63.11 – $76.00 – $37.00). FUI and SUI taxes are paid entirely by the employer (except in Alaska, New Jersey and Pennsylvania, which assess unemployment taxes on employees).
    B) $928.11 ($825 gross pay + $825 x .0765 for the employer's FICA match + $40 for unemployment taxes paid by the employer)
11) A – FICA taxable but not federal or state taxable
12) B – the 940 form is submitted annually (and is due by the end of January of the next year).
13) If the employer has the right to control not only what work will be done but how and when, then the worker is effectively an employee rather than an independent contractor.
14) No, the person is still employed by the temporary help agency.
15) ABC Company isn't required to do so, but if the state where the person works and the state where he or she resides have a "reciprocity" agreement, ABC can elect to deduct state tax for the state of residence.
16) Assuming no employee has more than the Social Security taxable wage limit in FICA taxable earnings for the year, each person should be paid $541.42 ($500 = Gross – Gross x .0765 or Gross = $500 / .9235).
17) ABC should make the tax deposit by Thursday the 24th (the third working day following the check date)

18) COBRA premium assistance payments can't be claimed as a tax credit on the 941 quarterly tax return; the employer must fill out and file a Form 941-X (941 correction form) in order to claim a deduction for COBRA payments.

19) $84.00 ($7,000 - $4,600 = $2400; $2400 x .035 = $84.00). Note: Louisiana, Minnesota and Montana don't allow carry-over of SUI wages – if Mary had been transferred to one of those states ABC Company would owe $245 ($7000 x .035).

20) $19,500 unless Ron turns 50 during 2021 – in that case he could contribute up to $26,000.

21) Form SS-4 (Application for Employer Identification Number)

22) Both the Income Statement and the Balance Sheet – an entry will be made to Vacation Expense on the 2019 income statement and an offsetting entry will be made to Vacation Payable on the 2019 balance sheet.

23) Zero – the cost of the vacation pay will be an expense on the 2019 income statement.

24) Vacation Payable will be debited.

25) Under accrual accounting the state unemployment tax expense will appear on the 2019 income statement.

26) The value of the housing allowance has to be added to the employee's wages for the workweek in order to calculate a regular rate of pay. To do that, multiply $500 by 12 and divide by 52 to get the weekly value of the housing - that total is $115.38. Add the weekly value of the housing to the employee's straight time wages of 45 hours x $14 per hour: $115.38 + $630.00 = $745.38. Divide $745.38 by the number of hours worked last week to get an effective rate of pay: $745.38 / 45 = $16.56. Assuming an overtime factor of 1.5, the employee's overtime pay would be 5 hours (the excess over 40 hours) x $16.56 x 1.5 which equals $124.20. Then the employee's total pay would be the effective rate of pay times 40 hours plus the overtime pay or $16.56 x 40 = $662.40 plus $124.20, which equals $786.60.

27) To "gross up" the amount of each pay check to cover FICA taxes you divide the amount of the bonus by 100% minus the FICA percentage. Assuming all the shop employees are under the Social Security wage limit, you would divide $500 by 1.0000 minus .0765 (which equals .9235), giving a gross amount of $541.42.

28) No. W-4 forms should be kept in the employee's file in case there is a question about their withholding tax.

29) No. Form 940 is an annual form, filed by the end of January for the preceding year. However, if your FUTA tax is $500 or more for the year you need to make quarterly FUTA payments.

30) There is no direct penalty, but the employer can be penalized for submitting incorrect or incomplete information returns such as W-2s.
31) $67.50 can be garnished (the amount by which disposable earnings exceeds the federal minimum wage of $7.25 per hour times 30 or $217.50). If the amount of disposable earnings was $290 or more then the garnishment couldn't exceed 25% times the disposable earnings, since that amount would be less than the difference between disposable earnings and $217.50.
32) Under FLSA rules, if the employer has expressly communicated to employees that work breaks may only last for up to 20 minutes, then you only need to count 20 or those 30 minutes as hours worked.
33) No, you don't have to pay extra for working a night shift – that's strictly a matter of agreement between employer and employees.
34) To calculate the employee's overtime pay divide the weekly salary by the number of hours the individual is expected to work in one week. Then multiply the resulting hourly rate by 1.5 and multiply that figure by the number of overtime hours worked: $550 / 40 hours = $13.75 per hour x 1.5 x 8 hours = $165.00 The total gross pay would be $550 + $165 = $715.00.
35) No, since the customer didn't have the right to determine the amount on the "tip line", the 10% charge is considered wages not tips.
36) Janice's Social Security tax will be zero since her FICA taxable wages were already over the $137,700 wage limit for 2020. Since the Medicare tax rate increases from 1.45% to 2.35% when an individual's taxable earnings reach $200,000, Janice's Medicare tax will be $3500 x .0145 + $1500 (the amount of FICA taxable wages over $200,000) x .009 which equals $50.75 + $13.50 or $64.25. Her employer's matching FICA tax for Janice will be $50.75 ($3500 x .0145) – since the additional Medicare tax applies to the employee only.
37) No. You must make at least $20 a month in tips for the tips to be taxable – tips of less than $20 in a month don't need to be reported to the employer.
38) The FLSA (Fair Labor Standards Act) covers overtime pay, minimum wage, and minimum age of workers but it doesn't cover paid time off.
39) C – withhold taxes based on the information provided by the IRS.
40) Karen's gross pay for the week is $650. Her straight time earnings are: 24 hours x $12/hour for the day shifts plus 24 hours x $13/hour for the night shifts or $600. To calculate her overall earnings you have to determine her "regular rate of pay"

which equals her straight time earnings divided by the total hours worked or $600 / 48 hours, which equals $12.50 per hour. Then her total gross pay is 40 hours x $12.50 plus 8 hours x $18.75 ($12.50 at time and a half), or $650.00.

41) Records concerning instances of an employee taking leave time under the Family and Medical Leave Act should be kept for at least 3 years.

42) False. Just because an employee is paid a salary doesn't automatically exempt him or her from minimum wage and overtime rules. The employee also has to meet specific job duty tests (and make at least $23,600 per year) in order to be considered "exempt".

43) Jonathan's gross pay is based on his "regular hourly rate" which is $525 divided by 35 hours or $15.00 per hour. For a 50 hour workweek Jonathan would be paid for 40 hours at $15.00 per hour and for 10 overtime hours at $22.50 (1 ½ times $15.00), or a total gross pay of $825.00.

44) The total tax percentage on Marion's bonus is 22.0 + 6.2 + 1.45 or .2965 (the supplemental federal withholding percentage plus the social security percentage plus the Medicare percentage). Then Marion's gross pay minus .2965 x her gross pay has to equal $2,000 – so her gross pay amount is $2,000 divided by (1 - .2965) which equals $2,842.93.

45) Except in certain special cases workers compensation payments to an employee are not considered taxable by the IRS.

46) No. Tim can get his overpayment refunded by claiming the overpayment as a credit on his year-end tax return.

47) Janice's net pay for the pay period is $1,429.56. Her Social Security and Medicare tax is $135.79 ($1,835 minus the $60 pre-tax cafeteria deduction times .0765). Her federal withholding tax is $165.69 (calculated from the federal tax tables as semi-monthly withholding for married individuals with zero deductions, based on gross taxable pay of $1,835 minus the pre-tax $60 cafeteria deduction and minus the pre-tax $40 401(k) deduction). Janice's net pay then is equal to $1,835 - $60 - $40 - $135.79 - $165.69 or $1,429.56.

48) The IRS considers severance pay provided in a separate check to be supplemental income and the federal withholding tax for that payment should be calculated as 22% of the gross taxable wages.

49) $7,650. Tom's employer has to remit Tom's Social Security and Medicare tax ($50,000 times .0765 = $3,825) plus the employer's matching share of $3,825. If Tom's FICA year-to-date taxable earnings total $205,000, his employer has to remit the employer

share ($137,700 in Social Security earnings times .062 + $205,000 times .0145 = $11,509.90). Tom however will have to pay $11,509.90 plus $5,000 times .009 for the Additional Medicare Tax on FICA wages over $200,000.

50) H-visa holders are not exempt from FICA or federal withholding taxes so the normal Social Security, Medicare and federal withholding tax should be taken out of the employee's pay.

51) The total cost of payroll to an employer is the sum of the gross pay (which covers net pay, voluntary deductions, company contributions and employee Social Security, Medicare, federal, state and any local withholding) plus the employer's matching share of Social Security and Medicare withholding plus federal and state unemployment taxes. Note: depending on the state where the employer does business, there may also be additional taxes such as disability or employee state unemployment withholding.

52) False. If an employee claims exemption from federal withholding on the W-4, that exemption expires at the end of January each year. If a new W-4 isn't submitted by the employee by February 15th IRS regulations require the employer to change the person's tax status to "single" with no adjustments until a new W-4 form is received.

53) Form SS-1.

54) To be classified as exempt an employee must be paid a salary of not less than $684 per week (Note: that threshold became $684 per week on January 1, 2020).

55) Even employees classified as temporary can participate in an employer's pension plan after completing 1,000 hours of service within a 12-month period.

56) Workers hired through a temporary staffing agency for short-term assignments are presumed to be employees of the staffing agency. However, temporary workers who have more than a short-term assignment with an employer are generally considered employees of that business, not the staffing agency, and must be included in the monthly employee counts and offered appropriate healthcare coverage.

57) Social Security, Medicare and FUTA (Federal Unemployment Tax), but not Federal Income Tax.

58) $800. Under FLSA rules an exempt employee must be paid his regular salary for a given work week regardless of how much he worked during the week- unless he misses the entire work week or voluntarily takes one or more days off.

59) The repairman.

60) In general, no. The only exception is a 401(k) plan.

61) The company's workweek. Under FLSA rules, a workweek is defined as seven consecutive 24-hour periods. The only other requirement is that the day of the week that the workweek starts stays the same and that the workweek is a fixed and regularly-occurring period of 168 hours. Once the workweek that applies to overtime calculations is defined, then the hours worked by the employee can be determined.

62) Imputed income is the value of cash or non-cash employee compensation. Examples of imputed income include: dependent care assistance or adoption assistance that exceeds the tax-free amount, group term taxable life insurance coverage over $50,000, personal use of an employer-provided vehicle, and non-deductible moving expense reimbursements. For payroll purposes imputed income is subject to FICA withholding but not federal income tax withholding (although an employee can elect to have federal income tax withheld) and must be reported as income in the appropriate boxes on the employee's W-2.

63) Yes, an employee can normally select both pre-tax and post-tax items from the company's Section 125 cafeteria plan options.

64) A full-time life insurance salesperson.

Appendix A – Useful Links

http://www.irs.gov (the Internal Revenue Service website - you can find forms, publications and additional payroll information here.

http://www.ssa.gov (the Social Security Administration web site)

http://www.payroll-taxes.com (payroll tax information, check calculators, a tax calendar and a discussion board)

http://www.payrolladviser.com (payroll blog)

http://www.payrolltalk.symmetry.com (payroll forum)

https://www.bna.com/payroll-blog/ (payroll blog)

https://www.patriotsoftware.com/payroll/training/blog/ (payroll blog)

http://www.irs.gov/pub/irs-pdf/f941.pdf (fillable Form 941 – Employer's Quarterly Federal Tax Return)

http://www.irs.gov/pub/irs-pdf/f941x.pdf (fillable Form 941-X Adjusted Employer's Quarterly Federal Tax Return or Claim for Refund)

http://www.irs.gov/pub/irs-pdf/f943.pdf (fillable Form 943 - Employer's Annual Federal Tax Return for Agricultural Employees)

http://www.irs.gov/pub/irs-pdf/f944.pdf (fillable Form 944 - Employer's Annual Federal Tax Return)

http://www.irs.gov/pub/irs-pdf/f940.pdf (fillable Form 940 – Employer's Annual Federal Unemployment Tax Return)

Appendix B – Glossary of Terms

125 Plan: Also known as a "Cafeteria Plan" or "Flex Plan" (see "Cafeteria Plan").

401(k) Plan: An employer sponsored retirement plan which allows employees to contribute part of their wages to the plan each pay period. Employee contributions (and employer matching amounts, if any) are not subject to federal income tax (and most state income taxes) until the money is withdrawn by the employee.

403(b) Plan: A tax advantaged savings plan covering self-employed ministers or employees of a public educational institution, a cooperative hospital service organization, or certain non-profit employers (Internal Revenue Code 501(c)(3) organizations). Tax treatment is similar to a 401(k) plan.

457 Plan: A retirement plan in the form of an annuity or mutual fund for employees of state and local governments and for tax exempt organizations.

1099: IRS forms used to report various types of income other than wages, salaries and tips on an annual basis (similar to W-2 forms). 1099 forms are normally used in connection with payroll to record payments made to independent contractors.

ABA number (routing number): A nine-digit number created by the American Bankers Association that identifies a specific bank or other financial institution within the United States. An ABA number is used for wires and electronic automatic clearing house (ACH) transactions such as direct deposit files and tax payments.

Abate: A term that means to decrease or diminish. Normally used in payroll in reply to a notification of penalty from IRS or some other agency, asking for a cancellation or reduction of the penalty.

Accelerated Deposit Rule: Also known as the "one-day" rule, it requires employers who accumulate a tax liability of $100,000 or more during a pay period to deposit the withheld taxes on the next banking day after the pay date.

AccuWage: A software program available from the Social Security Administration that can be used to test your electronic W-2 file for correct formatting before submitting the file to the SSA.

ACH: Automated Clearing House. A Federal Reserve Bank acting on behalf of an association of financial institutions. The Federal Reserve Bank serves as a clearinghouse for direct deposit or other electronic payment transactions, receiving and transmitting entries. Funds moving from Bank A to Bank B muse go through the Automated Clearing House.

Actual Contribution Percentage (ACP) test: One of two tests that companies sponsoring a 401(k) plan have to conduct annually to ensure that their 401(k) plans don't unfairly benefit highly-paid employees at the expense of other employees. Employers have to carry out the ACP test in order to retain the qualified status of their plans under IRS rules and to meet the requirements of the Employee Retirement Income Security Act (ERISA). If the plan fails the ACP test, the employer must take corrective action within the 12-months following the end of the plan year in which the oversight occurred.

Actual Deferral Percentage (ADP) test: One of two tests that companies sponsoring a 401(k) plan have to conduct annually to ensure that their 401(k) plans don't unfairly benefit highly-paid employees at the expense of other employees. Employers have to carry out the ADP test in order to retain the qualified status of their plans under IRS rules and to meet the requirements of the Employee Retirement Income Security Act (ERISA). If the plan fails the ADP test, the employer must take corrective action within the 12-months following the end of the plan year in which the oversight occurred.

Advanced Earned Income Credit (AEIC): Starting January 1, 2011 advance EIC payments will no longer be made to employees through payroll – employees who are eligible for the Earned Income Credit can still claim the credit when they file their year-end income tax return.

After-tax deduction: A deduction from an employee's pay that does not reduce the employee's taxable wages (as opposed to pre-tax deductions such as Cafeteria plans and employee 401(k) contributions).

Alien: An individual living in or visiting the United States who is not a U.S. citizen.

Americans with Disability Act (ADA): The ADA prohibits employers and employment agencies from discriminating against qualified job applicants and employees with a physical or mental impairment who can, with or without reasonable accommodation, perform the essential functions of the job they would be or are doing.

Annuity: A contract with an insurance company that pays you income in the future in return for a payment upfront or multiple payments over a period of time. Annuities are often used to provide retirement income; you buy an annuity by making either a single payment or a series of payments and your payout comes either as a lump-sum payment or as a series of payments at regular intervals.

Automated Clearing House (ACH): A Federal Reserve Bank or other financial institution acting as a clearing house for direct deposit transactions.

Backup Withholding: Federal income tax withholding on non-employee compensation required when the payee either fails to furnish the payer with a TIN (Tax Identification Number) or when the IRS notifies the payer that the payee's TIN is incorrect.

Base Annual Salary: An employee's minimum gross annual compensation excluding additional earnings such as overtime pay, bonuses, tips, commissions, use of a company car, health insurance or other benefits.

Base Period: When dealing with unemployment compensation the "base period" usually consists of the first four quarters out of the last five completed before the claimant's benefit year.

Biweekly: Once every two weeks.

BSO: Business Services Online – an internet wage reporting service for employers provided by the Social Security Administration.

Cafeteria Plan: A plan that offers flexible benefits under IRC (Internal Revenue Code) Section 125. Each employee covered by the plan can choose from various benefits which are generally paid for with pretax deductions from the employee's wages.

Carve-Out: A program separate from the primary group health plan, designed to provide a specialized type of care, such as a mental health carve-out.

Catch-Up Contributions: Elective deferrals made to a 401(k), 403(b), 457, or SIMPLE plan that exceed the usual contribution limit. Plan participants who are over or will be 50 years old in the current calendar year are eligible to make "catch-up" contributions up to a certain limit. For example, participants in a company's 401(k) plan can normally contribute up to $19,500 for 2021, but members who are or will be 50 in 2021 can contribute an additional $6,500.

CDAs: Consumer Driven Accounts. Benefit plans such as Flexible Savings Accounts, Health Reimbursement Arrangements, and Health Savings Accounts, that allow employees to pay for certain medical expenses with pre-tax dollars.

Circular A: IRS Publication 51, Agricultural Employer's Tax Guide. Publication 51 covers the regulations and instructions for withholding, depositing and reporting federal employment taxes for farm workers.

Circular E: IRS Publication 15, Employer's Tax Guide. Publication 15 covers the regulations and instructions for withholding, depositing and reporting federal employment taxes.

COBRA: The Consolidated Omnibus Budget Reconciliation Act of 1985. Under COBRA terminated employees have the option to continue their health insurance coverage with their former employer for a certain period of time following their termination. COBRA applies to any organization with 20 or more employees.

COD: Court Ordered Deduction. Any legal notice ordering an employer to deduct money from an employee's wages and pay that money directly to the court or to another agency (child support, garnishments, etc.).

CODA (Cash Or Deferred Arrangement): A retirement plan that allows employees to either have the employer contribute a certain amount to the plan or to receive that same amount in cash.

Combined Filing: A filing which includes tax liability and payments for more than on tax type. California for example requires combined deposits and filings for State Income Tax, State Unemployment Insurance, and State Disability Insurance.

Common Law Employee: A worker who is considered an employee because the employer has the right to direct how, where, and when the person's work will be performed, in addition to determining what work is to be done.

Common Pay Agent: Employers with multiple Federal Employer Identification Numbers (FEINs) who are allowed (under IRS rules) to consolidate their tax returns and tax payments under a single FEIN.

Common Paymaster: A situation where an employee works for two or more related companies at the same time and the related companies are treated as a single employer for employment tax purposes.

Compensatory Time: Paid time off given to an employee for working extra hours.

Constructive Receipt: "Constructive Receipt" of wages occurs when an employee's pay is available to him or her, free of any substantial limitation or restriction. **Note:** If a payroll has a pay date of say, 9-30 or 12-31 but one or more employees don't receive their check or direct deposit until after that date, then those employees' wages actually apply to the next quarter or the next year under the concept of constructive receipt.

Covered Wages: In general wages include all payments made to employees for services rendered, including salaries, bonuses, commissions, vacation allowances and many fringe benefits, regardless of what form the payment is made, when it's made or on what basis of production it's based. Wages also include the cash value of other forms of remuneration such as the reasonable value of food or lodging. Necessary business expenses reimbursed or advanced to employees such as per diem or traveling expenses are usually not considered taxable wages.

Credit reduction: Employers are not entitled to full credit for unemployment contributions made to states that have outstanding loans with the Federal Unemployment Trust Fund. Those states are referred to as "credit reduction states" and the credit percentages employers can claim for contributions made to those states are published annually in Part 1, line 6 of Form 940.

DBA: Doing Business As (the name under which an individual or business operates).

Deductions: An amount subtracted from an employee's gross pay. Deductions, other than taxes, can be taken before taxes are calculated (pre-tax deductions) or after taxes are calculated, depending on the type of deduction. Pre-tax deductions include items such as Section 125 cafeteria plan contributions.

Deferred Annuity: A contract with an insurance company that pays you income at regular intervals (or a lump sum) starting at a future date (e.g. after a certain number of years or at a specific age). Money in the annuity is tax-free until you withdraw it. A deferred annuity is any annuity that doesn't begin making payments to you within the first year after you purchase it; if you begin taking payments within the first year you have an "immediate annuity."

Deferred Compensation: Benefit plans under which employees may contribute a percentage of their wages to a tax deferred savings plan (usually a 401(k) plan). Employee contributions are exempt from federal income tax and, in some states, from state income tax but are not exempt from FICA (Social Security and Medicare) withholding. Employer contributions (if any) are tax-free. Contributions and earnings accumulate until distributed to the employee, at which point the employee must pay federal income tax (and state income tax if applicable) on his or her distribution.

Defined Benefit Pension Plan: A workplace pension plan that pays you a set benefit amount when you retire. Benefits are based on a formula that takes into account things like your salary, how long you were a member of the plan and how much you and your employer contributed to the pension plan.

Defined Contribution Pension Plan: A workplace pension plan where the amount you receive when you retire is based on the amount you and your employer have contributed, plus any investment earnings.

De Minimus Fringe Benefit: Any employer provided property or service having such a small value that accounting for it would be impractical and unreasonable, may be excluded from income as a "de minimus" fringe benefit.

DCAP: Dependent Care Assistance Program.

Direct Deposit: Electronic transfer of an employee's net pay directly into his or her bank account in place of printing a check.

Director's Fees: Fees paid to the director of a corporation. They are not subject to Federal income tax withholding, FICA tax or FUTA tax.

Director's fees are treated as self-employment income and a 1099 is issued to the director at the end of the year.

Disposable Income: The portion of an employee's earnings which is left after subtracting the deductions required by law (primarily taxes and mandatory dues).

Earned Income Credit (EIC): A tax credit available to low income employees which can be taken by the employee on his or her individual tax return. Advance EIC payments will no longer be made through payroll after December 31, 2010.

EBSA: The Employee Benefits Security Administration (EBSA) promotes and protects the pension, health, and other benefits of participants in private sector benefit plans. The main purpose of the EBSA is to help employees understand their rights and work benefits.

EEO-1 Report: A report filed annually with the federal government by employers with federal government contracts of $50,000 or more and 50 or more employees, or employers without government contracts but with 100 or more employees. The EEO-1 includes company data about the number of women and minority employees in specified occupational categories and subcategories. The EEOC (Equal Employment Opportunity Commission) uses the report to support enforcement of Title VII of the Civil Rights Act, which prohibits discrimination on the basis of race, color, religion or national origin.

EFT: Electronic Funds Transfer.

EFTPS: Electronic Federal Tax Payment System. An electronic system for reporting and paying federal taxes (go to www.eftps.gov for further information on enrolling and paying taxes using the EFTPS.

EIN: Employer Identification Number -- usually refers to an employer's Federal Identification Number (FEIN).

Elective deferral: A contribution to a deferred income plan such as a 401(k) plan.

Eligibility Period: The length of time you have to be a member of a group before qualifying for coverage under the group plan. For example, an organization whose health and dental plan has a 90-day eligibility period would require 90 days of qualified employment before coverage could begin.

Employee Leasing Company: A company that leases employees to another business on a contract basis. The leasing company handles all personnel matters and is generally considered the employer of the leased employees.

Employee Payroll Advance – Many employers will advance a certain amount of money to employee interest-free when the employee needs money quickly. The employer generally deducts a percentage from the employee's following paychecks until the advance is repaid.

Employee Plans Compliance Resolution System (EPCRS) - Allows employers to correct most problems involving qualified plans, 403(b) plans, SEPs, and SIMPLE plans. Mistakes that are often corrected using the EPCRS system include:
- Failure to allow eligible employees to contribute;
- Including ineligible employees;
- Nondiscrimination testing errors;
- Excessive or improper distributions; and
- Miscalculation of contributions.

Employee self-service – Allowing employees to change certain information about themselves (such as home address, marital status, or number of withholding allowances) using an online portal. Note: the same type of system can be used to let managers make changes to employee information for people in their department.

Employer's Supplemental Tax Guide: IRS Publication 15-A, which provides more detailed information than the Circular E (IRS Pub 15) regarding topics such as employee status determination, types of employee compensation, sick pay reporting, and rules for paying employment taxes.

ERISA: Employee Retirement Income Security Act of 1974 – sets protection standards for people in most private-sector retirement plans.

Escheat: The legal process involved in turning over unclaimed client checks (such as refund checks) to the state government.

ESOP: Employee stock ownership plans (ESOPs) are a type of deferred compensation plan in which the investments are primarily in employee stock.

ESPP (Employee Stock Purchase Plan): A type of employee benefit that allows participating employees to purchase company stock at a reduced price.

ETT: Employment Training Tax – a tax imposed on employers operating in California to provide funds to train employees in targeted industries in order to improve the competitiveness of California businesses.

EVS (Employment Verification Service): A free service provided by the Social Security Administration to verify the Social Security numbers of current or prospective employees. (www.ssa.gov/employer/ssnv.htm)

Excludable deductions: Deductions that are subtracted from an employee's gross earnings before a lien deduction is calculated.

Excludable earnings: Earnings that are subtracted from an employee's gross earnings before a lien deduction is calculated.

Exempt Employees: Employees who are exempt from the overtime provisions of the Fair Labor Standards Act (FLSA) because of their level of decision-making authority. In general, managers, supervisors, administrators and other in leadership roles can be classified as exempt employees.

Expatriates: U.S. citizens working in a foreign country. In general money earned by a U.S. citizen or a resident alien working anywhere in the world is subject to U.S. taxes (see https://www.irs.gov/Individuals/International-Taxpayers/Persons-Employed-Abroad-by-a-U.S.-Person for further information).

Federal Employer Identification Number (FEIN): The identification number assigned to employers by the Internal Revenue Service.

Federal information Processing Standard (FIPS) Code: The code on a child support order that identifies the agency receiving the payment.

Federal Reserve Bank: An independent agency of the U.S. government that deals with monetary policy, the regulation of financial institutions and the regulation of domestic payment systems such as Fedwire and ACH.

Federal Unemployment Tax Act (FUTA): A federal law enacted in 1939 which sets guidelines for the administration of unemployment compensation programs. All liable employers pay a federal tax to fund State and Federal unemployment insurance programs.

FICA: Federal Insurance Contributions Act (covers the combined payroll taxes for Social Security and Medicare).

FIT: Federal Income Tax.

FSA: Flexible Spending Account – An account funded by an employee through pre-tax contributions that can be used to pay for health care expenses not covered or only partially covered by the employee's medical, dental and vision insurance. Employers may make contributions to FSA's but aren't required to do so. Money contributed to a health care FSA must be spent within the current insurance plan year or forfeited.

FLSA: Fair Labor Standards Act (establishes minimum wage, overtime pay, record keeping and child labor standards for almost all full and part-time workers in the United States.

FMLA: Family and Medical Leave Act. The FMLA guarantees 12 weeks unpaid leave to most employees to care for newborn or newly adopted children or to deal with a serious injury or illness to the employee or member of his or her family.

Form W-2: Employee Wage and Tax Statement.

Fringe Benefit: Cash, services or property that an employer provides to employees in addition to their regular wages. Amounts paid by the recipient for the fringe benefit are not taxable – however the value of the fringe benefits are taxable unless specifically excluded by IRS regulations. The fair market value of a non-cash fringe benefit (less any amount paid for the benefit by the recipient) is considered wages and should be included in the employee's pay and taxed accordingly.

FUTA: Federal Unemployment Tax Act.

FUTA Tax: Federal Unemployment Tax

Garnishment: A legal process that authorizes an employer to pay part of an employee's wages to a creditor to satisfy a debt owed by the employee.

Group-Term Life Insurance: Term life insurance provided to employees, paid for by the employer, the employee, or both.

HCE (Highly Compensated Employee): An employee who receives compensation in the top 20% of all employees, is at least a 5 percent owner in the business and exceeds certain annual compensation levels as defined by the IRS.

HI: Retirees' health insurance. A federal government benefit program funded by Medicare taxes.

Health reimbursement arrangements (HRA): An HRA serves the same purpose as a Health Savings Account (see "HSA" below), but it's owned and funded by the employer. Any unused funds are returned to the employer when the employee leaves.

High Deductible Health Plan (HDHP): A health care plan with a high-deductible is designed to provide lower premiums, but requires more money up front before the insurance kicks in. The IRS sets the minimum deductible for an HDHP (the minimum is $1,400 for individuals and $2,800 for families for 2020). An HDHP works best for younger, healthy people who primarily need coverage in case of a serious medical emergency. HDHP coverage also comes with an annual catastrophic limit on out-of-pocket expenses for covered services from in-network providers. For 2020, the limit is $6,900 for an individual and $13,800 for a family.

Highly Compensated Employee (HCE): An employee who either, on any day during the current or preceding year, is or was a more than 5% owner or who received compensation in excess of the specified dollar limit for the preceding year ($130,000 for 2020).

HRIS: Human Resources Information System.

HRMS: Human Resources Management System.

HSA: Health Savings Accounts are tax-favored IRA-type trust accounts that eligible individuals - those covered by certain types of high-deductible health plans (HDHPs) - can use to pay for certain medical expenses incurred by themselves or their families. Money in the account not spent during the year stays in the account and generates tax-free interest. HSAs can be funded on a pre-tax basis through a cafeteria plan and in that case all employer contributions to the employee's account (by means of employee salary reduction) should be reported in Box 12 of the W-2 using code "W".

Imputed Income: The value of cash or non-cash employee compensation. Examples of imputed income include: dependent care assistance or adoption assistance that exceeds the tax-free amount, group term taxable life insurance coverage over $50,000, personal use of an employer-provided vehicle, and non-deductible moving expense reimbursements. Imputed income is subject to FICA withholding but not federal income tax withholding and must be reported on the employee's W-2.

Individual Retirement Account (IRA): A personal account set up at a financial institution that allows the owner to make contributions that are either tax-deferred (a traditional IRA) or are taxed up front and are tax-free when funds are withdrawn (Roth IRA).

IRC: Internal Revenue Code.

IRCA: Immigration Reform and Control Act of 1986. Prohibits employers from hiring individuals who are not authorized to work in the United States.

Independent Contractor: A non-employee contracted by a business to perform work of some type. The business species what work is to be performed but the contractor determines when, how and who will actually do the work.

IRS: Internal Revenue Service.

ISO (Incentive Stock Option): A statutory stock option that allows an employee to purchase company stock below current market price.

Key Employee – For 2018 a Key Employee as defined by the IRS, is an officer whose annual earnings are over $175,000, a 1% owner of the business with an annual earnings over $150,000, or a 5% owner in the business. Note: the terms "key employee" and "highly compensated employee" are used in annual nondiscrimination testing of retirement plans.

Leased Employees: Employers can lease highly skilled employees as a cost-saving measure. The leasing company hires and trains the workers and the employer pays a fee to the leasing company in return. Leased employees are usually employed on a long term basis.

Medicare: Federal hospitalization plan for U.S. citizens 65 or older, funded through Medicare tax withheld for employees' pay combined with matching amounts from employers. There is no annual wage limit for Medicare withholding.

Minimum Wage: The lowest hourly amount an employer can pay an employee under federal or state law.

MMREF (Magnetic Media Reporting and Electronic Filing) Specifications: A set of Social Security Administration specifications for filing W-2 and W-2C forms electronically.

NACHA: National Automated Clearinghouse Association.

New Hire Reporting: Required reporting of new or rehired employees to the appropriate state agency to help in collecting child care payments and in detecting abuse of the state's unemployment compensation or other assistance programs for the unemployed.

Non-cash fringe benefits: Benefits provided to employees in some form other than cash (e.g., health or life insurance) – benefits of this type may or may not be taxable.

Non-exempt Employee: Employees (hourly or salaried) who are covered by the minimum wage and overtime pay provisions of the Fair Labor Standards Act (FLSA).

OASDI: Old-age Survivor and Disability Insurance. A federal government benefit program funded by Social Security taxes.

ODFI: Originating Depository Financial Institution. A financial institution that is qualified to initiate direct deposit entries submitted by an employer.

Overtime: Hours worked in excess of the maximum set by federal or state law (generally anything over 40 hours in a given one week period).

Overtime Premium: An amount equal to one half of an employee's regular rate of pay times the number of overtime hours worked.

Partial Unemployment: Refers to a worker who is still an employee but, because of circumstances beyond his or her control, didn't work a full week and earned less than his or her normal weekly pay. Partial unemployment claims are usually filed by the employer.

Paycard: Debit cards funded by employers with the employees' net pay (can be used the same as a regular debit card).

Per diem: A daily expense payment, usually made for food or transportation.

Pieceworker: An employee who is paid per unit or number of pieces produced.

PIN: Personal Identification Number.

PIT: Personal Income Tax.

Plan Administrator: A person, group or entity specifically designated in a benefit plan document as responsible for managing the day-to-day activities of the plan.

Plan Sponsor: The entity that establishes a benefit plan. The terms employer and plan sponsor are often used interchangeably, but they aren't necessarily one and the same.

Pre-Note: A zero amount ACH transaction used to verify the accuracy of a person's bank account information before any actual transactions are processed for that person.

Pretax Deduction: A deduction from gross pay that reduces the employee's taxable wages (such as cafeteria plan or 401(k) plan deductions).

Qualified Employer: An employer who is eligible for a calculated tax rate due to having people actively employed during certain periods and having made all tax payments in a timely manner.

Qualified Nonelective Contribution (QNEC): If an employee who should have been eligible to participate in an employer's 401(k) plan wasn't given the opportunity to do do, a QNEC is one method to compensate the employee for that missed opportunity. The employer has to make a qualified nonelective contribution to the plan for the employee. The QNEC must be 100% vested and is subject to the same distribution restrictions as elective deferrals. The amount of the QNEC is equal to 50% of the employee's missed deferral which is calculated by multiplying the actual deferral percentage for the employee's group (HCE or NHCE) in the plan for the year of exclusion times the employee's compensation for that year.

Qualified Plan: A benefit plan that meets IRS requirements for tax-favored treatment (such as Cafeteria health plans or 401(k) retirement plans).

QRP: A Qualified Plan Participant in an employer-sponsored benefit plan.

Reporting Agent: Companies (not individuals) that perform payroll services (signing and filing certain tax returns and making federal tax deposits and other federal tax payments).

Resident Alien: In payroll terms, a resident alien is a person who passes either the "green card" or "substantial presence" test for determining resident status in the United States. Resident aliens are generally subject to federal income tax, Social Security and Medicare withholding taxes the same as any other employee.

Retroactive Pay: Wages paid for time worked in a previous workweek.

Sarbanes-Oxley Act: A federal law designed to provide protection for employees who report corporate and securities fraud by their employer.

SDI: State Disability Insurance.

Section 125: Section 125 is part of the IRS Code that allows employees to convert a taxable cash benefit (salary) into non-taxable benefits. Under a Section 125 program you may choose to pay for qualified benefit premiums before any taxes are deducted from your paycheck. Section 125 sets out rules and regulations regarding pre-tax deductions for some insurance premiums, un-reimbursed medical expenses and child/dependent care.

Self-Employment Contributions Act (SECA): Enacted in 1954, SECA authorizes the levying of Social Security and Medicare tax on the net earnings of most self-employed individuals. The basic tax rate for self-employed workers is 15.30 percent, twice that of regular employees due to the fact that employees pay one-half of FICA tax and employers pay the other half. If you are self-employed and your total annual income is $400 or more you have to file a Schedule SE and pay SECA tax on your net business income.

Severance Pay: A payment made to a terminated employee (usually an employee who has been terminated through no fault of his own).

Severance pay is normally intended to provide extra financial help for the ex-employee until he or she finds a new job and (unless specifically provided for in a contractual agreement) is at the discretion of the employer.

Shift Differential: Additional pay received by an employee for working shifts that are not as much in demand, such as evening or late night shifts.

Short term disability (STD): Short term disability pays a portion of an employee's salary if that employee becomes temporarily disabled due to illness or injury (except on-the-job injuries which are covered by workers compensation insurance). Typically STD policies provide payments for a period of 13 to 26 weeks.

SIMPLE 401(k): SIMPLE 401(k) plans combine the features of traditional 401(k)s with the simplicity of SIMPLE IRAs. Companies with 100 or fewer employees can establish SIMPLE 401(k) plans which work like traditional 401(k)s, but employee contributions are capped at a lower annual limit ($13,500 for 2020, with an additional "catch-up" limit of $3,000 for participants who are 50 or over or will be during 2020).

Simplified Employee Pension (SEP): An Individual Retirement Account (IRA) with special provisions, available to self-employed individuals or small businesses with less than 25 employees. Employers can contribute up to 25% of an employee's compensation (not to exceed $40,000 per year).

Social Security Administration (SSA): The federal agency in charge of administering Social Security.

Split Shift: A work shift divided into two periods of time with some time (usually several hours) in between.

SSA: Social Security Administration.

Standard Industrial Classification Code (SIC): When an employer applies for a federal employer identification number (FEIN) the government also assigns the employer a classification number that identifies the type of activity engaged in by the business.

State Disability Insurance (SDI): An insurance plan sponsored by a state to provide compensation for employees who are unable to work due to injury or illness.

State Unemployment Insurance (SUI): A state fund used to pay benefits to unemployed workers. Each state's SUI fund is accumulated from quarterly taxes paid by each employer operating within that state.

STD: Short Term Disability.

Stock bonus plan: Contributions are placed in a trust fund that invests in securities, including those of the participant's employer. This type of plan is financed by the employer or jointly by the employer and employee. When the employee retires or leaves the company, the proceeds from the trust fund are paid out in the form of company stock or cash.

SUB Plan: A SUB plan is tax exempt, Section 501 (c) (17) plan or trust established to provide severance pay to workers laid off due to a reduction in force or plant closing. SUB plan funds supplement state unemployment insurance benefits.

Supplemental Wages: Compensation received by an employee other than normal pay such as commissions or bonuses.

SUTA: State Unemployment Tax Authority.

Statutory Employees: Special groups of employees (such as full time insurance salespeople and certain homeworkers) whose wages are not subject to Federal Income Tax (FIT) withholding, but are subject to FICA (Social Security and Medicare) withholding and FUTA (Federal Unemployment Insurance) withholding.

Supplemental Executive Retirement Plan (SERP): A special non-qualified retirement plan for executives. Normally plans of this type aren't eligible for tax-favored treatment because they provide benefits over and above those provided by the company's qualified retirement plan.

Tax Levy: The attachment of a portion of an employee's wages (to the IRS or a state government) for payment of delinquent taxes.

Tax-Sheltered Annuity (TSA): TSAs are similar to 401(k) plans, but they have their own rules and are only available to certain types of employers. TSAs are governed by Section 403(b) of the Internal Revenue Code.

Third Party Sick Pay: Payments made to employees by a third party insurer because of non job-related injury or illness.

TIN: Taxpayer Identification Number.

Tip Credit: The "tip credit" provision in the Fair Labor Standards Act and many state wage laws allows employers to pay tipped employees as little as $2.13 per hour if their base pay plus tips brings their hourly rate of pay to at least minimum wage.

Totalization Agreements: Agreements with other countries entered into by the United States to avoid dual taxation. Also known as Binational Social Security Agreements, these arrangements generally mean that if an employee working in one of these countries is subject to their social security laws, then the employee and the employer are exempt from U.S. Social Security and Medicare tax.

Uniform Base Period: A base period that starts on the same calendar date for a new or transitional claim for all claimants.

USCIS: United States Citizenship and Immigration Services.

Vesting: An ERISA guideline that stipulates that employees are entitled to their benefits from a pension fund, profit-sharing plan, or employee stock ownership plan within a specified period of time, even if they no longer work for that employer.

W-2: Federal form that shows an employee's annual wages, taxes, and other information (such as fringe benefits) that affect the person's federal , state and local income tax returns.

W-3: Transmittal form to accompany paper W-2 forms when sending them to the Social Security Administration. The W-3 includes the total wage and tax withholdings for the W-2 forms being submitted.

W-4: Employee's Withholding Exemption Certificate. The W-4 is used to record the number of exemptions an employee claims (and any additional withholding amount desired).

Wage assignment: Committing a portion of an employee's future earnings to be used for scheduled payments such as union dues or a car loan.

Withholding: Subtracting amounts from an employee's wages for taxes or garnishments. These amounts are then paid to the government or other agency to whom they are owed.

Workers Compensation: A state administered insurance covering wokers' job related injuries or illnesses. Workers compensation insurance provides the employee with a percentage of his or her regular wages while unable to work.

Appendix C – Payroll Calendar for 2020

Note 1: If any date falls on a Saturday, Sunday or Federal holiday, use the next business day.

Note 2: Deposit dates for semiweekly depositors are not listed below – use the following rule to determine deposit dates: taxes on wages paid on Wednesday, Thursday or Friday must be deposited by the following Wednesday; taxes on wages paid on Saturday, Sunday, Monday or Tuesday must be deposited by the following Friday.

January 10th: Employees who received cash tips of at least $20 in the preceding month must report them to the employer on Form 4070, Employee's Report of Tips to Employer.

January 15th: Deposit payroll taxes for December (monthly depositors).

January 31st: W-2 forms distributed to employees and 1099-MISC forms to contractors. Also, the due date for filing W-2 forms either on paper or electronically (you must file electronically if you have 250 or more employees), and due date for filing 1099 forms if filed on paper or electronically. File Form 941 with the IRS for the 4th quarter of the previous year and annual Form 940 or 940EZ filed with IRS for the previous year. Deposit 940 taxes for the 4th quarter of the previous year (if liability is more than $100). NOTE: Fill out and attach Schedule A to Form 940 if you are a multi-state employer. Also, if you operated in a credit reduction state you won't be able to take the full 5.4% credit for your state unemployment tax paid; however, according to final figures from the Department of Labor there are no credit reduction states for 2018. File SUTA (state unemployment) forms for the 4th quarter of the previous year and pay the SUTA tax for the 4th quarter. Employers with tipped employees (who employed more than 10 employees on a typical business day) must file the annual report for employees' tip income (Form 8027). Also, this is the deadline for distributing ACA 1095-C forms to employees.

February 10th: Receive Form 4070 from tipped employees.

February 17th: Deposit payroll taxes for January (monthly depositors).

March 2nd: File Form 8027 (Employer's Annual Information Return of Tip Income and Allocated Tips) if there is tip income to report. File 1095-C forms with the IRS if filing on paper.

March 10th: Receive Form 4070 from tipped employees.

March 16th: Deposit payroll taxes for February (monthly depositors).

March 31st: Due date for submitting 1095-C forms to the IRS if filing electronically.

April 10th: Receive Form 4070 from tipped employees.

April 15th: Deposit payroll taxes for March (monthly depositors).

April 30th: File Form 941 for 1st quarter (May 10th if all taxes have been depositing timely, properly and in full), deposit 940 taxes if more than $100, and file SUTA (state unemployment tax) forms for 1st quarter.

May 11th: Receive Form 4070 from tipped employees.

May 15th: Deposit payroll taxes for April (monthly depositors).

June 10th: Receive Form 4070 from tipped employees.

June 15th: Deposit payroll taxes for May (monthly depositors).

July 10th: Receive Form 4070 from tipped employees.

July 15th: Deposit payroll taxes for June (monthly depositors).

July 31st: File Form 941 for 2nd quarter (August 10th if all taxes have been deposited timely, properly and in full), deposit 940 taxes if more than $100, file SUTA (state unemployment tax) forms and pay the SUI tax for the 2nd quarter.

August 10th: Receive Form 4070 from tipped employees.

August 17th: Deposit payroll taxes for July (monthly depositors).

September 10th: Receive Form 4070 from tipped employees.

September 15th: Deposit payroll taxes for August (monthly depositors).

October 1st: File Employer Information Report EEO-1 Form EEO-1 with the U.S. Equal Employment Opportunity Commission (for employers with 100 or more employees). Note: This deadline has been extended in the past and may be extended again for 2019 reporting.

October 12th: Receive Form 4070 from tipped employees.

October 15th: Deposit payroll taxes for September (monthly depositors).

November 2nd: File Form 941 for 3rd quarter (November 10th if all taxes have been deposited timely, properly and in full), deposit 940 taxes if more than $100, and file SUTA (state unemployment tax) forms and pay quarterly SUTA tax.

November 10th: Receive Form 4070 from tipped employees.

November 16th: Deposit payroll taxes for October (monthly depositors).

December 10th: Receive Form 4070 from tipped employees.

December 15th: Deposit payroll taxes for November (monthly depositors).

Appendix D – 2021 SUI Wage Bases By State

(State Unemployment Insurance wage limits

Note: The majority of states haven't announced their 2021 wage limit as of December 15tth, 2020.

Alabama - $8,000
Alaska - $43,600
Arizona - $7,000
Arkansas - $10,000
California - $7,000
Colorado - $13,600
Connecticut - $15,000
Delaware - $16,500
District of Columbia - $9,000
Florida - $7,000
Georgia - $9.500
Hawaii - $47,400
Idaho - $43,000
Illinois - $12,960
Indiana - $9,500
Iowa - $32,400
Kansas - $14,000
Kentucky - $11,100
Louisiana - $7,700
Maine - $12,000
Maryland - $8,500
Massachusetts - $15,000
Michigan - $9,500 (EST) ($9,000 for 2020)
Minnesota - $36,000 (EST) ($35,000 for 2020)
Mississippi - $14,000
Missouri - $11,500
Montana - $35,300
Nebraska - $9,000 ($24,000 for employers assigned the maximum rate)
Nevada - $33,400
New Hampshire - $14,000
New Jersey - $36,200
New Mexico - $27,000
New York - $11,800
North Carolina - $26,000 (EST) ($25,200 for 2020)
North Dakota - $38,500
Oklahoma - $24,000
Oregon - $43,800

Pennsylvania - $10,000
Puerto Rico – TBD ($7,000 for 2020)
Rhode Island - TBD (#24,000/$25,500 for 2020)
South Carolina - $14,000
South Dakota - $15,000
Tennessee – TBD ($7,000 for 2020)
Texas - $9,000
Utah - $38,900
Vermont - $14,100
Virginia - $8,000
Washington - $56,500
West Virginia - $12,000
Wisconsin - $14,000
Wyoming - $27,300

** TBD – To Be Determined
** EST - Estimated

Appendix E – State Tax Links

Go to: https://www.paycheckcity.com/ for information on state withholding tax, state unemployment insurance tax, additional state taxes, and new hire reporting, as well as links to various state agencies.

Appendix F – IRS Tax Forms

1099 Forms:

- **1099-A** – Acquisition of Secured Property.
- **1099-B** – Proceeds from Broker and Barter Exchange Transactions.
- **1099-C** – Cancellation of Debt.
- **1099-CAP** – Changes in Corporate Control and Capital Structure.
- **1099-DIV** – Dividends and Distributions.
- **1099-G** – Government Payments.
- **1099-H** – Health Insurance Advance Payments.
- **1099-INT** – Interest Income.
- **1099-K** – Merchant Card and Third Party Network Payments.
- **1099-LTC** – Long Term Care Benefits.
- **1099-MISC** – Miscellaneous Income.
- **1099-NEC** – Miscellaneous Income with non-employee compensation.
- **1099-OID** – Original Issue Discount.
- **1099-PATR** – Taxable Distributions from Cooperatives.
- **1099-Q** – Payments from Qualified Educational Programs.
- **1099-R** – Distributions from Pensions, Annuities, Retirement Plans, IRAs or Insurance Contracts.
- **1099-S** – Foreign Person's U.S. Source Income.
- **1099-SA** – Distributions from an HSA, Archer MSA or Medicare Advantage MSA.

Appendix G – Federal Holidays for 2021

Friday, January 1 – New Year's Day

Monday, January 18 – Birthday of Martin Luther King, Jr.

Monday, February 15 – Washington's Birthday

Monday, May 31 – Memorial Day

Monday, July 5 (July 4th observed) – Independence Day

Monday, September 6 – Labor Day

Monday, October 11 – Columbus Day

Thursday, November 11 – Veterans Day

Thursday, November 25 – Thanksgiving Day

Friday, Dec. 24 – Christmas Day

Appendix H – Sample Forms and Letters

Sample Letter Asking for Abatement of a Penalty:

Universal Supply Company
1000 S. Main Street Ste 100
Anywhere, USA 70000
(999) 999-9999

March 17, 2014

Department of the Treasury
Internal Revenue Service

Subject: Request to Abate Penalty

Reference:
  Notice Number: 999CG
  Date of Notice: March 3, 2014
  Employer ID: 77-1111111
  Tax Period: December 31, 2013
  Penalty Reference Code: 501

We have received IRS Notice 999CG, a proposed penalty for filing our 2013 W-2 forms on paper rather than filing them electronically. We understand that the W-2s should have been filed electronically since we had 259 W-2 forms - however we intended to file electronically (as we did in 2011 and 2012) but the paper forms were sent in by mistake. On the advice of our payroll provider we decided not to go ahead and transmit the electronic file once we realized the paper forms had been mailed.

We are requesting an abatement because there was no intent to deliberately file the forms on paper - it was a mistake and we fully intended to submit electronically (as we will again this year). We request that you please take this into account and adjust the penalty.

Thank you,

Sample Form Authorizing a Payroll Deduction:

Employee Name: _____   SSN: _____

Deduction Effective Date: _____

Payroll Deductions:
- 401(k)   % or $ _____
- 401(k) Loan $ _____
- Health Insurance $ _____
- Child Care $ _____
- Other _____ $ _____

I agree that my gross pay will be reduced by the amount of any deduction(s) indicated above. In the event of a deduction change during the year, my employer is authorized to deduct the new amount from my pay.

If a new Employee Deduction Authorization Form is not executed on or before the next year-end I agree that this form will continue to be in force for the succeeding year.

Employee Signature: _____
Date: _____

Sample Layoff Termination Letter:

Date _____

Reginald Parker-Hurst
888 Eighth Street
Anywhere, USA

Dear Reginald,

This letter confirms our discussion earlier today that you are being laid off from your employment with Acme Universal Widgets effective immediately. Unfortunately economic conditions in the industry have resulted in declining sale, forcing us to eliminate a number of job positions.

You will receive one week's severance pay for each year that you have worked here (12 weeks in your case). We will continue to provide health insurance coverage over that period. In addition you will receive payment for your accrued vacation time with your final paycheck.

You will receive the severance payment once you have signed and returned the enclosed release of claims document. You can also expect a separate benefits status letter outlining the status of your benefits upon termination, including information about your eligibility for Consolidated Omnibus Budget Reconciliation Act (COBRA) continuing group health coverage.

You will need to keep us informed of your contact information so that we can provide you with information you may need in the future such as your W-2 form.

You've been an excellent employee – if you want us to provide references for a potential employer and assist you in some other way please let us know.

Regards,

Sample Letter Providing Proof of Income:

January 14, 2015

Ronald Whistler
Universal Widgets
999 Main Street
Anywhere, USA

Mason Funsler
2nd National Bank
100 10th Street
Anywhere, USA

Re: Proof of Income for Tom Dooley III

Dear Mr. Funsler,

The purpose of this letter is to provide income verification for Tom Dooley III with regard to his application for a home mortgage through 2nd National Bank. As Human Resources Director for Universal Widgets, I can confirm that Mr. Dooley's current salary is $42,500. He also receives an annual bonus that has averaged $2,350 for the five years he has been employed by Universal Widgets. Mr. Dooley is an employee in good standing and I foresee no reason his income wouldn't continue at this level.

Enclosed is an earnings register of Mr. Dooley's earnings over the past 12 months along with a copy of his 2014 W-2 form. If I can be of further assistance please contact me at 1-800-999-9999 or by email at rwhistler@universalwidgets.com.

Sincerely,

Sample Separation Agreement and Release of Claims:

GENERAL RELEASE OF ALL CLAIMS

As consideration for the following (list here the severance pay, extended benefits, or other items you are agreeing to provide) offered to me by (business name), I release and discharge (business name), its successors, subsidiaries, employees, officers and directors (hereinafter referred to as "the Company") for all claims, liabilities, demands, and causes of actions known or unknown, fixed or contingent, which I may have or claim to have against the Company as a result of this termination and do hereby agree not to file a lawsuit to assert such claims.

This includes but is not limited to claims arising under the Age Discrimination in Employment Act or other federal, state or local laws prohibiting employment discrimination or claims growing out of any legal restrictions on the Company's right to terminate its employees.

This release does not have any effect on any claim I may have against the Company unrelated to this termination.

I have carefully read and fully understand all of the provisions of this agreement and release which sets forth the entire agreement between me and the Company, and I acknowledge that I have not relied on any representation or statement, written or oral, not set forth in this document.

Signed: _____   Date: _____
         (employee)

Signed: _____   Date: _____
         (for the Company)

Appendix I – IRS Form I-9

Section 1:

Employee Responsibilities for Section 1

Employees must provide their:

- Full legal name
  - If the employee has two last names (family names), include both. If the employee has two first names (given names), include both.
  - If the employee hyphenates his or her first or last names, include the hyphen (-) between the names.
  - Include his or her middle initial, if the employee has a middle name.
- Other names used, if applicable (e.g., maiden name).
- Current address, including street name and number (no P.O. Box), city, state and ZIP code
- Date of birth
- Check mark next to the appropriate box to indicate whether they are a U.S. citizen or national, lawful permanent resident of the United States, or an alien authorized to work in the United States.
- Alien Registration/USCIS or Form I-94 Admission number and the date employment authorization expires (if applicable)
- Signature and date

Additionally, employees may provide their:

- Social Security number (This is optional unless the employer uses E-Verify and the individual has been issued a number.)
- Telephone Number
- E-mail Address

Your employee must sign the form even if a preparer or translator helps them. The preparer or translator who helps your employee must provide his or her name and address and must sign and date the certification on the form. If more than one preparer or translator is used, have the additional preparers or translators fill out the certification on additional Forms I-9 and attach the forms to the initial Form I-9.

The date your employee enters next to his or her signature should match the date the preparer/translator signed the form.

Employer Responsibilities for Section 1

You must:

• Review the information your employee provided in Section 1.
• Ensure that your employee provided information in all required fields. (Note: Your employees are not required to provide a Social Security number in Section 1. However, a Social Security number may be required if you use E-Verify.)
• Ensure your employee signed and dated the form.
• Ensure the Preparer/Translator section has been completed, signed, and dated if your employee used a preparer/translator.

In addition:

• You should note whether your employees indicated in Section 1 that their employment authorization will expire.

• You may need to reverify your employee's authorization when his or her employment authorization expires. You may want to remind your employees, at least 90 days before their employment authorization expires and that they will need to present a List A or List C document to show continued employment authorization for reverification purposes. Employees must present these documents on or before the date their current employment authorization expires.

• Note that the expiration date for employment authorization provided by your employee in Section 1 may or may not match the expiration date of the List A or List C document your employee presents for Section 2, Employer Review and Verification. For reverification purposes, the earlier date should be used to determine when reverification is necessary.

Section 2:

Employee Responsibilities for Section 2

Employees must present unexpired original documentation that shows the employer their identity and employment authorization. Your employees choose which documentation to present.

Employees must present:

• One selection from List A; or

238

• One selection from List B in combination with one selection from List C. Note:

• List A contains documents that show both identity and employment authorization
• List B documents show identity only
• List C documents show employment authorization only
In certain circumstances, your employee may present an acceptable receipt in lieu of a List A, B, or C document. Receipts only temporarily satisfy the document presentation requirement for Section 2.

Employer Responsibilities for Section 2

An employer or an authorized representative of the employer completes Section 2. Employers or their authorized representatives must physically examine the documentation presented and sign the form.

The employer or authorized representative must:

• Ensure that any document your employee presents is on the Lists of Acceptable Documents or is an acceptable receipt.
• Physically examine each document to determine if it reasonably appears to be genuine and to relate to your employee presenting it. If you determine the document does not reasonably appear to be genuine and relate to your employee, you should allow your employee to present other documentation from the List of Acceptable Documents.
• Enter your employee's Last Name, First Name and Middle Initial (if provided) from Section 1.
• Enter the document title, issuing authority, number(s) and expiration date (if any) from the original document(s) your employee presented.
• Enter the date your employee began or will begin work for pay.
• Enter the name, signature and title of the person completing Section 2, as well as the date he or she completed Section 2.
• Enter the employer's business name and address. If your company has multiple locations, use the most appropriate address that identifies the location of the employer with respect to the employee and his or her Form I-9 completion (e.g., the address where the Form I-9 is completed).
• Return the documentation presented back to your employee.

Entering Dates in Section 2

Section 2 includes two spaces that require dates. These spaces are for:

• Your employee's first day of employment (i.e., "date of hire" which means the commencement of employment of an employee for wages or other remuneration).
• The date you examined the documentation your employee presented to show identity and employment authorization.

The Date the Employee Began Employment

The date your employee began employment may be a current, past or future date. You should enter:

• A current date
  ◦ If Section 2 is completed the same day your employee begins employment for wages or other remuneration
• A past date
  ◦ If Section 2 is completed after your employee began employment for wages or other remuneration. Enter the actual date your employee began employment for wages or other remuneration.
• A future date
  ◦ If Section 2 is completed after the employee accepts the job offer but before he or she will begin employment for wages or other remuneration, enter the date the employee expects to begin such employment. If the employee begins employment on a different date, cross out the expected start date and write in the correct start date. Date and initial the correction.

Federal contractors completing Form I-9 for existing employees as a result of an award of a federal contract with the FAR E-Verify clause:

• Enter the date their employees first began employment for wages or other remuneration from Section 2 of their previously completed Form I-9.

The Date the Employer Examined the Employee's Documents

This date is the actual date you complete Section 2 by examining the documentation your employee presents and signing the certification.

Section 3:

Employers may complete Section 3 when:

• Your employee's employment authorization or documentation of employment authorization has expired ("reverification").

240

• Your employee is rehired within three years of the date that Form I-9 was originally completed.
• Your employee changes his or her name.

Reverification

When your employee's employment authorization or employment authorization documentation (in most cases—see below for more information) expires, you must reverify to ensure your employee is still authorized to work. Look in Section 1 for the date that employment authorization expires and in Section 2 for the date that employment authorization document expires.

The employment authorization expiration date provided by your employee in Section 1 may not match with the document expiration date recorded by you under List A or List C in Section 2. For reverification purposes, the earlier date should be used to determine when reverification is necessary.

We suggest that you remind employees, at least 90 days before the date reverification is required, that your employees will be required to present a List A or List C document (or acceptable receipt) showing continued employment authorization on the date that their employment authorization or documentation expires. If your employee has a Form I-765, Application for Employment Authorization, pending with USCIS, and the application has been pending for 75 days, your employee may call the National Customer Service Center or schedule an INFOPASS appointment at a local office to request expedited processing.

Employers should not reverify:

• U.S. citizens
• Lawful permanent residents (LPRs) who presented a Permanent Resident Card (Form I-551) for Section 2
• List B documents
Unless reverification does not apply (as stated above), when your employee's employment authorization or employment authorization documentation expires your employee must present unexpired documentation from either List A or List C showing he or she is still authorized to work.

To complete Section 3, you must:

• Examine the documentation to determine if it appears to be genuine and to relate to your employee presenting it. If you feel the document does not reasonably appear to be genuine and relate to your employee, you should allow your employee to present other documentation from the List of Acceptable Documents.

• Record the document title, document number and expiration date, if any.

• Sign and date Section 3.

If you previously completed Section 3, or if the version of the form you used for a previous verification is no longer valid, you must complete Section 3 of a new Form I-9 using the most current version and attach it to the previously completed Form I-9.

Appendix J – 2021 Federal Withholding Tax Tables

The IRS introduced a new W-4 form in 2020, which should be used for employees hired after January 1, 2020 and for employees requesting a change in their withholding. Every 2020 W-4 that employers receive from an employee should have Step 1 (name, address, social security number, and filing status) completed and a dated signature on Step 5. Employees who only fill out Step 1 and Step 5 will have federal income tax withheld based on their filing status, earnings, and length of payroll period. Employees should only fill out information in Steps 2, 3 and 4 if they want to adjust the amount of tax that will be withheld from their paychecks. For details on how to fill out Steps 2, 3 and 4 look at Publication 15-T at www.irs.gov.

Employees who already have a W-4 on file won't be required to fill out one of the new forms unless they want to make a change in their withholding.

Note: The IRS has issued guidance to employers on how to compute federal withholding tax for employees whose current W-4 form dates back to 2019 or earlier. According to the draft version of Publication 15 (Circular E), this "computational bridge" works like this:

1. Select the filing status in step 1(c) of a 2020 or later Form W-4 that most accurately reflects the employee's marital status on line 3 of a 2019 or earlier Form W-4. Treat the employee as "Single or Married filing separately" on a 2020 or later Form W-4 if the employee selected either "Single" or "Married, but withhold at higher single rate" as their marital status on their 2019 or earlier Form W-4. Treat the employee as "Married filing jointly" on a 2020 or later Form W-4 if the employee selected "Married" as their marital status on their 2019 or earlier Form W-4. You can't convert an employee to a filing status of "head of household" using this computational bridge.

2. Enter an amount in step 4(a) on a 2020 or later Form W-4 based on the filing status that you determined in (1) above when you converted the employee's marital status on a 2019 or earlier Form W-4. Enter $8,600 if the employee's filing status is "Single or Married filing separately" or $12,900 if the employee's filing status is "Married filing jointly.".

3. Multiply the number of allowances claimed on line 5 of an employee's 2019 or earlier Form W-4 by $4,300 and enter the

result in step 4(b) on a 2020 or later Form W-4. 4. Enter the additional amount of withholding requested by the employee on line 6 of their 2019 or earlier Form W-4 in step 4(c) of a 2020 or later Form W-4.

New employees who received their first pay in 2020 and who failed to submit a Form W-4 will be treated as if they had checked the box for Single or Married filing separately in Step 1(c) and made no entries in Step 2, Step 3, or Step 4 of the 2020 Form W-4. However, an employee hired on or before December 31, 2019, who was paid wages in 2019 or earlier, should be treated as single and claiming zero allowances on a 2019 Form W-4.

Due to the number of options associated with the 2020 federal income tax withholding tables, the computer formulas and tables aren't included here. Please download the latest version of IRS Publication 15-T from www.irs.gov to make sure you have a current, detailed explanation of how to calculate federal income withholding for your employees.

(Currently you can download the 2021 draft version of Publication 15-T at: https://www.irs.gov/pub/irs-dft/p15t--dft.pdf)

Note: Be sure to take into account an employee's tax-deferred deduction amounts such as cafeteria plan deductions or 401(k) deductions - those amounts must be subtracted from the employee's gross pay to arrive at the taxable gross.

Appendix K – Workers Comp Requirements by State

Note: Sole proprietors, partners, most corporate officers, independent contractors, agricultural farm workers, domestic servants, casual laborers, real estate brokers and salespeople on commission, entertainers under contract, and volunteers in tax exempt organizations are generally not required to be covered by workers compensation insurance. For further details go to: https://quickbooks.intuit.com/r/hr-laws-and-regulation/workers-compensation-laws-by-state-rules-coverage-benefits/ or consult your state workers compensation agency.

Listed below are the general requirements for workers compensation coverage by state as of December 2019. Note: Each state has certain exceptions – be sure to check the particular exceptions for each state in which you operate.

Alabama – Compulsory for employers of 5 or more.
Arizona – Compulsory for all employees (although employees may reject coverage).
Arkansas – Compulsory for employers of 3 or more.
California – Compulsory for all employees.
Colorado – Compulsory for all employees.
Connecticut – Compulsory for all employees.
Delaware – Compulsory for all employees.
Florida – Compulsory for all employers of 4 or more (1 or more for construction-related trades).
Georgia – Compulsory for employers of 3 or more.
Idaho – Compulsory for all employees.
Illinois – Compulsory for all employees.
Indiana – Compulsory for all employees (corporate officers must also be insured).
Iowa – Compulsory for all employees.
Kansas – Compulsory for all employees (also required for corporate officers).
Kentucky – Compulsory for all officers (also required for corporate officers).
Louisiana – Compulsory for all employees.
Maine – Compulsory for all employees and for corporate officers owning less than 20 percent of the company stock.
Maryland – Compulsory for all employees and for corporate officers owning less than 20 percent of the company stock.

Massachusetts – Compulsory for all employees (no exceptions).

Michigan – Compulsory for employers of 3 or more.

Minnesota – Compulsory for all employees.

Mississippi – Compulsory for employers of 5 or more.

Missouri – Compulsory for employers of 5 or more (1 or more for construction-related businesses).

Montana – Compulsory for all employees.

Nebraska – Compulsory for all employees and for corporate officers who own less than 65% of the company stock.

Nevada – Compulsory for all employees.

New Hampshire – Compulsory for all employees.

New Jersey – Compulsory for all employees.

New Mexico – Compulsory for employers of 3 or more (all employees for construction-related businesses).

New York – Compulsory for all employees.

North Carolina – Compulsory for employers of 3 or more.

North Dakota – Compulsory for all employees. (**Note**: employers must buy workers comp insurance from the state agency).

Ohio – Compulsory for all employees. (**Note:** employers must buy workers comp insurance from the state agency).

Oklahoma – Compulsory for all employees.

Oregon – Compulsory for all employees.

Pennsylvania – Compulsory for all employees.

Rhode Island – Compulsory for employers of 4 or more.

South Carolina – Compulsory for employers of 4 or more.

South Dakota – Employers are not required to carry workers compensation insurance although employees may sue for compensation.

Tennessee – Compulsory for employers of 5 or more.

Texas – Employers are not required to carry workers compensation insurance but may still be liable for work-related injuries or illnesses.

Utah – Compulsory for all employees (5 or more for farm labor).

Vermont – Compulsory for all employees.

Virginia – Compulsory for employers of 3 or more.

Washington – Compulsory for all employees (**Note**: employers must purchase workers comp insurance from the state agency).

West Virginia – Compulsory for all employees.

Wisconsin – Compulsory for all employees.

Wyoming – Compulsory for all employees (**Note:** employers must purchase workers comp insurance from the state agency).

Appendix L – 2021 Minimum Wage by State

Note: If a state is not listed, then the federal minimum wage ($7.25 per hour) applies for that state.
- Alaska - $10.34 per hour
- Arkansas - $11.00
- Arizona - $12.15 per hour
- California - $14.00 per hour
  (some counties may have higher minimum wage amounts)
- Colorado - $12.32 per hour
- Connecticut - $12.00 per hour ($13.00 as of 8-01-2021)
- Delaware - $9.25 per hour
- District of Columbia - $15.00 per hour
- Florida - $8.56 per hour ($10.00 per hour effective 9-30-2021)
- Hawaii - $10.10 per hour
- Illinois - $11.00 per hour
- Maine - $12.15 per hour
- Maryland - $11.75 per hour (if 15 or more employees, otherwise $11.60 per hour)
- Massachusetts - $13.50 per hour
- Michigan - $9.87 per hour
- Minnesota – $10.08 per hour ($8.21 per hour for employers with less than $500,000 in sales per year)
- Missouri - $10.30 per hour (Higher rates may apply in Kansas City and St. Louis)
- Montana - $8.75 per hour (if sales of $110,000 per year or more)
- Nebraska - $9.00 per hour
- Nevada - $8.00 per hour ($8.75 per hour as of July 1, 2021)
- New Jersey - $12.00 per hour ($11.00 per hour if 5 or fewer employees)
- New York - $12.50 per hour (Higher rate in metropolitan areas)
- New Mexico - $9.00 per hour
- Ohio - $8.80 per hour
- Oregon - $12.00 per hour ($12.75 per hour as of July 2021)
- Rhode Island - $11.50 per hour
- South Dakota - $9.45 per hour
- Vermont - $11.75 per hour
- Washington - $13.69 per hour
- West Virginia - $8.75 per hour

Appendix M – FFCRA Paid Leave FAQ

Are all employees eligible for EPSLA and EFMLEA leave?
All employees of a covered employer are eligible to take EPSLA leave, but only those employed for at least 30 calendar days are eligible to take EFMLEA leave (subject to certain exceptions).

Are first responders and health care providers eligible for EPSLA and EFMLEA leave?
Under the FFCRA, employers "may elect to exclude" health care providers and emergency responders from EFMLEA and the EPSL paid leave.

Do employers have to continue their normal health care plans during the pandemic or do the EPSLA and EFMLEA replace that coverage?
Employees who take EPSLA or EFMLEA leave are entitled to continue coverage under their employer's group health plan on the same terms as if they did not take leave. During that leave, employers must maintain the same group health plan benefits provided to employees and their family members covered under the plan before taking leave. This requirement also applies to benefits provided through a supplement to a group health plan.

Can employers require employees to take a COVID-19 test as a condition of returning to the workplace?
Yes, the EEOC has stated that employers have that right, provided that the test is reliable and accurate.

If an employee's job is eliminated while the employee is on FFCRA leave, does the employer have to provide an equivalent position to the employee?
Not if the job would have been eliminated anyway, but the employer needs to be able to justify doing away with the employee's position.

Can employers who are re-opening fire employees who refuse to return immediately because their children's schools or daycare centers are still closed due to the COVID-19 crisis?
No. According to the Families First Coronavirus Response Act, those employees are entitled to take job-protected leave through December 31, 2020.

How are FFCRA qualified leave wages and CARES Act qualified wages treated for tax purposes?
Qualified wages paid under both programs are treated the same as normal W-2 wages. They're taxable income to employees and are subject to payroll taxes, the same as other W-2 wages.

If an employee is at home with a child because the school is closed or the childcare provider isn't available, due to COVID-19, is the employee entitled to both FFCRA sick leave and FFCRA expanded family medical leave?
Employees may be eligible for both types of leave, but only for a total of twelve weeks of paid leave. The Emergency Paid Sick Leave Act provides paid leave for the first two weeks (10 days) of emergency leave. After the first ten workdays the employee will receive 2/3 pay under the EFMLEA for the hours he or she would have been scheduled to work during the next ten weeks.

Can my employer deny a qualifying employee paid sick leave under the EMPSLA if the employee had already taken employer provided paid sick leave before the Emergency Paid Sick Leave Act went into effect?
No. The Emergency Paid Sick Leave Act imposes a new leave requirement on employers that is effective beginning on April 1, 2020.

Do employees not working in the United States count toward an employer's employee total?
Only if they're working in U.S. Territories.

Notes

(Add your own notes on the following blank pages)

Alphabetical Index

Made in the USA
Coppell, TX
10 January 2022

71345040R00142